Changing Lives

The "Postwar" in Japanese Women's Autobiographies and Memoirs

Asia Past & Present: New Research from AAS

Published by the Association for Asian Studies (AAS) "Asia Past & Present" features the finest scholarly work from all areas and disciplines of Asian studies.

For further information, please visit **www.asian-studies.org**.

- "Memory, Violence, Queues: Lu Xun Interprets China," by Eva Shan Chou

- "Scattered Goddesses: Travels with the Yoginis," by Padma Kaimal

- "South Asian Texts in History: Critical Engagements with Sheldon Pollock," edited by Yigal Bronner, Whitney Cox, and Lawrence McCrea

- "Beating Devils and Burning Their Books: Views of Japan, China, and the West," edited by Anthony E. Clark

- "To Die and Not Decay: Autobiography and the Pursuit of Immortality in Early China," by Matthew V. Wells

- "Collecting Asia: East Asian Libraries in North America, 1868–2008," edited by Peter X. Zhou

- "Prescribing Colonization: The Role of Medical Practices and Policies in Japan-Ruled Taiwan, 1895–1945," by Michael Shiyung Liu

- "Tools of Culture: Japan's Cultural, Intellectual, Medical, and Technological Contacts in East Asia, 1000s to 1500s," edited by Andrew Edmund Goble, Kenneth R. Robinson, and Haruko Wakabayashi

- "Modern Short Fiction of Southeast Asia: A Literary History," edited by Teri Shaffer Yamada

CHANGING LIVES

THE "POSTWAR" IN JAPANESE
WOMEN'S AUTOBIOGRAPHIES
AND MEMOIRS

RONALD P. LOFTUS

ASIA PAST & PRESENT

Published by the Association for Asian Studies, Inc.
Asia Past & Present: New Research from AAS, Number 10

The Association for Asian Studies (AAS)

Formed in 1941, the Association for Asian Studies (AAS)—the largest society of its kind, with approximately 8,000 members worldwide—is a scholarly, non-political, non-profit professional association open to all persons interested in Asia.

For further information, please visit www.asian-studies.org.

Published by:
Association for Asian Studies, Inc.
825 Victors Way, Suite 310
Ann Arbor, MI 48108 USA
www.asian-studies.org

Printed in the United States of America on acid-free, archival quality paper.

Library of Congress Cataloging-in-Publication Data

Loftus, Ronald P.
  Changing lives : the "postwar" in Japanese women's autobiographies and memoirs / Ronald P. Loftus.
    pages cm. — (Asia past & present: new research from AAS ; number 10)
  Includes bibliographical references and index.
  ISBN 978-0-924304-69-9 (pbk. : alk. paper) 1. Women—Japan—Social conditions—20th century. 2. Women—Japan—Biography—History and criticism. 3. Japan—Social conditions—1945–
4. Japan—Civilization—1945– 5. Japan—History—1945–
  I. Association for Asian Studies. II. Title.
  HQ1762.L64 2013
  305.40952—dc23

                                                    2012040656

Cover photo: Members of the Assembly of Japanese Mothers (*Nihon hahaoya taikai*) marching in Ampo demonstrations. Photo courtesy of Mainichi PhotoBank.

To my grandchildren

Leah Jo, Casey, Jackson, Emmett, and Luca

CONTENTS

Acknowledgments

I am indebted to many people, organizations, and institutions whose help was instrumental in completing this book. I began reading Japanese autobiographies almost thirty years ago. Professors Kano Masanao and Saeki Shôichi kindly met with me during the mid-1980s and helped guide my reading and thinking. Hôsei Professor Emeritus Nishida Masaru has been a mentor to me for over thirty years, and his advice and suggestions were always helpful. In 2007 the Japan Foundation provided financial support for seven months of research in Japan where I was affiliated with Ochanomizu Women's University. Professor Sakamoto Kazue was my colleague and host while I was there, and she helped me immensely. I have also received financial support from the AAS Northeast Asia Council (NEAC) and Willamette University's Atkinson Fund and Center for Asian Studies. Colleagues and administrative staff at our sister institution, Tokyo International University, provided much needed support at many stages in the evolution of this project.

Over the years I have presented various versions of my work at conferences, especially those of the Association for Asian Studies (AAS), Asian Studies on the Pacific Coast (ASPAC), and the Western Association of Women Historians (WAWH). Kyoko Mori was kind enough to read a portion of the manuscript and to offer valuable suggestions. Friends and colleagues such as Jan Bardsley, Barbara Sato, Barbara Molony, Carol Gluck, Chris Gerteis, and Laura Hein offered kind words and encouragement to me along the way. When I was in Japan in 2009, Yoshitake Teruko very kindly agreed to meet with me even though her health was not the best at the time. She is an amazing woman for whom I have the greatest respect and admiration. I am also very thankful for the time that Miki Sôko and Kusunose Keiko spent with me in Kyoto, also in the summer of 2009. They took me to the house where Okabe Itsuko lived, which is now a "by appointment only" restaurant; the owners were very generous and let us walk through the house and see where Okabe lived and worked. We had wonderful conversations, and I learned a great deal from these two women, who were very generous with their time and knowledge.

I also would like to thank the two anonymous manuscript reviewers who made very helpful comments as well as the Association for Asian Studies (AAS) editorial staff and editorial board. Jonathan Wilson, an excellent editor, worked diligently preparing the manuscript for publication and the copyeditors also enabled me to clarify many important points in the manuscript. Also, my colleagues at Willamette University, Miho Fujiwara, Juwen Zhang, Huike Wen, Mike Strelow, Cecily McCaffrey, Greg Felker, Pam Moro, Xijuan Zhou. and Roger Hull, all inspired or supported me in ways that of which I am sure they are not aware. Pamela Smith, the Administrative Support person for the Center for Asian Studies, helped in the preparation of the manuscript, although all the flaws and shortcomings are mine.

1

Endings and Beginnings

Addressing the Postwar Experience

Seldom has a nation experienced a more catastrophic defeat in war than did Japan in 1945. More than two and a half million soldiers and civilians died, and sixty-six major Japanese cities had been firebombed, rendering nearly one-third of the population homeless.[1] As John Dower characterizes the course of the war:

> From the Rape of Nanking in the opening months of the war against China to the rape of Manila in the final stages of the Pacific War, the emperor's soldiers and sailors left a trail of unspeakable cruelty and rapacity. As it turned out, they devoured themselves. Japanese died in hopeless suicide charges, starved to death in the field, killed their own wounded rather than let them fall into enemy hands, and murdered their civilian compatriots in places such as Saipan and Okinawa. They watched helplessly as firebombs destroyed their cities—all the while listening to their leaders natter on about how it might be necessary for the "hundred million" all to die "like shattered jewels."[2]

In the end, it was not necessary for all Japanese to die, but the wartime rhetoric about the destiny of the Yamato race and the splendors of the East Asian Co-Prosperity Sphere that had once held such sway over Japanese minds became bankrupt, virtually overnight. How did such a dramatic rupture affect Japanese people? How did they recall and reflect on the postwar years? Did women experience the end of the war differently from men? Memoirs and autobiographies often provide valuable clues for answering these kinds of questions, but how did writers reconstruct their memories and reorder the events of the past in order to turn them into coherent narratives?

Sharalyn Orbaugh argues in her book about Japanese fiction during the Allied occupation that narratives can be indispensable for the construction or preservation of identity in the midst of disruption and change. "Particularly in times of extraordinary cultural upheaval," she writes, "narrative is key to the reconstruction of some kind of identity that will allow a person to live through the traumatic rupture and into a viable present. . . . [T]he act of creating narrative is a way of bringing order to violence and unreason."[3] While Orbaugh's remarks refer primarily to fiction, I would argue that they are even more applicable to self-referential narratives, for autobiographies and memoirs remain a very compelling way in which we tell each other stories about our experiences: what we lived through and what we learned.[4] From these stories, readers are able to gain insights into how the world looked to Japanese women, and how they perceived the historical and social circumstances in which they found themselves.

Kano Masanao argues convincingly that men and women *did* experience the end of the war differently. For *men*, defeat in war shattered their self-confidence and their belief in a just and righteous war; for *women*, it felt as though an albatross, a "heavy weight" had been lifted from around their necks—this was the weight of the very concept of the Japanese "male" (*otoko*).[5] It may be that the very concepts of masculinity and femininity were not directly challenged until the 1970s with the appearance of the women's liberation movement in Japan, but there can be no question that notions of political equality, and equality in the schools and the workplace, were very much in the air during the early postwar years. The central argument of *Changing Lives* is that reading memoirs and autobiographies by Japanese women is a useful way to explore their reactions to the end of the war and to the challenges and opportunities that the early postwar years presented to them.

Who are some of the women whose narratives appear in *Changing Lives*? The remainder of this chapter contains excerpts from memoirs by four different women: Okabe Itsuko, Yoshitake Teruko, Shinya Eiko, and Sawachi Hisae. These authors all have something significant to say about what it was like to experience the end of the war and how that ending led them to embrace new beginnings. Yoshitake's memoir, *Onnatachi no undôshi—watakushi no ikita sengo* (A History of [Japanese] Women's Movements—and My Experience of the Postwar Years, 2006), is so compelling that portions of it will also be presented in chapters 2 and 3, as well as here in chapter 1. As her title suggests, she is intent on situating her experiences in the context of a postwar history of Japanese women's movements. She affirms what Kano suggests about the end of the war being experienced differently by men and women when she writes, "[D]efeat in war had been, for women, the most wonderful treasure imaginable." She sees the end of the war as having launched Japanese women on a trajectory toward greater opportunities for personal and political freedom, and she demonstrates this by documenting how postwar women engaged in social and political activism.

Following on the heels of the two chapters dedicated to Yoshitake's memoir, chapter 4 focuses on the story of newspaper reporter Kishino Junko's *Onna no chihei kara miete-kita mono: Joseikisha no jibunshi* (Things Visible from a Woman's Perspective: My Personal History as a Female Reporter, 1980), a narrative remarkable for the way it openly declares itself as postwar history writ small. Inspired by what she calls the ideals or "spirit" of postwar Japan, she traces her experiences in the workplace, her involvement with labor activism and the Ampo Movement, and finally her connections with the women's liberation movement in the 1970s. Chapter 5 features Kanamori Toshie's recollections of her career as a reporter for the *Yomiuri shinbun*, during which she consistently focused on women's issues. She questioned the direction being taken in postwar education and accurately perceived the significance of the demographic time bomb for the lives of Japanese women. Her memoir, *Waratte, naite, aruite, kaita: Josei jyaanarisuto no gojûnen* (I Laughed, Cried, Walked, and Wrote: My Fifty Years as a Female Journalist, 2006), includes a passionate appeal for Japan to transform itself as it adjusts to becoming an aged society in which elder care is a significant burden. How likely is it that this burden will be borne equally by men and women?

On Reading Women's Memoirs and Autobiographies

To believe that reading postwar women's memoirs is worthwhile for the insights it offers not only into women's lives but into the social conditions in which they were negotiating their subjectivity and historical agency assumes that the experiences of individual historical actors are, in fact, meaningful. Historians have been struggling with this issue for decades, ever since the "linguistic turn" made us aware that language is not neutral or transparent and actually structures and conditions our experience of reality. If we believe that reality is socially and linguistically constructed, can there be any room left for subjectivity and historical agency? Is there a historical or social ground from which an actor can chart his or her own life course, and craft his or her identity? Is it more difficult for women to assert their historical agency than it is for men? Some writers apparently think so.[6] "To be an agent," writes William H. Sewell, "means to be capable of exerting some degree of control over the social relations in which one is enmeshed, which in turn implies the ability to transform those social relations to some degree."[7] Did Japanese women feel that they had that degree of control over their lives? How concerned were they with transforming social relations?

In my previous work—*Telling Lives*—which focused primarily on women who were active during the interwar years, I argued that it was, indeed, possible for women even in the 1920s to discover and assert their historical agency. I was able to show that women were capable of fashioning a language and vocabulary with which they could conceptualize themselves as historical agents.[8] In *Changing Lives*, I carry this argument further by suggesting that we can discover within individual subjectivities as constructed in postwar autobiographies or memoirs a position—a moment—in which the narrator functions as a "site" consisting of differences (or tensions) between what is "given"—the historically and socially constructed reality—and how individuals might experience or process that reality. In the course of becoming aware of these differences, it is possible to turn this new awareness toward a transformation of society through either social or linguistic performance.[9] In other words, actors in the historical moment—and autobiographers who recall and reconstruct their experiences of being in the midst of unfolding events— have the potential to understand the situation in which they find themselves. By using the culturally given terms and definitions that surround them, but putting them to new and creative uses, they are capable of repositioning themselves in relation to historical events.

In order to accomplish this, though, they may need to develop new strategies for processing their experiences, and even for acting in the world, so that they will be able to see themselves in a manner, as Gabrielle Spiegel says, that is "constrained but not wholly controlled" by the conditioned reality in which they find themselves.[10] This argument does not deny the powerful constitutive effect of language, but it recognizes that by accepting the limitations of the social conditions in which one is enmeshed, one can do something to momentarily transcend these conditions and then proceed to find ways to work within the culturally constructed reality in which they find themselves. These moments of self-reflexivity—when narrators are able to hold the interactions among themselves, their past, and the social and political conditions in which they are enmeshed in a kind of suspended animation—are usually found in those passages in autobiographical narratives that grab our attention and lead us into a deeper appreciation of the era and human experience in general.

Therefore, this book focuses on how women address the postwar years in their self-referential narratives with an eye toward seeing how they situate themselves as narrating subjects in relation to significant postwar events, and how they reflect on and reconstruct these events for the printed page. How do their narrative strategies operate to pinpoint the spatial and temporal locations in which Japanese women managed to transform their consciousness? Did they encounter substantial obstacles to the establishment of their identity or subjectivity? If so, were they able to resist these forces and then reconstruct that moment of resistance in their texts? Did this become a pathway to negotiating their historical agency? The narratives examined in *Changing Lives* suggest that this is very much the case. Admittedly, history cannot be written simply by layering individual narratives one on top of the other. To be legitimate, to come up to the standards of the profession, history needs to be distanced from the individual's immediate, "subjective" experience and "told" from an objective and rational perspective.

On the other hand, as historians, we do value the individual stories out of which the larger public history emerges. As Jill Ker Conway notes, "We want to know how the world looks from inside another person's experience, and when that craving is met by a convincing narrative, we find it deeply satisfying."[11] The narratives explored in *Changing Lives* deliver this kind of satisfaction and also provide a useful corrective to the standard histories of postwar Japan. The fact that these women speak directly to us, in their own words, lends immediacy to their stories. Histories that stray too far from these kinds of stories, rooted as they are in the individual experiences of historical actors and agents, run the risk of overlooking important voices and ignoring the real issues and ideologies with which postwar women grappled.

The Day the War Ended: The *Gyokuon hôsô*

The "imperial broadcast" (*gyokuon hôsô*) of August 15, 1945, announcing Japan's acceptance of the terms of the Potsdam Declaration was one of the most transformative historical moments in modern Japan. People are not likely to forget where they were when they first heard the emperor's voice, nor how they felt at that moment. Distorted by the crackling of static and delivered in stilted, formal language, most listeners had great difficulty understanding what the emperor was actually saying. But the central message did eventually become clear: Japan was unconditionally accepting the terms of the Potsdam Declaration, and the war was over. Unconditional surrender—what had once been heretical and unthinkable—was now a reality. Surviving newsreel footage from this traumatic midday announcement, which the emperor delivered haltingly in a high-pitched voice, shows many of the emperor's bedraggled subjects, especially women, falling to their knees, covering their faces, and weeping. What lay behind these tears? Were they tears of shame and regret? Or were they tears of relief? In the beginning of the second volume of *Shôwashi, Sengohen, 1945–1989* (*History of the Shôwa Period, 1945–1989*), Handô Kazutoshi quotes from the reminiscences of five contemporary eyewitnesses who spoke to these questions. They expressed feelings of stupefaction and disbelief, as well as sadness, on hearing the news. But interestingly, not one of these commentators is female.[12] No doubt, any response to this event would be complex and multifaceted, but I think that significant insights can be gained by reading what women recalled about that day. Therefore, several excerpts from women's memoirs that recall the emperor's broadcast will be examined in the remainder of this chapter.

There can be no doubt that in addition to the traumatic rupture of the war's end, there were other historically and culturally significant moments that took place in the ensuing months and years as well. In general, the Allied occupation of Japan brought about many profound changes in Japanese society. Some would argue that nobody benefited more from these changes than Japanese women, who finally secured the right to vote, as well as equal access to education and jobs when the Supreme Commander for Allied Powers (SCAP) urged a policy of liberating Japanese women on the Japanese government. It should not be surprising, then, to discover that recollections about how education and employment opportunities were transformed appear frequently in women's personal narratives. As postwar society was reformed and reconfigured, especially after the era of high-speed economic growth began in the 1960s, concerns about women's social status and their relationship to politics and power, as well as their position within the family and their responsibility for both child care and elder care, have come in for increasing scrutiny.

There were also critical moments in the postwar years that had an impact on Japanese women, particularly the turbulent weeks during the Ampo[13] struggle in May and June of 1960, the student strikes and political activism of the 1960s, and the advent of the second-wave of feminism in the form of the "women's lib" movement in October and November of 1970. By the Ampo struggle, I refer to the roughly six-week period of intensive, highly-charged popular demonstrations against the 1960 renewal of the US-Japan Security Treaty. Although the protests were initiated primarily by radical students and representatives of left-wing labor unions, citizens from all walks of life, situated along all segments of the political spectrum, eventually took to the streets in order to protest an assault on what they perceived as the fragility of their new postwar democracy. A citizen-based movement on a very large scale, it appealed to many Japanese, and women of all ages played a critical role in the unfolding of events. But it was not a women's issue per se.

The same cannot be said about the advent of the "Lib Movement" a decade later in November 1970. Although it only involved a few thousand women in its initial phases—mostly younger women—it was definitely an epochal event for Japanese women. As historian Kano Masanao notes, even among practitioners of women's studies there has been notable reluctance to undertake a scholarly analysis of the Lib Movement. In part, he suggests, this may be because of the "scandalous image" associated with the participants in the movement as marked by their provocative behavior, their blunt and colorful language, and the confrontational tactics of the pink-helmeted members of Chûpiren (中ピ連), who opposed anti-abortion legislation and promoted the introduction of the birth-control pill. An unwelcome stepchild of the Left, the Lib Movement was perceived to have both "violent" and "destructive" tendencies and was sensationalized in the media for this.[14] Yet, as this book will make clear, the movement did succeed in transforming women's lives and altering the way they perceived Japanese society and their place in it.

I fully expected to find discussions of tumultuous moments such as the Ampo struggle and the women's lib rallies featured in the personal narratives of Japanese women, and while I certainly did encounter texts that probed these significant events, they were not as ubiquitous as I had anticipated. What was striking, however, was that almost every autobiography or memoir that I picked up went straight back to the moment when the war ended and discussed what it signaled for Japanese women about their future. Hence, this opening chapter has to do with endings and new beginnings; it will focus on the recollections of several female autobiographers about the day the war ended, beginning with Okabe Itsuko and followed by Yoshitake Teruko, Shinya Eiko, and Sawachi Hisae, respectively.

Okabe Itsuko

Nonfiction writer Okabe Itsuko, who passed away on April 29, 2008, was born in Osaka in 1923, the year of the Great Kantô Earthquake, as she likes to recall.[15] As her parents' youngest daughter, she claims that she was rather spoiled. She also makes a point of noting that her father frequently picked on her mother and made her cry in front of everybody, and that bothered her. She loved her mother very much and felt terrible for her. She even experienced suicidal feelings when she was just ten or eleven years old. Her mother recognized the signs, however, and begged her daughter not to abandon her prematurely. Although Itsuko grew up sickly and left school to recuperate from tuberculosis, she did survive and became a noted writer and cultural critic. After she left an unhappy marriage, she began to write on traditional Japanese arts and customs, cuisine, theater, war, the environment, and a wide range of other topics. In the course of her career as a writer, she published over 120 books. In her 2006 memoir, *Yuigon no tsumori de* (Intended as My Last

Will and Testament), she details the moment the war ended and the impact the war had on her life.[16] Here are some of Okabe's recollections of August 15, 1945.

We heard the news that at noon there would be the "gyokuon hôsô"—or the imperial broadcast—so we all dutifully assembled around the radio and listened. I gathered that the war was over at this point, although I really could not grasp the meaning of what was being said. But my father observed, "Well, there won't be any more need to dig this bomb shelter." Because that is what he had been doing.

My mother cried. I am sure she was thinking about Hiroshi [one of her older brothers]. I went with my cousins who lived across the way to the beach. The beach—up until then, since we never knew when or where the bombs might be falling, we couldn't just go out for a walk when we pleased. A group of us youngsters actually walking together to the beach? That hadn't happened in such a long time!

Somehow, when the war ended, I wanted to see the ocean. The ocean connects everything with everything else, and at that time I was thinking that Kunio [her fiancé] was still alive. So, when my cousins and I arrived at the beach, we could see people just sitting on the breakwater and watching the ocean. And this is something I will never forget—nobody was saying anything. It was strangely silent. Fishermen came and sat down, too, but still no one spoke. They just looked at the ocean. Quietly. Silently. . . .

I guess everyone was thinking the same kind of thoughts. Where are you? Are you alive? When are you coming home? Are you safe? I am sure that everyone was lost in thought about his or her loved ones. So many people, just sitting there, staring at the ocean; there was hardly any room to sit on the breakwater, but people were just staring out at the sea. And not saying anything.

I was able to squeeze myself in, and I just sat there, too, looking at the ocean. Kunio, where are you? That was the first thought in my mind: when are you coming home?

The war is over. I was just staring vacantly when, suddenly, I happened to look up and there was a full moon rising. It was an evening silvery moon. August 15. I will never forget it.

I said to the others that my mother would be worrying so we should get back. . . . And by the time we got home, it was already getting dark. We saw the lights being turned on in all the houses. Up until then, due to the blackouts, people had to cover their windows, so everything was always dark. Turning on the lights—that wasn't something we were used to. I thought to myself,

"Ah, the war is really over. We can turn on the lights!"

This was also a sight I will never forget. What a sense of contentment just to see all these lights come on—it was relaxing somehow. For human beings, light is some kind of proof that we are alive. (115–17)

Itsuko recalls an unforgettable moment, sitting in eerie silence on the breakwater, staring out at the ocean, underneath a rising silvery moon. This moment evokes a sense of longing: longing for the connectedness that the ocean can bring, longing for news of loved ones, longing for a return to some kind of normalcy. This passage also offers readers a sense of hope because on the way home, as lights come on in the houses around them, they offer some solace. They offer the contentment that comes from knowing that one is alive, and that there is enough illumination in the world to dispel the darkness and allow the young people—Japan's future—to find their way home. Two other significant narratives spin off of Okabe's initial recollections of that day, and they both serve to underscore a central theme in her memoir: the stupidity and destructiveness of the war, especially its devastating impact on families. The first is about the loss her older brother, Hiroshi, who was a pilot and a commissioned second lieutenant. She recalls the day his ship left the port of Kobe.

I could always say what I really felt to Hiroshi and he would understand me. I felt relaxed around him. When his ship left Kobe, we all went to see him off. My parents, my relatives, and I—everybody. . . . On November 10, 1941, his ship left port in Kobe; he was commissioned as a second lieutenant in the infantry. It was the last time I saw my brother.

This wonderful brother of mine died somewhere, exactly where I did not even know; somewhere near Singapore.

I am pretty sure the date that the news came to our home was March 15, 1942: *Hiroshi's plane was missing!* Just at that time, both my mother and my father were out, so I was the only one home to receive the phone call.

"Lt. Okabe Hiroshi has not returned," said the voice.

It seems that his plane took off on a reconnaissance mission and did not return. The phone call was from the local neighborhood association. In those days, the neighborhood association watched out for everything. You couldn't do anything without that organization knowing about it. . . .

Missing. All that could really mean is that he is dead. It was so sad for my mother. No one understood better than she what a splendid person her son was. How hard it must have been for her. But those were the days of militaristic education, and we were told that we must die in order to pay our debt to the emperor.

"He died a hero's death in battle then," she said, and she could not even shed a tear. She had to remain firm and resolute. And then the neighborhood association would come by and congratulate her on her son's glorious death in battle.

"Thank you," said my mother. I stood right behind her, bowing and saying the same thing.

But one of the neighbor women, who also had a son, Takuzô, came rushing right over, not even taking time to change. "Your Hiroshi was great. I am so sorry he had to die. Forgive us. He died for all of us," and she started crying. She was the first person to say anything like that. Both Mother and I, for the first time, burst into tears as well.

Up to that point, it had all been about people congratulating us on Hiroshi's heroic death and us replying with a "Thank you. We owe a lot to you." These were all just empty phrases that meant nothing. When I think about it now, we were just acting like idiots. It was comical, really!

Only our neighbor was being genuine. She spoke the truth from her heart. Because this was no time to be congratulating anyone about anything! At that point, Takuzô from next door was still alive. (49–81)

This passage is much more than just an account of the loss of a loved one. It offers a poignant critique of the entire prewar system of education, of the rhetoric of patriotic self-sacrifice, and of the peer pressure so eagerly and willingly applied by neighborhood associations. All the powerful forces that would suppress any discourse other than one laced with empty, patriotic slogans are clearly visible for readers to see. The conventions of the day dictated that the bereaved put away their personal grief and deep sense of loss and don a mask of pride and patriotism. Only the next-door neighbor is courageous enough to speak from her heart. And when she does so, Itsuko and her mother are deeply moved, and their true feelings overflow. All the unnatural stoicism and resolve demanded by the emperor-centered ideology collapse and are replaced with a flood of tears that is genuine and heartfelt. In retrospect, everything else had just been a ritualized, idiotic, public display, a comedic farce.

There is considerable power in this scene, but the second narrative embedded in Okabe's memoir—the story of the young man named Kimura Kunio, to whom she was engaged—constitutes an even more penetrating and full-blown critique of prewar ideology. She begins by explaining that after their engagement Kunio was permitted come to her house and they were actually allowed to be alone together in her room, even though her father and brothers were never far away, peering stealthily at them whenever they could.

> After our engagement, Kunio came over to our house and said, "Soon I'll be going off somewhere, so this is our last day to spend together." Now that we were engaged, it was finally all right for us to talk by ourselves. (87)

Itsuko's room occupied the third floor of the home, and Kunio remarks on her room.

> "Is this your room? You have a lot of books!" I could tell he was pleased to see so many books. In my room, near the door, there was a little glass window, so someone could look in from outside. I'd look up and see my father's face or my older brother peering in from time to time. Kunio was not aware of this, but I could see them from where I sat. So I am being watched, I thought. It would be terrible if we were to do anything, right? So we couldn't do anything. There wasn't any place where we could do anything. We were not allowed the time or the space. Not like today when young people can pretty much go anywhere and do anything they want. And we were running out of time.
>
> We both began to feel tense. I really had not been able to do anything for Kunio. I wanted to somehow show him something of myself, something good. So I got out my different, seasonal kimonos and was showing him how this one was for spring, this one for summer, and that one for winter. Kunio had a different way of showing me his feelings. He suddenly popped up and came over and put his arms around me and hugged me, and then he walked around the room with me. He said:
>
> "One way or another, I'd like to settle things before I leave." I wasn't sure exactly what he meant. In those days, young girls did not get to hear things like that. I was just barely twenty at the time. There was no such thing as sex education in those days, and he was not saying exactly what he wanted to do. It was sad, I guess, because nothing happened in the end. (87–88)

As she reconstructs his words and actions sixty years later, Okabe infers that Kunio probably wanted to be intimate with her somehow that night. But she did not know how to respond or how they could have managed any time alone, away from prying eyes. Hence the rising tension in the room. In the ensuing moment, though, Kunio shocks her not with his deeds but with his words.

> Anyway, while we were alone, Kunio lowered his voice and said to me:
>
> "I am opposed to this war. I think this war was a mistake. I do not want to die in this war. I do not want to die for the sake of the emperor or anything like that. You might be glad to die for the sake of your country, I don't know. . . ."

There he was, sitting in a cadet uniform with his high collar, saying things about the war being a mistake, about not wanting to die, even saying that the whole idea of dying for the emperor's sake was wrong. He spoke very clearly. This was a period in which you could not really speak frankly. This was the first time we had ever been alone, and these were the first words I was really hearing him say to me. It was something I will never forget. (89)

For the reader who knows something of prewar Japan, this story is poignant and powerful. Interspersed with thoughts of possible sexual transgression, here was the ultimate political transgression, a complete rebuke of the prewar code of the emperor system and everything it stood for. She continues with this.

Ah, it takes me back. He was just twenty-two; I was barely twenty. He was a good person. He was brave, he was straightforward, he was noble. He walked a straight line. He had spoken the truth to me, straight from his heart. In those days, if anyone had heard him say those things he would have been arrested and thrown in prison. And he was a soldier, no less!

And I spoke frankly back to him. I spoke my true feelings. This was the proof of the love between Kunio and me—to be able to say something you could not say to anyone else, not even someone in your family, nor a friend. Of course, it wasn't something you could say to a relative. These were words he spoke only to me.

However, I could not understand the significance of his words. Because all I had been taught was that one had to die in these circumstances. That's how I was raised, always hearing this phrase repeated. We were taught that we must be determined to die. Over and over again we were told, "Die for the sake of the emperor, die!" The neighborhood association, the school—it was the same everywhere. At school they told us, "Falling cherry blossoms— and the ones that remain will fall, too."

The education we received taught us to die willingly, so I could not comprehend the words Kunio was saying to me. The war was a mistake? I had never heard anyone say anything like that. In hindsight, it would have been best if I had asked him, "Why are you saying these things?" But there wasn't time, and all I could say was:

"If it were me, I would die willingly for the emperor."

Today this seems so sad, so harsh. He spoke to me so clearly—and to me alone; "it's a mistake," is what he said. Just a young, twenty-one or twenty-two-year-old Osaka man. And I heard the words he was saying. We were engaged, so I listened to what he said. But I could not understand the meaning of what he was saying. All I could say back to him was "What are you talking about? Of course, I would happily die for the sake of the emperor."

And so, in the dark of night, in Osaka station, waving a little rising-sun flag, I saw him off.

Waving my little flag, I sent him off to a war to which he did not want to go, a war he believed was a mistake. So I couldn't help but think of myself as a murderer.

He was only twenty-two, yet way back then he had the courage to say what he did. But I could not tell anyone about what he said. I couldn't even say anything to my mother. . . .

The truth was, we were living in times when if you said anything that might be offensive in public, or wrote anything, you would be picked up in a heartbeat and thrown into prison. So, if anyone had ever heard what Kunio said to me, he would surely have been imprisoned. That's the kind of era it was.

Figure 1.1. Okabe Itsuko and Kimura Kunio.
Used by permission of Fujiwara shoten.

I realized only much later, then, what a risk Kunio had taken, how great he really was. And back then I could not appreciate what he was doing. How sad for him. And we were not able to go anywhere together that night either. We just had so little time.

Moreover, in those days, young men and women didn't have the freedom to just go off to a hotel or anything. Just the two of us walking around together would attract attention from neighbors. That was the world we lived in. . . .

So how was it that in a time like this Kunio could have said those things to me? It really took me a long time to figure it out, but he had told his younger brother, "If I die, please look in the bookshelf and take care of what you find for me." So, after Kunio went off to war, his younger brother did as he was asked. He looked in the bookcase, and he found a place where books were stored in double rows. The front row had perfectly ordinary books that anyone could see, but behind them was a whole array of books on Marxism, books with various ideas that were considered "red" in those days. They all had lots of Xs marking the passages that had been censored.

Kunio had attended the commercial higher school, the Osaka City College of today, and he had probably gotten this kind of influence from Professor Kimura Wasaburô who was one of his mentors. Kunio had been drawn to the study of social science; he believed in equal rights for all, in antiwar thought, and in doing something to make the world a happier place; he wanted to make some contribution to the betterment of humankind. These were the things he had been thinking about for some time. That's why he believed the war was a mistake.

I didn't really know that he had been undertaking these kinds of studies until quite recently. We had never had the time to have that kind of in-depth conversation.

"The war is a mistake"—just that one phrase was all I had to hang on to for most of my life.

It would have been good if I could have asked him what that phrase meant. But I was so surprised that all I could say was, "If it were me, I would happily die for the emperor." How rude and thoughtless of me. I wonder how deeply my words hurt Kunio. . . .

I couldn't say anything more about all of this to Kunio, even though he had made the effort to say what he did to me. Because I could not understand what lay behind his words, I wound up saying something that was cruel and heartless.

And then I waved him off to war with my flag. (89–96)

Rhetorically, this passage makes use of the systematic repetition of the image of Okabe waving Kunio off to war with her little rising-sun flag while strategically interspersing the words Kunio spoke to her about the war being a mistake. The repressiveness of the era, the flaws in emperor system, and what a waste it was to throw one's life away for such a system—these were Kunio's core beliefs, which Okabe can see clearly now but could not at the time. Her litany constitutes an indictment not only of her own personal failing but of the entire prewar educational and political establishment's inability to see things as they really were, and to be open to a discourse about it. She learned only much later from his younger brother that Kunio had been a politically engaged young man who had taken significant risks. He had embraced left-wing ideologies and rejected the emperor system, neither of which were easy things to do in prewar Japan. It had cost many Japanese on the left their lives or landed them in prison.

Once she invokes this topic of the war as a mistake, though, Okabe does not let it go. In the following passage, she recalls the day she learned of Kunio's death.

"This war is a mistake,"

Kunio, you were so right to leave me with those words. If I did not have those precious, precious words to live by, then my life would have had no meaning. Such precious words. Today, in the times in which we live, they have become all the more precious.

The facts are now clear. One twenty-two-year-old youth, in January of 1943, right smack in the middle of the war, saw the conflict for what it was. He expressed himself directly: *this war is a mistake.* He said it so clearly. To be able to see it then, right in the midst of everything, that was something really great. I want some of the young people today to become this kind of person, the kind of person who can speak the truth, who can know his or her own mind, and can express themselves clearly.

For humankind, taking a stand against war is a step in the right direction. To do it right in the middle of a war must have taken so much courage. Kunio, you were right to do it. . . .

"This war is a mistake."

Because you left me with these words, I have my today. It is so sad that such a fine young man as you could have existed right here in the middle of Osaka, during wartime, and had those views about the war, and someone like me could not reciprocate.

Therefore, all I can do is repeat those words over and over. . . . If I want my own life to have any meaning, all I can do is work to preserve those words, to keep on repeating them, to keep them alive. In these days, in this world of ours, we need this more than ever. (118–27)

She repeats Kunio's words over and over not only for rhetorical effect but also because that is what she believes she must do. She claims that in order make it possible for her to have her today, and for her life to have meaning, she must let the world hear Kunio's words. Words had set traps for Itsuko; she had heard him utter words that she could not process because of what had been deeply ingrained in her. In turn, she uttered words that she wished she had not, words that spilled out of her because of an educational system and an ideological regime that had permeated her being. She had only an instant to respond, and she acted in the same mechanical, unfeeling way that she and her mother had when the neighborhood association "congratulated" them on Hiroshi's glorious death. Eventually, Itsuko learned that things were not exactly what they seemed: there was a whole side to Kunio that she knew virtually nothing about. Now it is incumbent on her to repeat what Kunio said to her and to share his story with the world. This is what enables her to (re)claim her "today."

What she did not fully grasp at the time was that her subjectivity had been so repressed that she had nothing with which to ground a response to Kunio. She realized that she needed to transform her life, to imbue it with meaning, not so much as a form of penance but as a way to make the world right. Or at least to make it a better place. By telling her story the way she does, full of repetitions and incantations, Itsuko not only condemns the mistakes of the past but also helps her readers develop their own agency so that they can become more capable of avoiding mistakes of the past, transforming the world into a better place in which to live.

Yoshitake Teruko

Okabe Itsuko's narrative illuminates a painful and difficult subject and does so with prose that is powerful and engaging. The second memoir I will introduce here is one of the most compelling that I have read, Yoshitake Teruko's *Onnatachi no undôshi—watakushi no Ikita Sengo* (A History of Women's Movements—and My Experience of the Postwar Years), which was published in 2006.[17] She begins with a rather dispassionate account of what the experience of war meant to Japan:

The Imperial Broadcast Flows from Radios on August 15, 1945

On August 15, 1945, Japan accepted the terms of the Potsdam Declaration and formally ended hostilities with the Allied powers. It was the end to a long war that had been going on ever since the year I was born, 1931, when, in September of that year, Japan dispatched troops to Manchuria (then a part of northern China).

As a result of the war, some 9.2 million victims suffered while some 23 million houses were either burned to the ground or destroyed, and 2.6 million people were killed while there were some 4.3 million casualties. Over 2.4 million members of the armed forces died in the conflict, and it is assumed from this that some 283,000 women were widowed. So it was not only a war in which Japan experienced the two atomic bombs dropped on Hiroshima and Nagasaki, while also suffering incredible damage and destruction [from fire bombings] throughout the country; it was also a war in which Japan inflicted a vast amount of pain and suffering on China and various countries in Southeast Asia. In the final analysis, this was not just the end of the war; it was total defeat.

I experienced the end of the war as an evacuee in Yamanashi Prefecture, in a small village surrounded by mountains. Exactly at noon, the village headman's radio faced toward us and began to play the imperial broadcast. Since the village was in the mountains, it was easy to get interference with the radio signal. There was so much static that it was practically impossible to clearly distinguish what was being said, so the broadcast ended without the central message being clear.

"So he said that we are to bear the unbearable and endure the unendurable, and fight until the last of the 100 million are destroyed, right?" someone asked.

"No, that was not it. He said that Japan has lost the war. We have to accept this reality and keep on living without losing our pride as Japanese." People were divided between those who were still looking for the final decisive battle and those who understood that Japan had lost the war, and they began to get into quite an argument in the garden right outside the headman's house. The headman himself, who had disappeared for a while, suddenly reappeared and in a pained voice said the following.

> Japan has been defeated. I just checked with the officials, and there is no mistake about it. People are to return to their houses and wait for the next communication. Remember that his majesty the emperor asked us to bear the unbearable and endure the unendurable. We should mind his words and not undertake any rash or hasty actions.

We were renting a small two-room, ten-mat house located some distance from the landlord where my mother's younger brother's family of five and our family of four were all living. When I got back to our little house I silently started to get out my futon because I felt so overwhelmed by a desire to go to sleep that I just could not resist it. I slept for thirty-six hours straight. I did try to wake up from time to time, but no matter how much I slept, in the deep recesses of my body there seemed to be an inexhaustible yearning for sleep, which continued to assert itself. So I just slept and slept.

We were the generation of children who did not know peace. The year I was born was when the Manchurian Incident occurred. Ever since that point, things had just escalated into the Sino-Japanese War and then the Pacific War, so we were raised right in the midst of the era of militarism. The duration of the war and my own age overlapped perfectly. When the Fifteen-Year War ended I was exactly fourteen years old.

Thanks to the thoroughly patriotic wartime education I received, I was raised to be a splendidly loyal young citizen. Many was the time that I would clasp a small rising-sun flag in my little hands and wave soldiers off to the battlefield. I would even take the initiative and stand out on the street with thousand-stitch good luck belts to send to soldiers and try to get the female passersby to cooperate and lend a hand. As an evacuee without enough food to eat, I never once complained. Because I thoroughly believed in the righteousness of the war and absolutely could not doubt that the outcome would be other than a victory. So when I heard the Imperial Broadcast, my frayed nerves were just split right in half. I am sure that it was this feeling of despondency that caused me to want to sleep so much.

Japanese Women Cooperated with the War by Protecting the Home Front

If this defeat in war caused even a child like me to feel despondent, it no doubt resulted in another whole level of complexity for adult Japanese women. As protectors of the home front, Japanese women had been co-opted into supporting the war effort by joining such organizations as the Patriotic Women's Association (Aikoku fujinkai), the Women's National Defense Association (Kokubô fujinkai), and the Greater Japan Association of Women (Dai Nippon fujinkai). Without these women's cooperation, it is highly unlikely that the war could have been continued for all those long fifteen years. Therefore, you could legitimately say that Japanese women unconsciously aided and abetted the assailants that invaded other countries.

In her autobiography, Ichikawa Fusae, who was the lifeblood of the movement to bring about the right of Japanese women to participate in politics, wrote the following passage.

> In the Yotsuya-Shinanomachi home of writer Nagata Mikihiko, we gathered in front of the radio with Nagata, his wife, and my friend Nagata Tsunehiko to listen to the emperor's broadcast. The emperor's voice, which we were hearing for the first time in this *gyokuon,* or imperial broadcast, was low but without any power. . . . Tears began

to roll down my cheeks. They were tears of frustration for
having lost the war, to be sure, but also peace was somehow
restorative. As waves of relief washed over me, I began to
think, well, what should we do now? Until the eighteenth
I met with people I knew in Tokyo and talked with them
about making a new plan.

It was not only Ichikawa Fusae; on the whole, women recovered from
the shock of defeat much more quickly than men. . . .

By creating a hierarchical system of control beginning with the
emperor on top—then the family—followed by males—and finally women,
one could say that the same call for the 100 million to rise and fight could
be transformed into the call for the 100 million to collectively repent. If you
look up at this control system from the bottom, you can see that it is a system
of repressive discrimination. Could not Japanese women, who occupied the
bottom rung of the hierarchy and were treated as though they were not even
human beings, find in the words "democracy" and "fundamental human
rights" the seeds of a brighter future? *In fact, defeat in the war was for Japanese
women the beginning of a new life.* (2–5, emphasis mine)

With these lines, Yoshitake affirms exactly what Kano Masanao suggests:
the end of the war *was* experienced differently by men and women, for whom
defeat was less a crushing blow than a new beginning. But even this new
beginning had its dark side. After talking about the establishment of the
RAA (Recreation and Amusement Association) as the government's feeble
attempt to protect Japanese women's virtue from enemy troops by enlisting
women to serve as prostitutes, Yoshitake goes on to reveal a shocking moment
in her own personal postwar history.[18]

In that same year of 1946, when my heart leapt at seeing Japanese women
cast their ballots for the first time, the very day after the election was held,
April 11, in a small corner of Aoyama Cemetery where cherry blossoms were
quietly falling, I was gang-raped by a group of American soldiers. Rape is
rather soon forgotten by the perpetrators, but for the victim it is as though
the victim is herself an assailant; rape has this extremely irrational aspect,
which makes the victim blame herself and her body throughout her life.

I tried committing suicide twice, and after failing what sustained me
was becoming engaged in the rising wave that was the dynamic women's
democratic movement.

The unruly sexual behavior of the American troops resulted in the rapid
spread of venereal diseases, but thanks to the policies of a GHQ [General
Headquarters] that had become very sensitive to the issue, they began to
spread to ordinary women information about disease prevention. It was

right in the midst of this effort that the incident I described elsewhere involving the inappropriate treatment of the two women from the Japan Motion Picture and Theatre Association took place.[19] Immediately, the women's departments of various unions made contact with one another, and there was wave after wave of protest against the police's handling of the incident. I do not suppose that there was any way for them to ignore such an outpouring of anger against this blatant violation of these women's human rights. The matter was even raised in the National Diet. (13–14)

For Yoshitake, there was an enduring connection between war and sexual violence, something confirmed by her own personal experience. A quarter of a century after her rape, she learned through her encounter with the women's liberation movement how to process and cope with her rape. In a later passage from her text she writes:

The origin of sexual violence can be found in that symbol of all violence— *war*. In order to eliminate war at its roots I have always believed that we must go to the deepest corners of society, even to all the four corners of the world, and see that gender equality can be realized so that we have true human equality. Ever since my student days when I was part of the student movement, my Tôei days when I was involved with union activities, and during the years after I left Tôei and became involved with Beiheiren—the Citizens League for Peace in Vietnam—I have worked to eradicate that peak of violence in the world, war.

However, just as with the emperor system, these kinds of pyramid-shaped movements always reflected male subjectivity, and they always, always made me feel uncomfortable. While I chanted repeatedly, as though I were intoning a sutra, that protecting the constitution means opposition to war, the fact that the movement was rooted in male subjectivity, something that today we would surely censure as sexual harassment, always seemed to get internalized into what was said so that while it was possible to protest right-wing policies, I could not help but feel strongly with each passing year that it was never going to go far enough to eradicate war at its roots.

On October 21, 1970, in the midst of an International Antiwar Action Day demonstration,[20] when Khalid, Tanaka Mitsu, and Asakawa Mari et al. raised their banner emblazoned with the Chinese character for "Resentment" and proclaimed their new organization, "Group: Fighting Women," I recall feeling such powerful emotions in my heart that it almost hurt.[21] I thought, "Aha, so the flag of the women's lib movement has been raised here in Japan, too! Finally I will be able to discover a place where I can feel comfortable." But I felt that in the eyes of these younger, radical "lib" women, I was just a forty-year-old woman who had raised a child within the existing marriage system and was working for the mass media, and therefore part of ordinary society, so I was just another elite woman who was entangled with and compromised by the system. Even in the midst of the lib movement, where I hoped against hope to find my female subjectivity, in the end I felt deep sadness at the fact that this was not a place where I could easily find solace or comfort either.

Tanaka Sumiko had the idea that she wanted to create a lib movement for middle-aged women that would raise some of the same type of women's issues, but with a way to feature slight variations in terms of age, occupation, and standpoint so that you could distinguish between such categories as "ordinary women" versus "special women" and "household women" versus "working women," as well as "married women" versus "unmarried women." This made my heart swell with the anticipation that even though such differences as age and viewpoint might exist, we could see the root causes of what makes it difficult for us to live as women, and, while joining hands and maintaining solidarity, we were able to launch an attack on those roots.

While I gave voice to these feelings, it felt like it was not my real voice, not a genuine voice that could cry out, "Yes! I have found a place where I can feel at home." I still felt diminished by trying to live in a male society, and I longed deeply for a space in postwar Japan where I could be free of these feelings of fear, for I had really been shaken severely by the aftereffects of my youthful exposure to sexual violence.

As I continued to live with the knowledge of how difficult it can be to recover control over one's mind and body after such an experience of sexual violence, it did not matter if I was at home or in the workplace, or even working with the union or being active in citizens' movements—I could not overcome this feeling of discomfort, this feeling of alienation, a feeling that there was no place in this world where I truly belonged. Moreover, whenever I overheard men talking in loud voices, telling people what to do, memories of the rape incident itself would come flooding back, and I would be enveloped in a sense of hatred and fear.

Trying to live my life while concealing my rape gave me a feeling of inferiority. The greater this sense of inferiority, the more I began to feel as though there was no adequate reason why I should be forced to live my life that way. When I would catch the sound of men talking, I could not help but feel sensitive to the inherent violence in their sense of superiority and, increasingly, more than men themselves, it was *male society* itself that I was growing to detest and feel isolated from. It was something that contributed to the overall sense of alienation that I was experiencing.

That I became able, under these circumstances, to begin to talk about my rape experience, and to write about it, *was due entirely to my encounter with women's lib*, because the movement helped me become aware of the existence of a female consciousness that resides inside of each one of us. Why had I lived for a quarter of a century trying to conceal the fact that I was a rape victim? Why had I continued to be plagued by a sense of inferiority? As I continued to probe this question, it suddenly became quite obvious. It was because I was, in the end, still governed by a stereotypical image of women that defined women's happiness solely in terms of getting married and being a good wife and mother.

By talking about my own rape experience, and beginning to write about it, I learned that rape is not simply a violation of the flesh; it is an infringement of the respect women should have as human beings. As such, it is the worst crime against humankind. And also I learned that a violation of this sort is not caused by animalistic instincts at all. It must be clearly recognized as a product of the culture of male superiority, and this recognition must become fully integrated into our feminine logic. Learning about all of this was part of my healing process. It was very gradual, but over time I began to feel my confidence and pride being restored. The first step toward my own personal liberation, then, began with recounting my rape experience and writing about it. (124–32, emphasis mine)

Although it remained a struggle for Yoshitake, and she had to find a subgroup of her own age cohort within the lib movement, she *was* able to find a voice with which to talk about what had happened to her as a teenager, and to discover a safe haven in which to explore her experiences and her consciousness as a woman. Initially, the movement did not seem to offer the "home" that she thought it might. She was older and more experienced than many of the youthful participants. But the consciousness-raising dimension of the movement—the part about looking inside oneself in order to ascertain what one believed and how one came to believe it—eventually led Yoshitake to make important discoveries about her feminine consciousness.

These were two important ways in which the women's liberation movement transformed Yoshitake's way of seeing and experiencing the world. The first was the very act of having the courage to write about it—both at the time and in her memoir. This was her way of using language in an active way not only to make sense of things but also to participate in the construction of a new social and political reality. The precise nature of the impact of the "women's lib" movement on women like Yoshitake and Kishino Junko will be explored in more detail in chapters 3 and 4 where the connections among student activism, the Ampo protests, and the women's lib movement will be closely examined. Suffice it to say here that in writing about the manner in which male subjectivity impinged on and conditioned everything she tried to do in her life constitutes a critical step in her ability to experience the impact of the patriarchy on her at the deepest level, and to begin to develop a strategy for asserting her own subjectivity in response.

The second way in which the Lib Movement affected Yoshitake was that it enabled her to discern "the root causes of what makes it difficult for us to live as women" and to develop a way "to attack those roots" as a strategy for transforming her consciousness and making the personal political. To write about feeling diminished, feeling fear and hatred, feeling alone and alienated, feeling full of loathing for both herself and the dominant male society, and coming to understand that she was oppressed by the stereotypical expectations of womanhood in Japanese society—these were such profoundly transformative moments of awareness that we as readers can appreciate how her consciousness shifted tectonically after 1970. As she re-presents these memories of her struggles and conflicts at the time, we can appreciate that she understood precisely what the socially constructed reality that she confronted had to offer her, and why it was insufficient. From this vantage point she was able to develop both personal and narrative strategies through which to assert her own female subjectivity as a necessary jumping-off place for developing her own historical agency.

Shinya Eiko

The third memoir to examine is that of film and stage actress Shinya Eiko (1928–) whose career began in an Osaka avant-garde theater group in the late 1950s and extended to films, television dramas, and half a dozen one-woman plays. She describes the process of coming to terms with the end of the war, the process that led her to the stage and screen, as one of "becoming ordinary." In psychological terms, becoming ordinary means to incorporate change into new ways of living, something many former Japanese imperial subjects were forced to do in 1945. In order to become ordinary, life has to be virtually begun anew and lived in a way that brings some coherence based on revaluating and reconstructing one's own experiences. It can involve "a process of convoluted passage during which people redefine their sense of self and redevelop self-agency in response to disruptive life events."[22] Shinya Eiko describes how she engaged in just such a reflective process in her 2005 memoir entitled *Joryū Shinya Eiko: Watakushi no rirekisho* (The Actress Shinya Eiko: An Account of My Life).[23]

Born in Osaka in 1928 and raised in the heart of the theater district, Shinya considered herself a typical militaristic young woman in the 1940s, "a loyal imperial daughter," one who was so enthusiastic about the war effort that she joined a women's auxiliary unit. However, the end of the war brought revelations that shocked her and brought her to what she describes as a "crossroad."

> In life, there are significant crossroads. August 15, 1945—the day Japan lost the war—was just such a day. My life was turned around 180 degrees when I was awakened from being a loyal "Imperial Daughter of Japan" to what it means to be an ordinary human being. The joy that accompanied the promise of never seeing war again still lives within me today. This was the starting point for my becoming a stage actor. "War is unacceptable." (6)

Becoming ordinary entailed a wrenching, 180-degree turn for Shinya, opening her eyes to the folly of war. Clearly, Shinya's experience of the end of the war was very similar to that of Yoshitake Teruko and echoes Kano's contention.[24] After the initial shock wore off, Shinya threw herself into "beginning a new life" and building a new Japan. Clearly, the end of the Pacific War caused her to reevaluate, reconsider, and reassess her perception of the world. As she explains it, the end of the war led her to reflect on her upbringing and youth, and she comments further on how these reflections put her on a pathway to becoming a stage actress.

> The fact that I could portray on stage for over thirty years an elderly Zainichi Korean woman in my one-act play *Shinse Taryon*, a play that exceeded two thousand performances, was no doubt aided by a number of objective factors, but it must also have had to do with the emotionally powerful landscapes that surrounded me in my youth and had such a powerful and disturbing impact on me. Moreover, that I was driven by a need to resolve things myself, and held a core belief, rooted very deeply in my soul, that "people are all people" (*hito wa mina hito de aru*) can also be attributed to these early experiences. I was never just playing a role. I think I was raised with the principles and passion necessary to confront the irrationality of prejudice and discrimination. (8–9)

In order to replace a belief in such things as a sacred, inviolable emperor, the Greater East Asia Co-Prosperity Sphere, and *kamikaze* (the divine winds), Shinya evinces a new faith: "people are all just people." Regardless of how insignificant they might appear, people matter. Prejudice, discrimination, and war are irrational and should have no place in the world. Shinya goes on to explain how the events surrounding the final cataclysmic end of the war came to affect her. In her auxiliary unit, she worked under a certain "lieutenant" who was apparently a Marxist with ties to the Japan Communist Party. Here is her description of the emperor's broadcast on August 15, 1945, and the events the followed.

The Emperor's "Gyokuon" Broadcast

. . . "Today, there will be a very important broadcast." The lieutenant had ordered everyone to gather at noon at the town hall, where there was a radio, to listen to the broadcast. Assuming that the message would be "fight on until the last person dies," I went to the town hall with anticipation and listened attentively. But there was a lot of static, and I could not understand what was being said. This was the first time ever to hear the emperor's voice, so as I listened I was practically stupefied by the solemn, dignified manner in which he spoke. However, not understanding a word he said, I returned to another room where the mobilized young students sat in gloomy silence. "We lost the war," they said, and I was surprised. The emperor's declaration of surrender was known as the *gyokuon* broadcast.

Since I had genuinely believed that the divine winds were going to blow and be Japan's salvation, I screamed in a loud voice, "There is no way he would say such a ridiculous thing!" However, the lieutenant took off his military sword and threw it down. "Japan has lost. Beginning today, it is our world." I thought maybe he had lost his mind. But, in fact, the lieutenant had been listening to a shortwave radio for some time, so he knew all about things like the Yalta Conference and the fact that the Allies were waiting to see what Japan would do. That they were already discussing ways to divide governing responsibilities for Japan; he even explained to me that "a huge bomb had been dropped, and this was an incredible thing." He explained to me about the August 6 atomic bomb on Hiroshima and the August 9 bomb on Nagasaki. And yet I still was unable to believe that Japan was in such a weak and vulnerable position.

But gradually, as more and more facts unfolded, I came to see the truth of it. I realized that I had been a brainwashed sixteen-year-old girl, so from that day forward, my life began to change in a major way. I began to become aware of the importance of *seeing with your own eyes and speaking from your own heart*.

Soon thereafter, we were all summoned back to the central office in Shirizaki, and in one day the army was disbanded. The war was finally over. (25–26, emphasis mine)

Suddenly, everything that Shinya understood about the world and believed to be true was being proven false. It was clearly a time to reassess and discover a new direction in life. It was time to learn to see with one's own eyes, to think for oneself, and to speak from the heart. The new pathway on which she would eventually embark involved joining a theatrical group and writing a one-woman play called *Shinse Taryon* about the discrimination faced by Korean Japanese women. But that was years later; first there were hardships to overcome and new experiences to undergo.

Immediately after the war, we had to endure real hardships. Right away my oldest brother contracted tuberculosis and died. He was only twenty-five years old. Just before the end of the war, he had started taking night classes at Ritsumeikan University. During the day, he helped out with household chores and in the evening took off for Kyoto for his classes. He was a very hard worker. When he took his physical for the army, he was incredibly thin and classified ineligible. "Don't be disappointed," he was told by the government officials. He had contracted tuberculosis once before, but in those days, unlike today, there were no effective medicines to prescribe; tuberculosis was "an incurable disease."

He entered a sanatorium at Kaizuka, and I followed him there to look after him. But he died within three months. I wonder what future he saw in his dreams. Our father's grief was very deeply felt. To see my father's retreating figure as he headed off to work—this man who had lost his wife and his two oldest sons—was truly a heartrending sight. (32–34)

Faced with substantial change and loss, and believing that the time had come for a new way of looking at the world, Shinya responded to a call for action. Part of her 180-degree turn from being a loyal imperialist daughter was to embrace left-wing ideology and engage in peace activities

What really brought about my new postwar motto—*see with your own eyes and think for yourself*—was a lecture meeting held for the people who had opposed prewar militarism but had been thrown in jail for years under the provisions of the Peace Preservation Law. These were people who did not change their views even though they were incarcerated, people like Tokuda Kyûichi and Shiga Yoshio. At the meeting, they were dressed in white turtleneck sweaters and khaki pants. I am not sure why, but it seems as though the occupation forces sponsored this rally. I strongly felt the purity of these brave fighters who stood up to the authorities and would not back down.

At the rally, "Tokkyû-san," (Tokuda Kyûichi's nickname) was joined by others such as Ichikawa Fusae and Kamichika Ichiko from the women's movement, and Katayama Sen and Nishio Suehiro from the labor movement. Their speeches were a huge hit with the audience. (33–34)

Shinya was most impressed to see women leaders sharing the platform with these left-wing heroes she admired. In the next section, She talks about her days as a fledgling reporter in the early postwar years and how what she encountered in those days helped her understand what was going on around her. The end of the war clearly brought not only shock but also a sense of liberation as Shinya was propelled into left-wing activities. However, disillusionment over the cancellation of the General Strike[25] brought an end to her Communist Party affiliation, if not her involvement with left-wing politics. Instead, she was drawn to the world of underground theater. Shinya next moves us forward to 1970 in order to explain how she came to write and star in her own one-act play.

The Birth of Shinse Taryon

In the 1970s, the popular wave of underground theater caught on in Japan, and I even tried going outside the company and performing in little coffeehouses. I created a one-act play based on the personal stories of older Zainichi Korean women—Harumoni, they were called, which means "grandmother"—titled *Shinse Taryon*. The first time I performed it was on April 29 and 30 at a little café in Umeda called Tsuji.

As far as the background of how I came to perform *Shinse Taryon* is concerned, at the theater troupe, if there was a play with, say, ten characters in it, at least seven or eight would be male roles with only two or three going to women. So, even if you were more talented than the male performers, you just could not get onstage. At the end of the day, we went around selling tickets while these rather unskilled men got to be onstage. So, under these circumstances, I started thinking about finding something that I could perform all by myself.

Shinse Taryon was the first work put on by the *Genten no Kai* and it was performed outside the theater group by independent volunteers. . . . The late Osaka producer Ozaki Akira reached out to me, saying, "Shinya-san, how about if you put together a show? I'll help with the production of it." We added Takahashi Masao and the producer Iwata Naoji of the Kansai Geijutsuza, and the four of us founded *Genten no Kai*. . . . Iwata-san had recommended to me this book by a group of six women called *Mukuge no Kai, Shinse Taryon: Zainichi Chôsenjinjosei no Hansei* [*Shinse Taryon*: The Lives of Korean Japanese Women Living in Japan] (Tokyo: Tôto shobo, 1972); when I read the book, I received such a strong impression that it felt like a bolt of lightning running straight through my body.

The six women who formed the *Mukuge no Kai* were Kubo Fumi, Hirabayshi Hisae, Sekiguchi Akako, Utsumi Aiko, Nakajima Akiko, and Kanma Kimiko. Kubo Fumi is still alive at age eighty-nine. . . . I called Kubo Fumi-san right away. "Go right ahead," she said, sounding very young and energetic. "Please use the material and make a good play out of it." So I had quite a challenge ahead of me to dramatize this work. I really did not know much about the history of Japan-Korea relations, and I knew little of the difficult times Japanese Koreans had faced. I had to start by studying these things.

Three months after first reading the book, I started to consult with Shin Gisu about the dramatization and costumes. He was currently the chair of the Film and Culture Cooperative. I also met with Kim Heeryo, who was chair at the time of the Osaka branch of the Zainichi Korean Literary Arts League. Then, with Mr. Kim's introduction, I went to Tsuruhashi to see Hon Jonjak, who managed the women's section of an ethnic clothing market. Hon-san advised, "Please wear a white Chima chogori when you perform." Her words penetrated to the core of my being.

Ever since, for thirty years, I have continued to perform in the white Chima chogori that she sewed for me. For the two-thousandth performance, she made me a new one and said, "Please wear this one for the commemorative performance."[26]

The reason that I have been able to continue to perform this play two thousand times over more than thirty years, all across Japan, is because of the generosity of the wonderful people of the Zainichi Korean community, and because of the great people in the audiences who have come to see the play over the years. The first time I performed it, the play was twenty-eight minutes long; today it runs one hour and twenty minutes.

The experience of performing this play has created many powerful memories that continue to live on inside of me. (53–55)

Figure 1.2. This photo, found in Shinya Eiko, *Enji Tsuzukete Hitori Shibai Shinse Taryon*, 127, is used by permission of Kobashi Kazushi and Kawase Kôji.

In order to "become ordinary," Shinya had to process and reevaluate things about Japan's past of which she had never been aware. Her concern with uncovering and representing this past was not limited to the experiences of Zainichi Korean women; she was also drawn to stories about other minorities who suffered discrimination and poverty such as *buraku* (outcaste) women and Korean A-bomb victims who just wanted to be treated the same as any other *hibakusha* or A-bomb victims.

Learning about Korean A-bomb Victims

About eight years after I had started performing *Shinse Taryon*, I first learned about the Korean A-bomb victims and was shocked! Someone cried out, "Japanese people are not the only victims of the bomb!" Then, about two years later, I began to meet Zainichi Korean A-bomb victims in Hiroshima and Nagasaki; I listened to their stories, even spoke with members of a research group, and read any number of books on the subject.

"There was an incredible flash and then a powerful explosion. I was stunned!"

"I was knocked down, and when I stood up, there was this sound, then a flash; before I realized it, my body was all tattered, and my hair was gone. And I couldn't hear anything. There was no sound. Even today I am still weak and anemic." . . .

One A-bomb victim, Kim Bunsen, from Taegu, came to Japan to see the play *The A-bomb Victim in the Chogori* when it was performed at the Osaka YMCA. After he had finished watching the play, Kim-san said to me, "I definitely want you to do this play in Korea, because I want everyone there to know about the pain and hardships experienced by the Korean A-bomb victims." So five months later, on December 14 in Pusan, and the next day, the fifteenth, in Taegu, and finally on the sixteenth in Seoul, we performed the play. That was our first overseas performance. Since the *hibakusha* problem was not very well understood in Korea, I was delighted that we could connect with so many people in this manner. We performed twice to completely full houses at the Hanmadan Theater.

> *I don't really want anyone to do anything special for me. I just want to be treated as a human being.*

When those lines were delivered, I could see white handkerchiefs waving in the dimly lit theater.

> *We want nothing more than to be treated the same as the Japanese who experienced the bomb.*

I will soon be approaching two thousand performances of this one-person play—and no lines bring flesh and bone to the experiences of these Korean women more than these. (71–73)

Wanting nothing more than to be treated as an ordinary human being: this obviously resonated deeply with Shinya. In a play written for her by her husband, Uzuno Akihiko, Shinya also took up the issue of *buraku* women.

It has now been more than fifteen years, but I played a role in another of the plays written and produced by Uzuno, the story of an older *buraku* woman called *The Legend of Himiko*. To date I have performed this role over 430 times. . . . The main character in this play was based on the real life experiences of Murata Himiko; she sits on a park bench and recalls her life story, the legend of Himiko. She is taking a break from her job of sweeping up in the park when she starts to tell her story.

Himiko spent her early childhood years in the Taishô era (1911–26) and so was raised on stories of the Rice Riots and the Great Kantô Earthquake. She married twice, each one ending in failure; she changed jobs, experienced the war during the first half of the Shôwa era, and experienced economic recovery in the second half, during which time she raised her son as a single mother. The season is fall, leaves are all around her, and while she sweeps them up she recounts her life story. When she opens a little amulet pouch left to her by her late father, inside she discovers a soiled copy of the Declaration of the Buraku Liberation Movement, carefully cut out of paper by her father. I can barely describe how difficult it was for me to portray the life of this old woman who had survived so much pain and discrimination throughout her life as a *buraku* woman.

Toward the end of the play, Himiko delivers these lines.

> *OK, everyone, listen to what I have to say. I may not have all the education that you do, but I have lived as a woman through all these years—the Meiji, Taishô, Shôwa, and Heisei eras—and I have survived unspeakable things. Somehow, this body of mine knows deep down what is right and what is wrong.*

In the play, her son's wife reads the Buraku Liberation declaration aloud. These lines have come to symbolize *The Legend of Himiko* as it narrativizes the tenacious and unyielding nature of Himiko. I absolutely love that paragraph! . . .

I wanted to play the part of this *buraku* woman authentically, with all her blood, sweat, and tears, and with the groans of pain that were wrung from her body. When it came to the end of the play, and the reading of the [Declaration of the] Buraku Liberation Movement, I tried to do it with as much pride as if it were the world's first declaration of human rights. I wanted these lines to give the play its lifeblood, something that would come from my own heart, from my own flesh and blood. . . .

The reason I decided to continue performing plays is simply that I love the theater, and the opportunity to play so many different kinds of people really makes me happy. There is also the joy of transcending racial, ethnic, and national boundaries. For this is a way to better understand history, the feelings of other people different from yourself, and human nature in general.

The genesis of all my performance art is the notion that war is wrong. I had experienced directly with my own physical being the fact that war crushes human beings and destroys their spirit. I came to where I am today through theater, and I will continue the journey. I may perform in a wide variety of dramas, but always at the core of my being will be the idea that war is unacceptable. (134–38)

Deep down, at the very core of her being, Himiko's body *knows* what is right and what is wrong. She has learned. She has lived through history—*herstory*—across four different imperial eras and survived. By portraying her onstage, night after night, Shinya partakes of that truth as well. Portraying not only Himiko but Japanese Korean women, and Korean atomic bomb victims as well, night after night, year in, year out, in small halls and cafés for thirty years—this was the pathway Shinya chose. Her journey was not an easy one. It never is when you seek to transcend national, ethnic, and racial boundaries in order to better understand the present through the past that shaped it. You need grit, determination, and some hope that it is possible to transform the "social relations" in which one is "enmeshed."

In a manner reminiscent of Okabe Itsuko, Shinya holds herself accountable for believing in the lies that she was taught as a sixteen year old. Until the day the war ended, her subjectivity had been molded to ensure that she would be a loyal and patriotic imperial subject. She attended the imperial broadcast fully expecting to hear that she would soon die and her soul would join the hundred million ancestors and contemporaries. From August 15 on, Shinya had to work in order to recover her humanity and reconstitute her subjectivity. She had to work at her craft, and she had to discover roles—and even create them herself—that would allow her to express with passion her belief that war is wrong. Acting is a methodology that brings mind, body, and voice together to create a new awareness, a new kind of consciousness. Hers is not specifically the *onna-ishiki*, the "feminine consciousness," to which Yoshitake Teruko and Kishino Junko will refer in subsequent chapters, but it is a consciousness that demands a place for former imperial subjects who were systematically stripped of their identity and subjectivity by the prewar thought system, remnants of which obviously persist right down to the narrative present. By using her voice and body to represent subjects who had been denied a voice and an identity, Shinya makes her one-woman plays function as sites where history and ideology are contested and where she can offer new avenues to her audience and her readers so that they can become ordinary human beings who are capable of seeing and thinking for themselves.

Sawachi Hisae

The final memoir discussed in this chapter is Sawachi Hisae's *Watashi ga ikita "Shôwa"* (The Shôwa I Lived).[27] Unlike the other women considered in this chapter, Sawachi (1930–) was not even in Japan when the war ended. She was living in Manchuria, where her family had emigrated in 1935, so she does not record being summoned to assemble in front of any radio to listen to the imperial broadcast. But the end of the war had no less an impact on her. From her vantage point in Manchuria, she has much to say about the conduct of the once vaunted Kwantung Army and what life was like for former conquerors when their army lost. Much of her memoir is given to reconsidering the process by which the military seduced the Japanese government and press to support its incursion into Manchuria.

> The origins of the Manchurian Incident itself were unmistakably in a fabricated plot. The second phase of the plot, to spread the flame of battle and seize all of Manchuria, involved the dispatch of troops to Kirin and the arbitrary decision to pull troops in from across the Korean border into Manchuria. It was a perfect example of the strategy the military favored: kill two birds with one stone. First, the Wakatsuki Cabinet decided on September 19 on a nonexpansion policy.
>
> According to the Army Regulations, chapter 2, the crime of arbitrary use of power is explained.
>
> > Article 35: The penalty for General Staff initiating a war with foreign powers without cause is death.
> >
> > Article 38: The punishment for failing to wait for orders and without cause launching a battle is death or imprisonment for not less than seven years. . . .
>
> According to these Military Regulations, General Honjô, chief of the General Staff, should not have been able to escape the death penalty. But in the history of the Japanese Army, there has never been a single commander executed for arbitrary use of power. . . .
>
> Schemes, plots, arbitrary violation of borders, and irresponsible deployment of military power—these were the hallmarks of the age. However, if there were circumstances requiring arbitrary decisions, then it would be impermissible to not act arbitrarily. What rendered the Military Regulations ineffectual was that only the military was allowed to construct explanations of circumstances in the field.

With regard to the conduct of military affairs, civilian officials had absolutely no right to interfere with the right of the imperial high command. However, at the time of the Manchurian Incident, the government did have some leverage because it needed to approve the budget without which dispatching troops would have been a practical impossibility.

Nevertheless, at 3:00 a.m. on September 21, Chief of Staff General Honjô decided to deploy troops to Kirin and commenced military hostilities. At 3:22 p.m., the commander of troops in Korea, Hayashi, received the following cable from Kanetani Hanzô of the General Staff.

> Troops of the Kwantung Army have begun to conduct military operations in the area of Kirin, and due to an extreme shortage of manpower we request supplemental forces from the Korean Army. Urgently request you to dispatch the Mixed Brigade unit from Shingishu and cross the Yalu River. . . .

Headquarters had already dispatched troops from Port Arthur to Mukden. With Chief of Staff Miyake and high-ranking staff officers Itagaki and Ishihara as the nucleus of the hard-line group, General Honjô decided to dispatch troops to Kirin, and he launched the operation, informing General Headquarters after the fact. The reason given was unrest among the troops at Kirin and the need to protect Japanese residents. To what degree would political decisions be influenced by this fait accompli? Reflecting on later historical developments, this choice was seemingly a turning point. As Wakatsuki Reijirô notes in his memoirs:

> Before troops were dispatched, or even afterward for that matter, expenses had to be appropriated. The troops could not last one day, they could not eat, if there were no appropriations. . . . At that point, regardless of whether the cabinet members agreed or not, I went straight to the imperial palace and reported to the emperor about payment for the movement of troops from Korea. As soon as I left, Kanetani secured an imperial audience and obtained imperial approval for the dispatch of troops. . . .

Domestically, Japan was not yet in the era when declarations by military authorities were absolute. But arbitrary military actions, which should have been held to the standards that were included in military regulations, were aided by newspaper articles that swallowed the military position hook, line, and sinker. Sending troops into Kirin should have been seen as a real milepost in the process of the era's downward spiral.

Ignorance is a powerful and frightening thing. When my parents decided to immigrate to Manchukuo [Manchuria], I doubt that they seriously discussed what political problems might be likely to arise. When my father took the test to enter the South Manchurian Railway Company and move to Kirin, I doubt they read any newspaper articles from 1931. In our family, perhaps only my uncle had any reservations about what was going on.

When the dispatch of troops from Korea occurred, the possibility of participating in war became a reality even for the engineering unit that my uncle was with in Hyoen. Being involved in a battle meant that there was a distinct possibility of dying. For these young people—my aunt and uncle—who had been nurturing their love since 1928, dying in a war was definitely not something they wanted to do.

On the evening of September 24, 1931, the imperial government made an official announcement about the Manchurian Incident. No matter how extensive a debate may have occurred within the cabinet, or among the people at large, or even if there had been efforts to stop the arbitrary actions taken by the Kwantung Army or the army in Korea, they would have been to no avail. Because once an imperial government declaration was issued, opinion was, in effect, unified. . . .

Beginning in the early years of Shôwa, all the way up to December 8, 1941, and the beginning of the war with the Western powers, the historical record is one of a march to war. How much blood was shed as a result of these deceptions by those elite military bureaucrats who were in power at the time? How much influence did they exert on the course that the nation followed? The Manchurian Incident was based on a string of continuous deceptions. The creation of Manchukuo, which followed the incident, opened the door to Japan's ambitions toward China and ultimately to a large-scale war that encompassed all of China. The war with the United States and Britain was simply a political extension [of Japan's policy toward Manchuria].

Deception is still with us. It is not limited to Japan. Why is this pattern repeated in various countries, wherever soldiers don uniforms? Even if it is not the result of oppression as a result of the arbitrary decisions of a ruling military clique, civilian society has always been powerless in the face of lies perpetrated by the military. In most cases, at least one or more lives have to be sacrificed for the sake of these lies. When those who die are citizens of the same country, the effect of their sacrifices is that much greater. It means that one more step has been taken toward illegal conduct by the military and the loss of innumerable lives both within and outside the country.

History is like the air; it is like the ocean. Rare is the person who lives in a specific era and can ascertain exactly where she is. Even when something is nearby, or right in front of one's eyes, one cannot always observe the nature of its direction and progress. (57–81)

Accountability is important to Sawachi, and she argues effectively that the military elites in prewar Japan lacked a sufficient amount of it. This meant that military leaders were free to deceive civilian political leaders, the press, and ultimately the people. Once the decision to enter Manchuria and engage in hostilities received imperial sanction, it was irreversible. The result was too much death and destruction. Writing about the day the war ended, Sawachi recalls:

Fifty years ago, on August 15, with the acceptance of the Potsdam Declaration, the war came to an end. On this day of unconditional surrender, I was fifteen years old (actually fourteen years and eleven months).

At that time in our house in Jilin we had living with us a young couple that had fled from the city of Mudanjiang after the Soviet Union entered the war. The husband was an employee of the South Manchurian Railroad; when winter came they were required to move to the south, so they left us.

Therefore, in and around the time of August 15, our little house was overflowing with people. There were five of us and the couple from Mudanjiang, plus we had numerous Kwantung Army soldiers who were billeted at the school for Chinese children who were coming in and out of our house to use the bath. They were just a small unit with no commanding officer around, so there was always a lively conversation taking place with a variety of perspectives represented.

In January of that year, my grandmother had died. My father was temporarily assigned to the Jilin Agricultural Construction Office, so he was not there. We received a telegram, and that evening my mother set out for Hyoen. Left behind, I watched her leave from the window. The light from the window made a little square patch of light in the darkness. A fine, powdery snow was falling.

When my mother returned, she talked about my aunt and uncle's youngest daughter, who had just been born, and how when my aunt was pregnant her heart condition worsened and she became very bloated (it is speculated that this may have been one of the reasons they decided to commit suicide in the postwar period).

The collapse of the southern front was complete, and on April 5, the Soviets announced their intention not to renew the neutrality pact with Japan. On May 8, Germany surrendered unconditionally. Once the European front had started to collapse at the end of February, the movement of Soviet troops toward the eastern front was more active. The days when Manchuria (and neighboring Korea) would become battlefields for Soviet troops were getting closer day by day.

When the "peerless" elite fighting troops of the Kwantung Army were diverted to the southern front, things began to get shaky. Their place was taken by troops who were not prepared for combat either physically or in terms of their training. Their weapons were inadequate as well. In order to round up these supplemental troops, there was a grassroots mobilization of Japanese all across Manchuria. Even one of the teachers at the girls school was called up this way (there were teachers from our school who never returned from battle), and they even took men from agricultural development projects. This was around the end of May. . . .

After the Soviets entered the war, troops were transferred to Jilin by train. . . . But the commanders were nowhere to be found. So the troops just wasted time at the Chinese elementary school, and after Soviet troops occupied the city on August 19, they quietly put down their arms, formed up in their ranks, and were led off singing battle songs. Their destination was internment camps in Siberia. For several days we intermingled with these troops that the Kwantung Army headquarters had abandoned, offering them farewell cups of water and seeing them on their way.

If there had been any serious attempts to follow impractical slogans like "offering one million lives" and "resist to the end, continue the war indefinitely," it wasn't evident in Manchuria where the soldiers' mission was to get rid of their uniforms as quickly as possible and pose as civilians. I chose to frankly oppose this idea of resistance to the end, and I elected to follow the path of recognizing defeat and suing for peace. But the last of these Kwantung Army soldiers who were led off like sheep were a pathetic sight.

Wasn't it a soldier's supreme duty to protect the *tatemae*—the fiction for which they were fighting? What a deception! These were supposed to be the Emperor's Soldiers, who were to never surrender, but their leaders did nothing to avoid capture. What makes me want to denounce the whole thing as "Complete Lies" is the fact that the useless Kwantung Army contrived a battle plan that abandoned the civilian population and its own troops.

The very next day after they had laid down their arms, soldiers who were deserting ran around to all the houses warning us that "the women will be violated," so we ran outside and watched the uniformed troops pass by, their tanks making a deafening roar.

I was able to figure out what this warning meant without anyone having to explain it to me. I sat on the steps in our *genkan* (entryway), undid my hair, which was tied up in three places, and let it hang down. My hair fell in clumps on the floor of the *genkan* as the scissors worked frantically to cut it all off. I had tried dressing in boys' clothing, but that did not fool the Red Army soldiers, so I was very afraid. I felt like I had no country. We had to face reality by ourselves, as individuals or as a family, as naked as the proverbial white rabbit of Inaba. No one was going to come to help us.

Around this time, my uncle and his whole family decided to commit suicide in the mountains near Subun [in Korea]. It is said that they used some kind of explosive device. As of February 1945, the Engineering Corps to which my uncle belonged was to be diverted to the southern front, so he was to leave Hyoen. The idea was the he was to leave his family behind and go off to die, perhaps on Truk Atoll or in Luzon or maybe even Taiwan. However, since he was a member of a special company, he was to be left behind with a rearguard unit that would probably face the Soviet army.

Fourteen years had passed from the time he first donned a uniform to the time he committed suicide. This pretty much corresponded exactly with the time from the outbreak of the Manchurian Incident to unconditional surrender. It is as though in choosing a military career he knew that his final destination was an appointment with death.

He might have died at the southern front or died of illness (or starvation) on the battlefield or maybe even drowned in the ocean when his troopship was sunk. It was even possible that he would be killed fighting the Soviets. But there are many things unclear about his decision to die with his wife and children. We never really understood what his wife and children were doing with him so near the front. But amid circumstances in which avoiding death would be difficult, perhaps their decision to die together as a family made some sense. After his death, my uncle never once appeared to me in my dreams. . . .

Japanese people were completely unprepared for the reversal of fortunes that was brought about when people who had formerly been rulers in another country were now defeated. They were without a plan. But still it seemed that their quality of life determined the nature of their experience of defeat. . . .

The war was over. At the time, we did not know how disastrously things had gone at home; thanks to the Allied bombings, we were returning to a Japan that was thoroughly burned out. . . . Like my parents, I wasn't particularly stricken with homesickness for Japan, but I felt I was obligated to return home, so I felt as though I was in suspended animation. At the instant I learned of our defeat in war, I fell into a kind of daze, entering a life without much focus after I realized—very seriously—that the "divine winds" had not come to save us. Besides having an instinctual fear of being violated, I became a girl whose heart was basically not moved by anything. Since crying on August 15, 1945, the day the war ended, at the ceremony disbanding the corps of volunteer apprentice army nurses, when everyone was crying as the army doctors and nurses were saying goodbye to the sanitation workers, I had forgotten how to cry. . . .

We lived this way, as refugees, for four months from April to August.

The latrine was built in sight of where we boiled our water. In the same area where there had been a cholera outbreak, the patient's dirty clothes were thrown away. They covered them with lime, but there were still plenty of flies around. It was impossible not to feel frightened. But there was no other place to prepare our daily meals. . . .

I recall one day when I was having a particularly heavy menstrual flow and I went into the latrine. It was a flush toilet. Mr. S came back from somewhere outside and knocked on the toilet door with the light on. I was the only one at home. Since I didn't want to have to leave the bathroom with a strong scent of menstrual blood, I made sounds with my mouth to simulate a bowel movement and Mr. S left.

That was the last time I had my period in Manchuria. Having started my period in the fall of 1945, it was really painful to go through this in a place where you had no privacy. I worried about getting my period in a place like that. But fortunately I was spared from having my period further until we left. . . .

When Japanese people hear the term *refugee*, they undoubtedly think of other people in some faraway country. However, fifty years ago, some Japanese, reaping the seeds that they had sowed, became refugees themselves. They were saved by the compassion of people from other nations.

In our case, after we got back to Japan, things were all right. So I do not need to write about the hardships of our postrepatriation days. How do the people feel who were oppressed by Japanese, who were forcibly removed from their lands and their homes? And how about the workers and the comfort women who died, people who wanted to return to their homes but could not? It has taken them more than fifty years to rebuild their lives. How do we answer these people who would want to drag up and revisit the past?

I have no desire to hear people claim that they are young and had nothing to do with the war. All Japanese people who have lived in the Shôwa period are involved. A Japan that cannot confront its own history honestly and without deceit will never be able to graduate from its own past. The Nakamura family died out, and the postwar era began for my parents and my two siblings and I. My father died at age fifty-one, and my mother died when she was sixty-four. Now there is just myself and my two siblings. I have already lived longer than my mother. (207–36)

Analysis

Recovery from the trauma of war and defeat is no easy matter, but Japanese women seemed to evince a particularly resilient spirit in rediscovering themselves and "becoming ordinary." All four women discussed here were thoroughly indoctrinated and such loyal imperial daughters right up to the moment of the *gyokuon* broadcast that they never questioned their belief in the sacredness of Japan's mission and the power of the divine winds to save them. Later they were shocked to learn how weak and vulnerable Japan had become. Out of their dismay and bewilderment grew a determination to probe history, reevaluate the present, and establish their agency.

Okabe Itsuko was moved to try and redress the harm she believed she had visited upon her fiancé by placing his story—their very private story—in the public realm. Kunio spoke to her privately, as a lover would, but what he said would have been considered treasonous. She places herself in the narrative not as an innocent but as a murderess, an aggressor, a destroyer of something good in the world. One lasting image she imprints on the minds of her readers is of her waving Kunio off to war with a little rising-sun flag in her hand. Many Japanese did this time and time again, and so we may conjecture that there were many other stories like Itsuko's. But then again perhaps not, because there do not appear to have been very many Japanese males quite like young Kimura Kunio. At any rate, Okabe confesses not in order to expiate but in order to teach. She wants readers to learn from her mistake. But in the moment she confesses and brands herself a murderess, she launches an assault on the entire prewar regime of thought.

Yoshitake Teruko was stunned by the message delivered in that "jeweled voice," so distraught that all she could do initially was retreat into sleep. But it did not take long for her to emerge from her somnolence and realize that defeat meant that the days of the imperial "hierarchical system of discrimination" were numbered. This in turn meant that there was a tremendous opportunity for Japanese women to remake themselves. As she writes, "[D]efeat in the war was for Japanese women the beginning of a new life." Hence her primary textual strategy is to weave her own personal narrative in and around the story of women's movements, the story of women becoming engaged in political and social activism as a path toward establishing one's identity and subjectivity. The postwar years began in a shockingly difficult way for this young woman when she was gang-raped by American GIs. But the women's liberation movement offered her both solace and a pathway to recovery. There she found the voice and the vocabulary to name her dilemma, and the cultural space she needed to come to grips with the jarring and deeply disturbing experience of sexual violation. Speaking and writing about her experiences—bringing them into language—made it possible for her to discover her own subjectivity and thereby reclaim her historical agency.

Shinya Eiko speaks directly to the process of becoming ordinary, becoming human again. She was shocked to discover what an unthinking imperial subject she had become. Owen Evans "mapped the contours of oppression" in his study of recent German autobiographical treatments of the past and found that the need of "totalitarian regimes . . . to mould a new consciousness and recast the relationship between the individual and the State" left citizens with psychological gaps and even wounds that needed to be addressed, and autobiographical narratives were a useful tool in the process of recovery.[28] Shinya discovered her path to recovery in performance art. By portraying onstage the lives of women who had suffered a great deal more than she had, she created the opportunity to transcend national, cultural, and ethnic boundaries. She stood before crowds—some small, some large—night after night, depicting the inhumanity of discrimination against Korean Japanese and *buraku* women. Her voice and body spoke directly to her audience, and in writing and delivering her lines, she was able to discover her own subjectivity and repair and reconstitute her identity. By dealing directly with topics from Japan's past, she was likewise able to assert her historical agency. What drove Shinya Eiko to seek transcendence of war, as well as of national and ethnic boundaries, was her unflagging desire to demonstrate that, in the end, "people are all people." It may be a simple truth but one that many in our world still struggle to comprehend and embrace. She also constructed a new motto for herself, one that became her mantra: *see with your own eyes and speak from your own heart.* If postwar Japanese could learn to do this, they would have taken the first step toward becoming historical agents.

Finally, for Sawachi Hisae, the moment of defeat exposed the hypocrisy of Japanese militaristic adventurism and transformed the former colonial masters into refugees stripped not only of their belongings but of their status and identity as well. She writes of being a refugee. Her textual strategy is to characterize herself as an outsider seeking to find her way home. Given that she spent most of her youth in Manchuria, recovery for Sawachi entailed coming to understand the Manchurian Incident, the historical moment that launched Japan on its long road to war, and to come to grips with the forces that drove someone like her father to leave Japan for Manchuria in the 1930s. Sawachi's bitterness about the lies and fictions of prewar and wartime Japanese ideology is a palpable force in her text. The once vaunted Kwantung Army was redeployed elsewhere, leaving unprotected the civilian population that it had placed in danger in the first place. She witnessed troops deserting and officers shedding their uniforms in order to save their own lives. Sawachi shed some tears on August 15 but never again; she was still very young, but circumstances forced her to "forget" how to cry. Her family and her countrymen had been abandoned. "I was very afraid. I felt like I had no country. We had to face reality by ourselves," she writes. She depicts the squalid conditions in which they had to live while awaiting repatriation, such as having to prepare meals not far from the latrine. Privacy was limited, and she even refers to the embarrassment of experiencing a particularly heavy menstrual flow during her final month before repatriation as if to say that she was leaving part of her essence behind in this land, which Japan had once subjugated and ruled.

The whole experience took a toll on her family and that is what she wants readers to take away from her text. Her uncle and his family committed suicide together in Korea, and her parents died rather young. As she puts it, the Nakamura family died out. But her look at the end of the war is unflinching, and she will not accept the excuse of younger people who did not live through the war years that they bear no responsibility for what transpired. She asks something difficult of her younger readers: do not confuse ignorance with innocence. History is there to tell a story, and all the generations, whether born in the Shôwa period or afterward, have an obligation to come to grips with it. It is not simply a matter of those who cannot remember the past being condemned to repeat it. Rather, it is a warning that those who refuse to immerse themselves in their own history may be unable to find the ground on which to construct their subjectivity and historical agency. In recalling her experiences as a young refugee, the daughter of a defeated nation-state, Sawachi begins the process of bringing the past into language in the only way she can: by narrating the story of the "Shôwa that [she] lived."

2

CONTEXTUALIZING HISTORY

YOSHITAKE TERUKO'S "ONNATACHI NO UNDÔSHI—WATAKUSHI NO IKITA SENGO"

By integrating her personal narrative with the story of what was taking place in the larger social and political world around her, Yoshitake Teruko effectively contextualizes her memoir, translated as *A History of Women's Movements—and My Experience of the Postwar Years*, within a narrative of the history of postwar Japanese women's movements. Her assumption is that the actions, events, and discourses in which she participated can best be understood if we can grasp what William H. Sewell calls the "logics of history." "We cannot know," he writes, "what an act or an utterance means and what its consequences might be without knowing the semantics, the technologies, the conventions—in brief, the logics—that characterize the world in which the action takes place"[1] The result is a narrative that touches on many of the movements that attracted and mobilized Japanese women in the postwar period: the League to Acquire Women's Right to Participate in Politics, the Women's Democratic Club, the Federation of Housewives, the Assembly of Mothers, and the Japan Federation of Women's Organizations. Yoshitake also mentions the Zengakuren (Zen-Nihon Gakusei Jichikai Sôrengô or the All-Japan Federation of Student Self-Governing Associations), the radical student group located on college campuses, which she joined; the tumultuous Ampo struggle; and, finally, the women's lib movement of 1970. Interspersed with these stories are more personal accounts of her education, her college years, her entry into the workplace, and her involvement with women's groups and women's issues throughout her career.

Her narrative, then, moves back and forth between objective descriptions of political and social movements, as well as the historical context in which they were situated, and the deeply personal, subjective passages, which reveal the narrator struggling to create some sort of ground on which she can integrate her experiences of the world—the world in which she both stands and writes—and generate a new identity and subjectivity in which a sense of historical agency can be rooted. In this chapter, I open with her account of the early postwar initiatives to acquire the right to participate in politics for Japanese women, but the reader should recall that the first five pages of Yoshitake's chapter 1 were introduced in the previous chapter, so the excerpt below begins in a later subsection.

The End of the War and Women's Participation in Politics: Ichikawa Fusae as a Pioneer

The earliest initiative to be organized in the years immediately following the defeat was the Committee for Postwar Women's Policies. The leadership was provided by Ichikawa Fusae.

In 1924 Ichikawa Fusae organized the League for the Acquisition of Women's Right to Political Participation (later known for short as Fusen kakutoku dômei), and ever since she was selected as its executive director; for sixteen years, she led the movement to acquire political rights for women. But, in 1940, Ichikawa suddenly dissolved the league and joined the All Japan Women's Association, which was under the umbrella of the right-wing political association, and went to work as the executive director of the All Japan Association to Limit Freedom of Speech. She claimed that it was in order to cause women's abilities to be recognized with the aim of acquiring the right to political participation within the framework of national policy. This approach resulted later in the expulsion of some public officials from office. But in her autobiography, there is not a single word of reflection or explanation of this wartime defection.

[F]or Ichikawa Fusae, who burned with a passion for establishing women's political rights, the Potsdam Declaration, which she had read, convinced her that it was essential for the occupation forces to grant women the right to actively participate in politics. No doubt, having worked for so many years in the movement, she probably felt strongly that rather than being given this right, Japanese women should take it for themselves. So, on the very next day after Japan's defeat was announced, Ichikawa called together like-minded people such as Yamataka Shigeri, Kawasaki Natsu, Akamatsu Tsuneko, Yamamuro Tamiko, Miyawaki Sumako, Senbongi Michiko, Ôno Kiku, and Muraoka Hanako, and on September 24, 1945, the political subcommittee on the acquisition of political rights for women drafted a petition under the supervision of Executive Director Ichikawa Fusae.

After the cabinet of Prince Higashikuni Naruhiko fell, the Shidehara Cabinet received the petition, and the next day, after the decision was made at the cabinet meeting on October 11, 1945, GHQ issued its revolutionary order to liberate Japanese women, permit the organization of labor unions, liberalize education, and democratize the economy, with MacArthur specifically saying, "Give Japanese women the right of political participation."

So technically the right of Japanese women to participate in politics was something granted by the occupation authorities, but, in reality, we can also say that it was the result of Japanese women taking matters into their own hands and demanding this right. The October 13 announcement by the Shidehara Cabinet that Japanese women would have the right to participate in politics went into effect on December 27. (5–7)

Exercising the Right to Political Participation for the First Time, April 10, 1946

When the Lower House passed the reform of the election law on December 25, and it became law on December 27, it meant that the right of political participation for which Japanese women had been yearning for so many years had finally been granted. That this came about was due in part to the push for democratization coming from GHQ, but also from the fervent demand by Japanese women for this right, which had been steadily growing in intensity with each passing day. . . .

The first opportunity that women had to exercise their newfound right was during the year following Japan's defeat on April 10, 1946, a day that should go down as a pivotal moment in Japanese history. On that day, even though I was just fifteen years old, I dragged my mother—who never liked to go anywhere—to the polling place; I was not about to stop crying unless she came along with me.

In the yard outside the school that served as a polling place, I could see lots of young women like myself there, even though we were too young to vote. This was probably because we young people could not help but shudder at the prospect that women like our mothers, who did not really appreciate how important a single vote could be, needed to know that "If you do not exercise this important right, then the status of women is likely to revert to what is was in the prewar period." I could not help but feel an intense passion well up inside me as I watched women filing into the voting booths right alongside men. I thought, "Today, a new pathway to the future is being opened, one that is very different from the path that women had taken in the previous era." Many politicians of that day overlooked the position that Japanese women were now able to occupy. Moreover, they underestimated the commitment of many women to avoid walking on the same path that our mothers had trod.

So the commitment of women to get involved, and their daughters' resolve not to live their lives the same way their mothers had, no doubt increased the rate of voter turnout among women. The number of women voters at that time was around 21,500,000. On election day, 13,760,000 women, or nearly 67 percent of eligible women, turned out and voted.

The final number of women candidates in the election was eighty-three. Among them, thirty-nine, or 45 percent, were elected. Those numbers remain the highest on record right down to today. . . .

Women, motivated as they were by a strong resolve not to return to the past, and entrusted with the vote for the first time, were all of one mind. Whether they were voting themselves or exhorting others to vote, they burned with an intense passion to stand up and participate in politics in order to build something out of the ashes of defeat in war. (7–9)

The Encounter between Ethel Weed and Japanese Women

One of the people who played a significant role in unleashing the wave of the women's democratic movement was Lt. Ethel Weed of the Civil Information and Education section of GHQ. After graduating from college, this feminist activist was determined to play a positive role in advancing the cause of liberating Japanese women. In order to gather opinions for the purpose of forming an effective policy toward Japanese women, she immediately asked Kato Shidzue and Hani Setsuko to her office.

At one point, when the three of them were talking, she wanted to know why the vast majority of Japanese women had blindly cooperated with the aims of an aggressive war without expressing even the slightest doubt. And she also delivered a serious critique of the Women's Patriotic Association and the National Women's Defense Association. She further argued persuasively that if Japanese women were committed to never going down the same path again, there must be an awakening of a fundamental awareness of human rights, and that one by one, they should establish as soon as possible a women's democratic movement rooted in individual autonomy. Present on that day and acting as interpreter was Matsuoka Yôko, along with support from Kato Shidzue and Hani Setsuko, and together they formed the nucleus of a new women's democratic movement.

Kato, Matsuoka, and Hani were soon joined by Miyamoto Yuriko, Sata Ineko, Yamamoto Sugi, Akamatsu Tsuneko, and Yamamuro Tamiko so that before we knew it these eight key figures were launching a new movement. With these eight women as the core, preparatory meetings were frequently held with the result that on December 10, 1945, the movement finally took shape and was called the Women's Democratic Club. (10–11)

An epochal moment in postwar history occurred on December 25, 1946, when the Association to Protect Women was established after a shocking incident took place. One evening, on November 15, near Ikebukuro Station in Tokyo, two female employees of Nippon Eiga were suddenly arrested off the streets on their way home and taken to Yoshiwara Hospital, where they were forced to undergo a medical examination. This kind of treatment, which was justified in the name of protecting American soldiers from venereal disease, was now beginning to be extended to ordinary women. I think we could say that the existence of these kinds of sexual issues with American troops marked the beginning of a dark episode in postwar Japanese women's history.

On August 15, 1945, in anticipation of the arrival of the first occupation forces, people in the Tokyo and Kanagawa areas fell into a total panic. Wild rumors to the effect that "All the men will be sterilized and forced into hard physical labor while the women will violated" circulated freely. The governor of Kanagawa Prefecture, Fujiwara Takao, went so far as to grant a three-month severance package to all female employees and urged them to flee to the countryside. The municipal offices for Yokohama and Yokosuka soon followed suit. Neighborhood associations were even posting notices ordering females to evacuate. Young women were being told to darken their faces with soot and cut their hair short like a boy, while older women were being urged to evacuate.

After August 16, the evacuation of women intensified, and the transportation ministry was even planning for special trains from Shinjuku and Ueno stations on which women could ride for free. Newspapers repeatedly ran announcements warning women to dress in *monpe* (cotton trousers) or their air raid shelter uniforms. At the time, I was staying in Yamanashi Prefecture with my mother and older and younger sisters, where we had been evacuated, and following our father's warnings, we delayed our return to Tokyo by three months.

Claiming that it was acting to protect Japanese women from sexual assault by American troops, the Higashikuni Cabinet established "facilities near the bases of occupation forces for the safeguarding of women." On August 18, a cabinet order was issued to establish such a facility. On August 26, a special Recreation and Amusement Association was created, and a month later it became known as the RAA. Prostitutes who worked at the RAA were dubbed the Special Volunteer Corps. The RAA, which was really nothing more than a gift of Japanese women's sexuality from the vanquished to the victors, symbolized the ugly side of Japanese men's sexual consciousness—after all, these were the men who had declared bombastically during the war that "the soldiers of a strong army will by definition commit rape" and had gone ahead and created practice of ensconcing comfort women to service Japanese troops in the field.

So the existence of the RAA could hardly become a successful barricade to protect Japanese women. Beginning with the rape incident that occurred in Yokosuka, rapes became a regular occurrence. (11–13)

On March 9, 1947, in the People's Square (as it came to be known after the creation of the Society to Protect Women) outside the imperial palace, more than a thousand women gathered to celebrate International Women's Day. Under such banner slogans as "Let us get rid of this corrupt government, which cannot control the black market or inflation, and start to enjoy a bright and pleasant life" and "Let us destroy all the restraints that enslave women and make their lives miserable," and while singing "Unite the World in a Circle of Flowers," these women marched and sent a message of solidarity to the International Democratic Women's League. International Women's Day had to overcome numerous obstacles, but it has continued right down to the present day. The Women's Democratic Club has always been at the core of these celebrations. There is no doubt that this is a testimony to how significant the women's democratic movement was to the development of the women's movement in Japan. (14–15)

It is important for Yoshitake to begin her narrative with a recapitulation of the story of how Japanese women secured political rights in the immediate aftermath of the war. She asserts that despite the role played by the occupation authorities, Japanese women did step up and assert their claim to the vote. Also Yoshitake makes the point that young girls of her generation were determined to see their mothers exercise their franchise because they did not want to see things revert to what they had been during the prewar period. One of the other significant transformations of the early years of the occupation was educational reform and how it affected women. Yoshitake takes up that part of the story in section 3 of her chapter 1.

Women begin no longer putting up with insults

One of the most valuable treasures that Japanese women received after Japan's defeat was "equal rights for men and women in education." In the prewar period, the differences between men and women were taken to be a matter of blood, that is, it was believed that men had, from the moment of birth, superior blood running through their veins while women's blood was inferior, so that no matter how much women might try they could never become like men. Whether it was from the viewpoint of the entire educational system or from the content of textbooks, women were thoroughly discriminated against. As for higher education, with the exception of Tôhoku University and perhaps one or two others, doors were firmly closed to women.

The gates of Japan's universities were opened to women for the first time on December 4, 1945. On that day, the Ministry of Education, responding to GHQ directives concerning the liberation of women and the democratization of education, proclaimed, "In order to open high schools to Japanese female students, it is important that middle-school education be standardized for males and females and a policy of coeducation established. To this end, the following procedures shall be enacted."

This seemed like a 180-degree turnabout for a Ministry of Education that just six short months ago had been trying to elevate the prewar "good wife, wise mother" approach to education by running around promoting the "mother of a deified soldier" and the "Yasukuni shrine widow"; but GHQ had mandated revolutionary changes in education. Since fanatical militarism and an exclusivist patriotic spirit were the dominant characteristics of the prewar Japanese identity, and they supported a premodern system of social hierarchy that would have to be completely swept away if any postwar radical democratic reforms were to take place, radical educational reform would have to be given top priority.

In the first place, an education committee was created to decentralize the educational system, which had been responsible for propagating state-centered nationalistic ideology from the center to the local areas. Then the old-style educational system, which separated boys and girls and reinforced social distinctions and rank order, had to be replaced with the new 6-3-3 system, which offered a single educational track with equal opportunity for all.

In March of 1947, the Fundamental Law of Education (Kyôiku kihonnhô) and the School Education Law (Gakkô kyôikuhô) were promulgated. In April, under the auspices of the new educational system, new primary and middle schools were established. Then, at an astoundingly rapid pace, the education revolution was set in motion. . . . My postwar democratic education began in the burned-out ruins of Tokyo, where all the passages dealing with militarism and discrimination against women were being stricken from the textbooks by marking them out with black ink. These were actually wonderful, exuberant days for me! . . .

July 15, 1948, an Educational Commission charged with democratizing education was established, the Education Committee Law was passed, men and women had equal rights to participate in elections and were eligible to stand for election as well. First, on January 15, 1949, Education Committee members were elected from the five major urban centers and the prefectures, and 38 women were elected. In 1952, some 850 Education Committee members were elected from urban areas, wards, and villages. But in 1956, the Education Committee members became appointed, and gradually the road to democratized education was increasingly obstructed. (19–22)

Prospectus for a New Educational System for Women

The issuance of the order to create an outline for a new educational system for women, while it was directed toward scholarship and learning, undoubtedly gave great encouragement and courage to women who had previously been jettisoned by the educational system. On April 22, 1946, the first three women passed the entrance exam to enter the economics department at the University of Tokyo, and by May the entrance figure for all departments was eighteen female students, something that became a topic of considerable discussion.

I was definitely one of those people who were moved and inspired when I saw the photographs in the newspaper of the smiling faces of these young women, blooming like large roses, brimming with pride, confidence, and enthusiasm as they walked through the gates of this great university, shoulder to shoulder with the male students, entering an arena that had been closed to women for so long.

I believe that there were many women who directly experienced the reality of their own lives being improved because there were women in the previous generation who, when given an opportunity, rose to the occasion and took advantage of it. I believe it meant that we postwar women, who survived these years, could embrace a robust and flexible kind of frontier spirit that saw these opportunities as not just there for somebody but there for us to take advantage of. (22–23)

There follows a brief section on Beatte Sirota and her role in dismantling the patriarchal *ie* system and creating the new constitution. I resume with excerpts from chapter 2 that discuss the role of Oku Mumeo and the Japan Housewives Association.

The Founding of Shufuren

September 15, 1948, is when the movement that took a large rice paddle as its symbol, known for short as Shufuren, or the Federation of Housewives, began. The food shortages that occurred immediately after Japan's defeat were really a continuation of what people had put up with during the war. Burned out of our own house and forced to live in a relative's two-mat room on the second floor of a salaryman's home, we obviously did not have the resources to buy any black market goods; we had to make do with two small portions of rationed rice to feed a family of five. There were also continuing poor harvests so that people in the large metropolitan areas lacked basic staple foods and would have to eat things, like potatoes and cornflour, that other people were throwing away. Sometimes we would even have to eat crystal sugar that was infested with insects in place of regular staple foods. So if there was a late postal delivery or we had to wait for the next mail, we young children would have to go around starving with our stomachs empty. My younger brother, who was five years old at the time the Japan Federation of Women was started, was probably afflicted with tuberculosis as he became incredibly thin.

Amid these food shortages, it is not surprising that the anger and indignation of housewives boiled over when, in order to survive, they had to indulge in a "bamboo shoot existence," which meant they had to sell their clothing and household goods in order to purchase necessary foodstuffs to stave off starvation.[2]

On August 24 of that same year, some 15,000 housewives from Katsuhika Ward in Tokyo rushed into four distribution centers and sat down with a strong show of force. Meanwhile, representatives of some 2,000 women rushed to the ward office and demanded to speak directly to the head of the ward. After being made to wait for a very long time, they were able to obtain 300 grams per person of rice and dried bread. Again on September 6, 500 housewives set out for city offices to negotiate and were soon successful in receiving additional distributions of food to some 55,000 households within the ward.

That year, the salaries of the lowest-paid public employees went from a low salary base of 1,800 yen in January to 2,920 in March, then to 3,700 yen in May, 5,300 in November, and finally 6,370 in December. From this, it is pretty easy to gauge how severe inflation was at that time. By the way, the price of rice on the black market in February was 200 yen for 1.8 liters, and the prices for other goods were skyrocketing, which meant that the pressure on household budgets just continued to mount. Under these circumstances, the housewives who stood up demanding better access to staple foods were not about to be deterred, and there were even occasions when, fearing an outbreak of violence, armed policemen intercepted them on their way to remonstrate with government officials.

Women even came frequently in large numbers to Oku Mumeo's office, a member of the Upper House of Councillors, to demand that food staples be made more available and that policies be implemented to lower prices. Oku Mumeo had been born in Fukui in 1895, and after graduating from Japan Women's University, she developed a strong interest social and labor problems during the height of the Taishô Democracy Movement. After responding to a request from Hiratsuka Raichô, she took part in the founding of the New Women's Association (Shin fujin kyôkai) in 1920. She poured all her energies into amending the Public Police Safety Law, an endeavor in which she was ultimately successful.[3] In 1923, she formed an organization for working women and published a journal called *Shokugyô Fujin* (later *Fujin undô*), and for many years she continued as an activist advocating for working women, even establishing "settlement houses" for women. She took this same energy and commitment and applied them to making inroads for women in the political world. . . . Oku was concerned about the lack of women's groups that made everyday problems their central concern, and she was willing to take on the leadership of the Federation of

Housewives in order to address the problems facing housewives.

In the inaugural issue of the official organ of the Federation of Housewives, called *Shufurendayori,* which appeared on December 5, 1948, the lead article, "A Pleasant Battle," made clear the federation's character and the aims of its policies. The following is an abbreviated version of the inaugural statement.

> *The greatest success of the Federated Housewives' movement to date has been the establishment of a pipeline into government officialdom so that the voice of female consumers can be heard in quarters that have heretofore been reserved for business elites only. Let us raise our voices and loudly proclaim* the *difficulties that we are facing in our daily lives. This deeply rooted movement is aimed at responding to our rights being trampled upon. All the pain and frustration that many thousands of women have experienced in these very difficult circumstances after Japan's defeat in war lead us to unite and stand up for our rights.*
>
> *The Federation of Housewives is a cooperative organization formed for the purpose of uniting women around issues directly connected to our daily lives. Let us join together as one and raise our voices boldly in order to protect our livelihood.*
>
> *Let us also work joyously in order to establish a bright and positive life. Whether it is in the cities or the countryside, we want to have chapters of the Federation of Housewives formed far and wide. I also believe that our federation should become an organization that advocates the lowering of prices and the enhancement of the value and importance of housewives. . . .*

Under the leadership of chairwoman Oku Mumeo, who was determined to expand the reach of the organization, housewives took to the streets. For twenty full days, from morning to night, women boarded trucks and made the rounds of the squares and public spaces in front of railroad stations, and under clear blue skies proclaimed the inauguration of the Federation of Housewives.

> *"Laborers in the kitchen! Housewives! Let us all band together and leave no one out!"*

All this passion and energy was bound to mobilize people. This Federation of Housewives, which was born in the center of Tokyo, had, in a very short time, propelled itself forward and developed branches throughout the entire nation. This was precisely the right time to move, and this is how the All Japan Federation of Housewives came into being.

Food May Day

The organization of women teachers into a single unified body would have to wait for the formation of the Japan Teacher's Union, known as Nikkyôsô, in June 1947. Prior to the formation of Nikkyôsô, there were two national organizations in place, the All Japan Teacher's Union Cooperative, and the All Japan League of Teachers. They were responsible for carrying forward the postwar labor movement to eliminate hunger, which spread like a wildfire. Specifically, female workers who had been inspired by GHQ's order to liberate Japanese women participated in the labor movement enthusiastically. Women's branches of labor unions began to be formed one after another, and local women also joined hands and protested against the food and commodity shortages.

On May 19, 1946, three hundred thousand people jammed the square in front of the imperial palace and inaugurated the People's Assembly to Obtain Rice, known for short as "Food May Day." They called for ordinary people to manage food distribution and were resolved that a truly democratic government featuring a place for both Communist and Socialist Party representatives be established. One after another woman with an infant strapped to her back mounted the podium and protested the food shortages, and, bolstered by support from the women labor organizers, women issued desperate pleas for the distribution of milk to young children, food to schoolchildren, and increased nutrition to pregnant women. It was this Food May Day that helped bring about a substantial bond between female laborers and local women.

On January 1, 1947, Prime Minister Yoshida, who was fearful of close ties developing between the labor movement and the people, criticized one group of labor leaders as "a lawless gang." The labor leaders, who were determined to confront this challenge to the labor movement by the government, immediately started to organize an General Strike for February 1, which would involve all public and private employees across the board. On January 28, the appeal went out to workers from all across Japan to join the General Strike, topple the Yoshida Cabinet, and convene an emergency national assembly to help overcome the current crisis.

Meanwhile, the current level of inflation seemed to know no bounds. A female teacher who had spent many years on the job would receive an average end-of-year payment of 280 yen, but if she were to go out and buy some sugar or daikon radish, she would soon find that she had used all her money up. In addition, the metropolitan rice ration came in eight-day portions. This was the only way to stave off starvation. Conditions were so desperate that if they did not do this, people would be dying of starvation one by one. So the unions, which were calling for wage increases and better food distribution, naturally earned the sympathy and support of the citizenry because these demands were exactly what each individual citizen needed. Would there be any way to interfere with the General Strike, which had garnered such wide support among the populace?

Women Teachers Lament GHQ's Decision to Ban the General Strike

The Cooperative Council of the All Japan Teacher's Union, known for short as *Zenkyôkyô*, was the organization capable of bringing together 320,000 teachers under the direction of the Central Struggle Committee. The *Kyôzenren* opposed the General Strike. But the women's branch of the Tokyo Metropolitan Teacher's Union—or *Kokkyô*—stood their ground with a strong sense of mission and said they would not abandon the children and pledged to protect the teachers' position even to the death. For nights and days on end, these women worked hard planning for the strike. Naturally, since it was a General Strike, all public transportation would be paralyzed. Among the *Kokkyô* union members, some had bicycles and some did not. Those who did not have bikes decided to spend the night at their schools, and the numbers of people involved were reported to the women's branch of the union. There were even some schools where the teachers were split three ways among prostrike, antistrike, and those who did not really feel strongly. Whether they supported or opposed the strike, everyone still felt the pressure of the desperate conditions, not knowing whether they would be able to eat or not, so some pointed their fingers at supporters of the General Strike, calling them "Reds," while others were ridiculed for being government toadies. Under these kinds of circumstances, where it seemed that bloodshed was likely to ensue, some union members were unable to withstand the pressure and defected.

On January 31, the day before the General Strike was to go into effect, General MacArthur himself announced the order that GHQ was canceling the strike. The head of the strike committee, Mr. Ii, heard the news of the strike's cancellation in the middle of the night. When the women teachers heard the profound sadness in his voice, they could not help but break down and cry as well.

For me, this was a shocking event because I had believed with certainty that the General Strike would be carried out. Urban trains were plastered with signs on the sides, declaring, in bold letters, "Carry Out the Strike, Get Rid of Hunger!" One would see the same slogans on banners at the post office; in fact, these signs were ubiquitous all over Tokyo. At the girls school that I was attending, they had decided to close the school on February 1. Anxious to see what would happen, I had been eagerly anticipating and looking forward to this day. This is because I had fully embraced the notion that this revolution—being carried out, as it was, not from above by GHQ but by the Japanese people themselves—would radically transform Japan and bring an end to the era of chaos and confusion. But this dream was smashed to bits by just one word from MacArthur when he canceled the strike. On this fateful day, we could not fail to recognize that, in the end, just like Sun Wukong from the Chinese tale *Journey to the West*, when he was being held in the palm of Kannon's hand, our very existence was firmly in the hands of the occupation forces. Even a relatively removed third party such as myself could not fail to realize that all of us were subject to the maelstrom of the occupying authority's substantial pressure. (30–43)

For many of the women whose narratives are featured in *Changing Lives*, a note of disappointment is sounded whenever the hopes and ideals of postwar democracy are chipped away or left unrealized. Yoshitake's chapter 3, "Things Taken from Us by Force during the Korean War," discusses the idea that the onset of the Korean War and Japan's support of the United States thrust Japan into the middle of the Cold War and therefore represented a decisive blow against the ideal of a postwar pacifist Japan. But her narrative here becomes more personal as she discusses her admittance and entrance to a prestigious Japanese private university, a privilege denied women in the prewar era.

Gaining Admission to the Literature Department at Keiô University

In April 1950, overflowing with hopes and dreams, I took my first steps toward being a college student at Keiô University. Although my parents hoped that I would abandon the idea, I forged ahead and was accepted by the literature department. On the day I received word that I had been admitted to the university, I was on a night train on my way back to Nagoya where my family was living. My father, who had received the "Cherry Blossom Blooms" telegram and knew that I had been admitted to Keiô, was sitting there respectfully as he ceremoniously placed a thick brown envelope on the table in front of me. "All of a sudden you are going to need money for your entrance fees, your class enrollment costs, as well as your room and board. This envelope contains the money you will need. From the beginning, I was not very fond of the idea of a woman attending university, therefore I am not *giving* you this money. It is a loan. Please take the time to read and sign the loan papers for me." In my father's voice I could hear resonating the rigid, stubborn streak of a Meiji man. Since this was the first time in my whole life that my father had ever treated me like an autonomous individual, I was very happy. But I also felt quite nervous. I can still remember that day just as though it were yesterday, how thrilled I felt when I grabbed the loan papers and signed them without hesitating, Yoshitake Teruko.

On the day of the university entrance ceremony, I passed through the university gate by myself and slowly made my way up Mita Hill. Here and there, one could see a few female students mixed in with the males. These female students who had to break down the negative stereotype that women who pursue scholarship will somehow be unhappy actually looked forward to this day as they embraced a sense of common purpose and solidarity with other women. Meeting their gazes, I could not keep from wearing a big smile on my face, something equivalent to a suppressed cheer. Since the other women probably felt that we shared a similar way of seeing things, they returned my smile with equal cheerfulness.

On both sides of the pathway, male students were lined up, calling out to the female students, vying for their attention. They were recruiting for the various "circles" or activity clubs. Since we females were in such a minority, they seemed to be making a substantial effort to persuade us to join their circle. If it is a buyers' market, then the buyers have the right to choose.

At the top of the hill there was a large cherry tree, and standing underneath the canopy of fully blooming cherry blossoms stood a lanky young man holding his lunch in his hand, lost in thought. He showed no indication of being a violent type of person, and as I approached him he mumbled something, hemmed and hawed, and handed his lunch to me. When I looked at the lunch box, it was an invitation to join the university theater group.

My guess was that these were young people who had spent many long years feeling incapable of expressing themselves adequately and were now seeking to liberate themselves from their dark past. In the midst of this age of confusion, and seeking to find a place in society that would affirm their existence, these young people had thrown themselves into the theater movement. Anyway, this is what I came to understand after I had joined the theater club. The first thing that drew me to the theater club was seeing this skinny, stalklike young guy who was dispatched to recruit for the club. I intuited that if these were the kinds of students in the club then there was not likely to be a lot of strongly pious types involved.

Anyway, this cheerful young scout for the club hurried me off to the gym right away. In the middle of this big classroom, with all the desks and chairs pushed off to one side, the members of the theater group were practicing a realistic interpretation of the Camus play *The Just Assassins*. It seems as though they did not have a female student to dress up for the role of the terrorist Maria, so at this stage they still had a male student playing the role. Therefore, it was in these circumstances that, before I knew it, the career of actress Yoshitake Teruko was born!

And from that day forward, I was so busy every day that my head was swimming. In the daytime, we had rehearsals for *The Just Assassins* in between classes. In the evenings, I was working at a Shinbashi cabaret called Showboat, which was located near Tsuchihashi. Trying to balance these three roles, student, actor, and hostess, was exhausting, but I felt so energetic and full of life. Looking back I can be both amazed and thankful for my youth.

It was my first major role, and when I was awarded the top prize for a lead female actress among the university students, I was thrilled, and once again I was made to feel strongly that Japan's defeat in war had been, for women, the most wonderful treasure imaginable. If the prewar education system had continued, wherein women were deemed to be without ability and were spiritually and intellectually shackled by the "good wife, wise mother" educational philosophy, I would never have learned that I had any talent as an actress or that I had any ability at all. Instead, I would have no doubt proceeded with timid and hesitant steps forward lamenting my lack of talent and ability all the way.

Moreover, I would not have had the space to learn to appreciate that both men and women can be vehicles for cultural expression. Also I believe that peace and democracy had a role to play in enabling us, through the theater, to shine some light on the ways in which men and women live, and the connections they develop, so that when people tried to trample on our rights, or deny us the experience of peace and democracy, I was able to stand my ground and express a decisive "No!"

On June 25, at the public lecture hall on campus, we performed our play, *The Just Assassins*. The hall was filled to capacity, and the play was well received; the experience brought the actors and the audience together so that after our final performance, the energy among our theater troupe did not dissipate. However, the very next morning, the faces of the students in the drama club, as they gathered in our little room, turned uniformly dark. It was because the newspaper headlines that morning boldly declared that the Korean War had begun. Members of the theater club included many students who had been called up in the final stages of the Pacific War and were sent overseas but fortunately returned home safely and were able to resume their studies. Since these young people had experienced war directly, their abhorrence of war was probably even stronger than everyone else's. One student, "O," had been detained in Siberia, and he said in a deeply sad voice:

> *This incident will surely escalate into war. This will be the end of postwar democracy for sure. It seems apparent that the hawks at GHQ who want to turn Japan into their Far East forward base are ascendant. I am sure they will take advantage of this opportunity to reestablish militarism as a priority in Japan, and this will alter the very nature of the state structure.*

I could say nothing but only stare closely and intently at his face as he spoke. It turned out that O's words about the Korean War were prophetic.

Korean and North Korean Troops Open Hostilities

On June 25, 1950, a Sunday, just before dawn, the Korean Peninsula was engulfed in the flames of war. At the thirty-eighth parallel, which subsequently became the border between North and South Korea, North Korean and South Korean troops clashed. It was a conflict that erupted in one small corner of the Far East but eventually expanded to include the introduction of United Nations troops and also troops from the People's Liberation Army in China and would require a full three years to resolve.

During this period, Japan, which had become the base for the UN troops, benefited from an influx of foreign capital funds as part of what was called "special procurements" (*tokuju*), which, coupled with the Dodge Deflationary Policy, swept aside in one easy motion the economic stagnation that had been plaguing Japan and laid the foundations for the subsequent era of high-speed economic growth. But also, as O had predicted, the predecessor of the Self-Defense Forces, the National Police Reserves, was established and the process of remilitarization began.

The Korean War dragged out over a long period, and North Korea was blamed for starting it. At that time, MacArthur wanted to change American Far Eastern policy, and he was especially hoping for a new Taiwan policy in order to isolate China. I imagine that he was thinking about a joint defense perimeter involving Japan, Korea, and Taiwan.

America from the outset had placed emphasis on Korea as a base for its Far Eastern policy, continuing to exercise economic, material, military, and psychological influence over all aspects of Korean life. America's influence over Korea just before the outbreak of the Korean War was virtually absolute.

It is really difficult to discern which side may have actually initiated the war, but it was a conflict that, in terms of the escalation of the ideological hostility between East and West, was bound to occur.

Hiratsuka Raichô Calls for Peace and Disarmament

With the outbreak of the Korean conflict, the first people to fully appreciate its real dangers and start acting on those concerns were Japanese women. The Japanese government was eager to conclude a separate peace with the United States. However, most women who desired peace in their hearts felt that in this atmosphere of escalating East-West conflict it was not time for a separate peace, but a comprehensive peace, including numerous countries but especially China and the Soviet Union.

On the very next day after the outbreak of hostilities, June 26, the senior leader of the women's movement, Hiratsuka Raichô, joined four other women, Ueno Yayoiko, Uemura Tamaki, Gauntlett Tsune, and Jodai Tano, to issue the following declaration: "We hereby resolve to protect to the bitter end the commitment established in Japan's constitution to eliminate armaments and war." In so doing, they created a "Petition by Japanese Women concerning the Problem of Concluding a Peace," and they decided to hand a copy of the petition directly to Secretary of State Dulles, who was visiting Japan at that time.

Hiratsuka Raichô, who was in her mid-sixties at the time, published a brief article on July 29, 1950, in the *Women's Democratic Newspaper* entitled "An Unarmed Peace."[4] It said, in part:

> In the end, we need to preserve our neutrality. This is how we can preserve the peace. The principle is deeply engraved upon my heart, and that is why I want to launch this movement. Of course, we fully recognize that to be caught between two worlds and to resist choosing either side is not easy. . . . From here on out, commensurate with the situation in the rest of Asia, there will be a certain amount of acceptance of Japan's rearmament. But, needless to say, this is a violation of the constitution, and since this is all tied up with the war, it means that Japan has lost its neutrality. This is something that we absolutely must oppose. And we need to consider carefully just how we can take a clear stand on a host of other issues and contemplate how to avoid war and preserve peace. Our enemy is war and war only.

Unarmed neutrality is the central underlying principle of our constitution. When I read Hiratsuka's article, which was permeated with her commitment to this fundamental principle, I was still in my teens, and my heart was instantly moved and inspired by her commitment. The fact that I have continued to hold fast to this principle of unarmed neutrality is because, at the time of the Korean conflict, when the Japanese government was poised to cast aside the fundamental principle of the Japanese constitution and start rushing down the road to rearmament, someone like Hiratsuka Raichô was able to courageously express her own beliefs in this short but powerful article. An important starting point for me, I believe that this article constitutes a classic statement of the antiwar and peace position that Japan should embrace. (50–56)

GHQ Initiates the Red Purge

Japan was embarking on the final stages of its postwar democratic era. The winds of the Red Purge (a major sweep of Japanese Communist Party members and its supporters during the U.S. occupation of Japan), which came upon us like a storm, were the harbingers of the death of postwar democracy. The Red Purge clearly reflected GHQ's desire to convert Japan into its base in the Far East, and the Yoshida Cabinet, which was determined to conclude a US-Japan Peace Treaty in order to secure Japan's independence, began to suppress freedom of expression in the leading newspapers and magazines of the day.

In terms of the Korean conflict, the Yoshida Cabinet's policy was to positively assist the United States. In order to make Japan a military outpost in the Far East, at some point a military would again have to become a necessity. An unarmed Japan could hardly be the United States' surrogate in one corner of the Far East capable of keeping an eye on the activities of communist countries.

In a letter dated July 8 (1950), MacArthur instructed Prime Minister Yoshida to create the National Police Reserves (seventy-five thousand men) and the Japan Coast Guard (eight thousand men). With these orders in hand, the National Police Reserves was publicly announced as early as August 10, and on the same day the first unit, with seven thousand police officers, was created.

This sudden movement to the right hit like an avalanche. Lacking the capacity to respond rapidly to such a frontal assault with an effective opposition movement, and given that the energy of the union movement was being decimated by the Red Purge, the overall response to these developments was very sluggish. And thanks to the restrictions on freedom of expression, the public did not have access to accurate information, so they could not muster sufficient energy to mount an opposition movement either.

Nevertheless, a group of women, heeding Hiratsuka Raichô's appeal that young people oppose these developments, poured their energies into the development of an antiwar movement. On July 16, the Women's Policy Bureau of the Socialist Party held an All Japan Women's Policy Conference and came up with the slogan "Protect the Constitution and Popular Independence, Oppose Wars of Invasion and Internal Violence." On this basis, organizations designed to "protect peace" were created in locales throughout Japan, and on October 6, "An Evening of Young Women's Culture" was held, where voices raised against war resounded high into the night sky. On July 17, refusing to buckle under to fierce pressure, the women's section of the Japan Communist Party announced an appeal to all women who love peace.

On August 5, under the auspices of the All Japan Federation of Labor, an "Assembly of Women Activists Committed to Protecting Peace" was convened, and some fifty women representing twenty different organizations attended and pledged cooperation, while on August 14, the young women's section of the National Railway Workers' Union (*Kokutetsu Rôdô Kumiai*, or

Kokurō for short) and the Japan Teachers' Union (*Nikkyōsō*) held a "Peace Celebration" at Yomiuri Hall; a large number of passionate, dedicated union people and democratic women's youth groups participated and strongly expressed their antiwar sentiments. Soon local "Protect Peace" organizations were created everywhere, and these women's passion for peace drove them to embark on a movement to get signatures for the Stockholm Appeal [to ban nuclear weapons].

On university campuses there was also a movement to collect signatures. Since mass meetings and demonstrations on the campuses were being very strictly regulated, I guess you could say that gathering signatures for the Stockholm Appeal seemed like an appropriate way to express a resounding "No!" to the reactionaries. I myself became active collecting signatures. Among the hostesses at the Showboat there were a lot of people who were willing to sign. Many among them were war widows themselves.

The All Japan Widow's Association was launched on November 29, 1950. At that point, there were some 1.8 million widows, and among them, war widows numbered some five hundred thousand. Families in which single mothers were raising young children represented a serious problem in those early days of postwar chaos. Feeling strongly that they needed to organize in order to protect their livelihoods, widow's associations began to appear throughout Japan, and the fact that they were able to pyramid up into a national association was because they took on the character of an organization seeking compensation for widows. Unfortunately though, the Widow's Association was soon co-opted by the government.

However, many of the individual war widows had lost their husbands when they were very young, and so they possessed strong feelings of hatred for war. There were many hostesses like that who took the lead in gathering signatures for the petition. . . . The outbreak of the Korean conflict changed the meaning of peace advocacy in Japan a great deal. Especially for women, this was the first time they were motivated by a strong aversion to seeing their husbands, sons, brothers, and loved ones sent off to war again, and this is why they were engaging in antiwar activities for the first time.

Peace signatures were not only in favor of banning nuclear arms. One could also say that it was a way for Japanese citizens, still under the occupation and therefore unable to express their opposition to the Korean War, to take the first step toward expressing national sentiments against war. On January 10, 1951, starting with the Women's Democratic Club but extending to numerous other women's organizations, a petition calling for peace was sent to the heads of state of many nations. The writer Miyamoto Yuriko drafted the petition, but she passed away on the twenty-first of that same month at the age of fifty-three. Neglecting her own illness and dedicating herself to the peace movement—I wonder how many other women she inspired with her courage.

Prime Minister Ashida Hitoshi, who succeeded Yoshida Shigeru, continued to follow the will of GHQ and push for rearmament. At the time of a speech in Fukuchiyama City, Prime Minister Ashida said, "Japanese women oppose rearmament, so we will proceed secretly." This remark was so inflammatory and confrontational that the angry women's groups presented him with a formal document of protest, which said, in part:

> We Japanese women demand that you make a formal retraction
> {of} the slip of the tongue you made recently and that it be widely
> distributed to the citizenry. Furthermore, Japanese women oppose
> rearmament in favor of peace. And we demand that you dedicate
> your efforts to securing a comprehensive peace with all the countries
> of the world.
>
> Signed

The Japanese Women's Peace Roundtable, the Women's Democratic Club, the League of Japanese Women Workers, the League for the Preservation of Democracy, the Nakano Women's Peace Association, and the Japan Democratic Women's Association.

This is a document that clearly expresses a strong desire for and commitment to peace among Japanese women. The torch of the movement opposing the Korean War continued to be passed from this point forward from woman to woman. (56–59)

Female Students and Zengakuren

The Korean conflict (later War) broke out on June 25, 1950, and with the ceasefire on July 27, 1953, at last entered its final stages. This war, which endured for a full three years, took the lives of many people. When the war broke out the entire population of Korea was around thirty million. They say that approximately three to four million people died. The greatest number of people who died were from North Korea. The number of North Korean civilians who died was more than two million, while some half a million soldiers were killed. On top of that, some one million Chinese soldiers died.

South Korean civilian deaths were approximately 1 million, while some 53,629 Americans lost their lives, and among them 33,629 were killed in combat. Other UN troops, excluding Koreans and Americans, who died in combat numbered 3,194, and of those 686 were English. Other UN troops with high casualty rates included those from Turkey, Greece, and France.

The responses of both parties to this conflict give it its special character. Both sides claimed victory, but in reality both sides believed that they had lost. To be sure, both sides did both win and lose. However, in terms of political and military results, each side's experience was not the same. This war that began as a conflict was, for both the North and South Korean peoples, a calamity from which it was very difficult to recover. The civil war was not something that could be resolved through the efforts of the North and South Korean peoples. Rather, it was something frozen by external forces. Ever since, the Korean people have been divided between North and South with the prospects for conflict ever deepening.

Among the principal countries involved, most consider Japan to be the primary beneficiary of the Korean War. On September 8, 1951, Japan signed a peace treaty with the United States, as well as the US-Japan Security Treaty, and on April 28 of the next year, they went into effect and the abolition of GHQ was announced. On that day, Japan became independent, if in form only. One could say that the fact that Japan was able to sign a peace treaty and achieve independence at a considerably earlier point in time than even the government had imagined was due to the Korean War.

Japan was assigned a significant role in the Korean War by America. For the American military, Japan was an indispensable territorial base, and airfields began to dot the countryside of the Japanese archipelago. [General Matthew] Ridgway was later quoted as saying, "We did not fight the Korean War from a base on the Asian continent. We used Japan as our base."

The 1950 Treaty of Friendship between China and the Soviet Union was believed to be for Japan the biggest threat to stability in the Far East. America was strongly lobbying for the resurrection of Japanese military power, and in response to this push, the predecessor to the Self-Defense Forces, the National Police Reserves was created. The National Police Reserves was secretly mobilized in Korea. As Coast Guard director Okubo Tsutsumi later noted, "The conclusion of the peace treaty with Japan was based on the fact that Japan cooperated with America. If Japan had not performed minesweeping duties for them, the United Nations countries would probably not have signed treaties with Japan. In other words, we could say that the peace treaty was the direct result of the work Japan's fleet of 'special minesweepers'."

If you look at this peace treaty with Japan in name only, it may well read like a harmless document that promises peace, but to North Korea and China it was not such a simple matter. The North Koreans and Chinese were looking at the resurrection of men who just a scant six years ago had been war criminals guilty of perpetrating massacres on a large scale against the people of Korea and China. The peace treaty with Japan, which served as a trigger for turning the Korean War into a stalemate, also was responsible for ripping from the hands of the Japanese people the postwar democracy for which so many people had died. If the peace treaty with Japan was the reward for Japan's military cooperation, then inevitably Japan was going to begin marching down the path of militarism. By establishing what was, in effect, a military treaty in the US-Japan Security Treaty, Japan was taking the first step toward becoming a country with compromised independence, a semi-independent country with US military bases attached. (60–62)

The Bloody May Day Incident

The morning of independence day dawned. On that morning, at each school, the principal offered his morning instructions and edification to the children while he saluted the rising-sun flag and mindlessly chanted "Banzai." It was a day full of blessings.

However, Japan's road ahead was by no means unequivocally bright. The Zengakuren students declared on that day, "The Peace Treaty is an insult to Japan. We call for the abrogation of this treaty." They also called for opposition to the Subversion Prevention Law and convened a strike conference. It was a challenging day that called for "vigilance and determination." This is how it was reported in the *Mainichi Shinbun* of April 28, 1952.

On that day, I attended the Zengakuren Protest Conference, held at Waseda University. Ever since, in a blatant attempt to eradicate opposition movements, the government had introduced a bill reminiscent of the prewar Peace Preservation Law, called the Subversion Prevention Law, the energy of the Zengakuren had been dedicated to stopping the passage of this legislation. The excuse used by the government for hurrying to pass the Subversion Prevention Law was the "Bloody May Day" that had occurred just three days after the peace treaty was signed.[5]

Many ordinary citizens had grave misgivings about the government's undertaking of the "reverse course," including signing the US-Japan Security Treaty, which made Japan even more subordinate to America, and then sponsoring legislation to control the public peace and regulate labor. The reverse course was merciless in its assault on the rights of working people, and especially on women's rights. It is a fact that by the time of the first May Day after the signing of the peace treaty, working people were filled with anger and resentment. First, at the central May Day demonstration near Jingû Gaien, some four hundred thousand laborers assembled and demonstrated on behalf of workers' rights while also calling for opposition to rearmament.

This year the government declined to grant permission to use the public square in front of the imperial palace for a demonstration. The Sôhyô, the General Council of Trade Unions, sued for use of that space, but the case remained unresolved. Because there was a strong feeling that the square in front of the imperial place was "the People's Square," there was immense pent-up anger and resentment about the way in which the "reverse course" was callously withholding permission, and this feeling exploded spontaneously into a heated demonstration. The demonstration was divided into five different routes and on route number 2, the demonstrators were banging a war drum, had long wooden staffs, threw rocks, and waved their placards as they rushed into the ranks of waiting police. The police threw tear gas canisters and fired their pistols randomly, and in the course of a three-hour pitched battle both sides continued to attack and inflict damage on the other in a genuine melee; there were many casualties and even, regrettably, some deaths.

As a result of being lured by the police, the demonstrators entered the square. They were provoked by the authorities and fell right into the trap. From this incident they learned the importance of remaining cool headed when engaging in this kind of activity.

A Zengakuren Student Wearing Black Slacks and a Bright Red Jumper

It was on September 18, 1948, that the All Japan Association of Student Councils (Zennihon Gakusei Jichikai Sôrengô, or Zengakuren for short) was formed. Established initially with the aim of democratizing universities from within, Zengakuren gradually became more radical and was ready to meet head-on the antidemocratic political circumstances that it was facing. The name Zengakuren not only became famous inside Japan, but it became widely known internationally as well. The focal points for the Zengakuren movement was Waseda University, while one of the central locations for the struggle against passage of the Subversion Prevention Law was Keiô University. Keiô had experienced internal demonstrations in which most of the students participated, but factions within the movement that wanted to stop these demonstrations began to fight with one another. I even participated in some of these demonstrations.

A bright red jumper and black slacks. This was my trademark apparel. I became familiar with other female students from various universities, so I began to develop a loose network of female student acquaintances. Thanks to all the wonderful treasures that Japan's defeat in war brought home to women, we students who had the privilege of studying freely to our heart's content possessed a deep appreciation for just how precious peace can be, and it penetrated to the depths of our beings. I think that is why I participated as diligently as I did in the organizational meetings and the distribution of posters.

Since there were not many female students, we were easy targets for the police. On one occasion I joined a bunch of students who had gathered outside the Shibuya Police Station, where a student had been arrested for selling copies of Red Flag (Akahata). We were seeking his release on bail, and we sat in front of the police station all night. Along with several other coeds, I joined some of my friends on the sit-in. Just a little before dawn, suddenly the police burst right into the midst of our little group of students and started attacking us. "It's that woman in the red jumper," I heard someone say, and I barely had time to make a run for it. I was thrown face down onto the street. All of the female students were taken to the Shibuya Police Station.

The whole time they were interrogating us they were hurling insults and obscene language in our faces. Even though we were fighting for peace and democracy, just as the male students were, we had to endure in silence their diminution of us as women by throwing foul language at us. Since we were only guilty of a misdemeanor, they held us overnight and then released us. But psychologically the feeling of worthlessness was akin to being raped, so, in the end, it was a step propelling me along the path toward joining the women's liberation movement. . . . (60–65)

Launching Fudanren: Opposing War and Protecting the Constitution

What the women who were trying to stand up and confront these adverse winds wanted most of all was a single, umbrella organization that could unite all the strong-willed women who aimed to oppose war and protect the constitution. So, on May 2, 1949, a single organization based on women who supported peace and designed to unify many women's organizations was established. It was called the *Fujin dantai kyôgikai*, or *Fudankyô* for short. After the Korean War started and in the midst of suppression of the peace movement, internal conflicts deepened, and the one thing that all the participating organizations could endorse was the idea that war was awful, so this became the unifying principle, which led to the suggestion that this position be adopted and the meeting brought to a conclusion. And so the next year, on July 5, Fudankyô was disbanded.

But ever afterward, whenever there was an opportunity, women continued to talk about the need for a unifying organization. The realization of this desire could only be accomplished by means of the great courage and conduct of Kôra Tomi, an elected member of the House of Councillors who had traveled to Moscow by herself to participate in an international economics conference.

Kôra Tomi was born in 1896 in the city of Takaoka in Toyama Prefecture. Her mother, Kuniko, had entered Tsuda College at age forty. Raised in this kind of family environment, Tomi entered the English department of Japan Women's University and after graduating attended graduate school at both Columbia and Johns Hopkins Universities and in 1927 started to teach child psychology at Japan Women's University. Two years later she married the psychiatrist Kôra Takehisa and continued with her teaching career.

But she hardly kept herself locked up in an ivory tower. She participated in a number of social movements, including the movement for women's suffrage, because she had been a devoted follower of Rabindranath Tagore's philosophy of renunciation of war as something opposed to humanity.[6] In 1947 she was elected to the Upper House at large, and she was active as member of the Democratic Party.

As someone who believed in the renunciation of war, Kôra Tomi advocated for a comprehensive peace, and when it came time to cast her vote on the US-Japan Security Treaty, she voted against it. Since at this time even the Socialist Party was split into left- and right-wing factions, many were very surprised at her courage to vote as she did.

Just after this, news came to her that the Soviet Union was interested in lifting the iron curtain and inviting people from all over the world to an International Economics Conference in April of 1951. Since it was still a time when normal diplomatic relations with the Soviet Union had not yet been reestablished, the Japanese government had no intention of formally participating. However, Kôra was a member of the Overseas Repatriation Committee so she saw a chance to negotiate directly by herself and she ignored the prohibitions of the Foreign Ministry. So, after attending a UNESCO [United Nations Educational, Scientific, and Cultural Organization] meeting in Paris she decided to go entirely by herself and breach the iron curtain.

It was quite an undertaking. Based as it was on a strongly held belief that the true road to peace was to sign a comprehensive peace treaty with all the countries, including China and the Soviet Union, how much courage and energy did it impart to other women who continued to oppose the separate peace and the US-Japan Security Treaty?

On July 27 at the Hibiya Public Meeting Hall thirteen groups and four thousand people participated in a welcome home reception for Kôra Tomi. Since diplomatic relations had not been reestablished and the Foreign Ministry would not grant permission to visit communist countries, there was some concern that Kôra might be arrested when she reentered Japan. In order to ensure that she not be arrested, women like Hiratsuka Raichô, Kamichika Ichiko, and Ueno Yaeko joined forces in support of Kôra, and quickly organized an action committee that planned for Kôra's welcome home party and got everything prepared in advance.

Kôra Tomi set the tone with her passionate appeal to women to join in a unifying organization: neither China nor the Soviet Union were going to invade Japan. Most of the nations of the world were hoping that Japan would find its own road to peace. Japanese women needed to be of one mind and ensure that these hopes would be realized.

Responding to her appeal, on August 2 more than thirty women's organizations, including the women's department of the Consumer Cooperative Union, the Women's Democratic Club, the Assembly of Mothers, the Kansai League of Housewives, and the Working Women's Cooperative Association, established the Preparatory Committee for the League of Women's Organizations, and on April 5 of the following year, they formally established the Japan Federation of Women's Organizations, or *Nihon fujindantai rengôkai*, known as *Fudanren* for short. Hiratsuka Raichô was elected chair, and Kôra Tomi was selected as vice chair.

With "Retain the Peace Constitution and Oppose Rearmament" as their watchword, Japanese women were organized so their voices could be heard from this point forward. During the next election for members of the House of Representatives, they circulated posters telling people "Do Not Vote for Candidates who Support Rearmament," thus beginning *Fudanren's* long career of standing up for positive currents in an era when the winds of change were blowing against them. (72–76)

The exhilaration of entering Keiô University, a former male bastion, and joining the theater club, where she stood out in performance of a Camus play, gave way to a certain amount of darkness when the Korean War started pushing Japan inexorably down the path toward rearmament and abandonment of any pretense of neutrality in the Cold War. But, in Yoshitake's eyes, Japan's defeat in the war had been, for women, "the most wonderful treasure imaginable." It enabled them to enter the university and organize and agitate for peace under the slogan of protecting the constitutional principles embodied in Article 9. The next chapter in her memoir takes up Yoshitake's story of the other significant transformation that the occupation had brought about: better access to employment opportunities for women as she tells her story of job seeking and beginning her career after graduating from Keiô University.

The Birth of Japan's First Female Advertising Producer

Near the main gate of Keiô University they had put up a bulletin board where various companies posted their guidelines for applying for jobs. Perhaps reflecting the prosperity of the procurement boom sparked by the Korean War, the board was plastered with job announcements.

I was with an upperclassman from the theater club. K., who was a graduate student, and we were diligently looking at the job posters. Ever since the night we were arrested at the Shibuya Police Station, K. and I had been living together. K. wanted to be a journalist, and I was looking to become an assistant film director.

While K. was intently taking down job application information and writing it in his notebook, I was standing there becoming increasingly irritated. An assistant film director was an artistic position. However, in all the film companies, artistic positions were classified as "women ineligible," which would be written in big, bold letters. It was not only film companies. In fact, among all the job announcement posters that were hanging up on two different bulletin boards, more than two-thirds of the positions were women ineligible.

K. tried to console me by pointing out, "Well even if male students are eligible, it does not mean that all of them get to take the entrance examination."

"I understand that," I said. "But there is a world of difference between the circumstances of those people who are given the opportunity to take the test and those who are denied that same chance. Article 14 of the new constitution states unequivocally that there should be no discrimination based on sex, so shouldn't that be clear enough? I do not care what anyone says, but to deny a woman the opportunity to take an entrance exam because she is a woman violates the constitution. I believe that equality of opportunity is the very foundation of democracy."

But no matter how much I tried to make my case, K. kept insisting, "Even though male students may get to take the test, there is no way that everyone who takes the exam is going to pass it. Reality can be tough," he kept insisting, repeating the same words over and over. And all our friends in Zengakuren had exactly the same response.

Fortunately, one film company, Tôei, had not plastered "women ineligible" across all their job categories. So, feeling that I was placing all my hopes for the future on this one company, I applied to take the entrance examination. At the test site for an artistic position, there were some twenty women assembled. But when it came to the second round of interviews, I was the only female remaining. My name was called right about in the middle, so I did as I was asked and sat in the chair in front of me. I sat there very nervously as they hurled one question after another at me.

However, these questions had absolutely no connection with either film, my view of work, or my understanding of human nature. Rather, in the end, they all had to do with private matters about my relationships with members of the opposite sex. There was even one guy who kept asking rather suggestive questions without the slightest trace of embarrassment, such as:

"What kind of men to do you like?"

"Is there a type of man that you like among this group?"

"Do you have a boyfriend?"

One fat guy sitting right in the middle who was laughing as he spoke said to me quite frankly, "Actually, in our company, since way back, artistic positions have only been filled by males, so we did not think we needed to go to the trouble of writing 'women ineligible' all over our job announcements." When I heard these words, my tension level rose accordingly, but at least I understood now exactly what was going on.

"You people invited me to the interview stage not because you were impressed with my abilities as demonstrated on the written test but because you were only going to be interviewing men and you wanted to sandwich in a woman just to amuse yourselves and stave off the boredom. Now I imagine that some of you men must have daughters. I would like you to imagine just for a moment how you would feel if that daughter of yours, staking her dreams for the future on a written exam to enter a company, which she passes, shows up for the personal interview stage, full of hope and expectations, only to find that she is there solely to amuse the interviewers. If you learned that such a situation exists, wouldn't you find it inexcusable as a father? As far as I am concerned, I am rejecting this undemocratic company."

I stood up to leave, my heart beating fast, the sound of my footsteps loud as I started for the door. But suddenly there was a man standing right next to me, saying, "Miss Yoshitake. Please wait a minute." When I looked into his face, I saw it was a gentle-faced man who had been sitting all the way over on the right. He had sat quietly through the entire interview up until this point.

"My name is Y., and I am the head of the advertising department. To be sure, everyone has been very rude and inconsiderate of you. You definitely have a lot of guts. What do you say? Maybe it is about time that we have a woman come to work in a creative position. Won't you be the pioneer that helps create this new era and come to work in my department?"

Mr. Y's sincere response brought back a sense of calm to my heart, which had been stirred up by feelings of anger, disappointment, and the sense that I had been insulted.

So I entered the advertising department of Tôei Studios. A film company may appear to be a very modern enterprise, but this one retained the prewar value system that privileged males. The wage differential was one thing that jumped out right off the bat. Even though they may have graduated from the same university and entered the company at the same time, the woman's salary would be only two-thirds of the male's salary.

On the first payday, when I realized how great the differences were, I lost my temper and took the salary envelope that I had just received and threw it out of the fifth-floor window to the street below. Other members of the department collected all the money, put it back in the envelope and handed it back to me.

Mr. Y., my department head, said to me, "Miss Yoshitake, I understand your frustration very well. However, you cannot change people's consciousness and values all at once. Change is something that people have to create. Just because someone works hard to bring about change does not necessarily mean that change is going to come about. You cannot be so impatient."

My department head was a genuine prewar "old liberal" who had spoken out against the war and spent time in jail as a consequence. Therefore, he had been genuinely waiting for the flowering of postwar democracy. Thanks to this Mr. Y., I was the first woman selected to be an advertising producer. Since I felt I should heed Mr. Y.'s encouraging words, I threw my self wholeheartedly into my work and made it my motto to work three times as hard as the men. (77–81)

The Sunagawa Base Advertising Campaign and Joining the Struggle against the Bases

Three years later I was in charge of the advertising for the film by the well-known socialist director Sekigawa Hideo, *The Sunagawa Base.*[7] This became the occasion for me to get involved with the struggle over US bases in Japan.

America was an occupying country, and once it had acquired the right to have bases, it was not about to abandon them. In 1969 there were 148 US bases in Japan. The amount of area they covered was approximately 365 square kilometers. In addition, there were also some 24 maritime sites where the United States was entitled to conduct maneuvers. The Self-Defense Forces had 1,688 bases occupying a total area of 836 square kilometers. And it also had 23 marine bases.

The space occupied by US bases in Japan was considerably larger than the twenty-three wards (-*ku*) that make up the Tokyo metropolitan area minus the area of Itabashi-ku and five other of the eastern wards. If you add the Self-Defense Forces' bases as well, then the total area is about twice the size of the twenty-three wards plus an additional space equivalent to the size of Chiyoda-ku.

At the end of the war, the old army bases and naval yards included 14,443 places comprising about 2,970 square kilometers of space. Among these, after the war, more than 2,500 square kilometers were excluded as farmland and land to be opened up to cultivation, so what was able to be transferred directly to the occupation forces of the old military bases was approximately 60 square kilometers.

During the Korean War, the Americans continued to utilize their bases and in fact needed to strengthen and expand them. The land liberated from the former imperial army bases was reacquisitioned while farmers were forced to give up their lands. Since this was a matter of life and death, farmers and fishermen began to stand up in order to resist, and this was the beginning of the struggle over the bases.

Since independence, the very first fierce, protracted struggle to occur was the fight over the firing ranges at Uchinada.[8] Uchinada was a fishing village that faced the Japan Sea in Ishikawa Prefecture. It was in September of 1952 that the Americans issued the notification that they wanted to annex land for a firing range. The sand dunes that ran along the village (480 hectares) and the ocean that was adjacent were acquired on a four-month lease. So they ran about ten thousand meters of barbed war separating the fishermen from the sea, and from 8:00 a.m. to 5:00 p.m. there were four shells launched every five minutes, making the place seem much like a battlefield.

This village had very little in the way of cultivated fields; it was just a very poor village with a boss who lent out nets and boats to fishermen and a few meager stores. The men of this village normally spent between eight and ten months working elsewhere in places like Hokkaidô or Kyûshû while the women who stayed behind tilled their tiny fields and tried to support their children and elders by making fishing nets and selling fish.

These people started saying, "This is insane! We cannot take any more of it," and they began to courageously stand up and resist. Very soon thereafter, a Committee against the Uchinada Firing Range was established, and all across Japan a fierce antibase movement began to develop. The peak of the struggle came in June of the following year.

Dressed in *monpe* and laborer's *tabi*,[9] and wearing white headbands emblazoned with "Oppose the Requisition," these mothers grabbed straw mats and set off for the prefectural offices. They were accompanied by gnarled old grandmother types and daughters in the ten-year-old range. Even though they were beaten and kicked by over three hundred policemen, they vowed to stay and "Protect until They Die." These women persevered for a full year, but in the end the fight to stop the Uchinada Firing Range ended in defeat. (78–83)

"You Cannot Drive a Stake into Our Hearts": The Fight over Bases

The women of Uchinada, who had such firm resolve that they were willing to risk their lives and livelihoods in order to preserve peace, were able to hand down to another generation of women the will to fight the existence of the bases.

It was May 4, 1955, when the announcement came to the Sunagawa City mayor's office from the Tokyo Goods and Services Bureau that the Tachikawa Air Base would be expanding. The area that was going to have to be evacuated in order to accommodate the expansion included about 140 houses.

Dating from the prewar years and continuing into the postwar, the farmers of Sunagawa had already had some 250 hectares taken from them in order to provide for a former army infantry base and then for the Americans.

On May 6, 1955, the farmers of Sunagawa got together with officials from the municipal organization to form the Sunagawa City League to Oppose the Expansion of the Base. That they were able to rally such support was no doubt due to the long history of oppression and having their land confiscated, which generated much anger and frustration.

"You may drive a stake into our lands, but you cannot drive a stake into our hearts." Drawing inspiration from these words, born amid the struggle against the Sunagawa Base, the fight soon reverberated in places all over Japan. Especially noteworthy was the solidarity of the women.

Up until this point, the problem of the military bases had largely been approached from the angle of the increase in prostitution and the corruption of morals in the areas around the bases, as well as the impact this had on the education of children, so in this environment it was possible to galvanize women to focus their energies on a movement designed to protect the children. This is what provided the motivation to establish the Committee to Protect the Children.

However, after the peace treaty between the United States and Japan was signed in April 1952, it became possible to approach the problem of the bases from a different angle. The treaty allegedly made Japan independent, but because it was a bilateral treaty with America only, Japan was independent in name only and was forced to be subordinate to the United States. When the women realized that the leases of the bases were being done in semiperpetuity, it sparked them to launch a movement to have the bases withdrawn in their entirety.

At the time of the Uchinada struggle, many women offered their support to the women there. The Women's Democratic Club took the lead in organizing campaigns to raise money and gather signatures, and several times its members visited Uchinada and conducted sit-ins with the local housewives near the artillery range.

Also at the time of the Uchinada struggle, the response of the women was quite rapid. It came just at the time when more than sixteen organizations were cooperating and in the midst of preparations for the

First Assembly of Japanese Mothers. These women's organizations included the League of Japanese Women's Organizations (Fudanren), the Society to Protect Japanese Children, the Women's Democratic Club, the Consumer Cooperative Union, the Tokyo Mother's Association, the League to Regulate the Cleaning Up the Environment, the Japan Teacher's Union, the Women's Department of the Tokyo Regional National Railway Workers Union, and the Women's Coal Mine Cooperative Association to name a few.

From the members of the Assembly of Japanese Mothers' action committee came the following message of support and encouragement.

"With all the love and support from the point of view of a mother, we pledge to work on behalf of peace."

When this language was read to the entire assembly, there was a thunderous roar of applause. The Fudanren immediately set about seeking support for the Sunagawa struggle from its member organizations.

Generally speaking, when you mention a movement to oppose bases, you think of a fairly specialized group of people getting involved. But, in the case of the Sunagawa struggle, they really wanted to ensure that the real picture of what was happening to the mothers and children of Sunagawa would become widely known, and they wanted people to recognize that this was a struggle to bring about real peace for Japan, so they wanted to expand the circle of women's solidarity. For this reason, Fudanren sought widespread cooperation and even planned a special volume of essays called *An Anthology from the Sunagawa Women and Children*. So, from a very busy late fall until New Year's, mainly the members of the Women's Democratic Club began a series of visits by Fudanren women to Sunagawa.

In their spare time, between the intense and busy struggle in which they were engaged, the women of Sunagawa joined forces in order to create their essays, and by the end of January 1956 they had completed a manuscript called "Trampling on Wheat: A Collection of Essays from the Women and Children of Sunagawa." The anthology included the passionate outcries of as many as fifty women and middle-school students. Their writing really pierced your heart, and it was a major contributing factor to raising awareness about the problem of the bases.

"The blood that must flow, must flow." The head of the women's committee wrote these words very clearly after the police had cracked her skull with a police baton and blood was running down her face.

The women who wanted to come to their aid began heading to Sunagawa. Sometimes they would stand with the Sunagawa women shoulder to shoulder and join them in their sit-ins. On other occasions they would take a turn cooking or, at their request, washing the women's mud-caked clothing for them. I guess one could say that the reason the fight against the Sunagawa Base lasted as long as it did, all the way up until the struggle against the Vietnam War began, was the passionate support that these women received.

I had the experience of working with the film *The Sunagawa Base*, which depicted these women's fierce and determined appeal for peace.[10] At a preview showing of the film, I felt as though my heart was being gripped so fiercely, and I felt both shock and tension, to the point that I could not move a muscle or do anything. Even after the film was over and the lights came up, I could not rise from my seat.

The Shibokusa Mother's Group and the Struggle against
the North Fuji Practice Range

In later years, I became involved with the struggle to oppose the North Fuji Practice Range, and this, too, was an outgrowth of my responsibilities for promoting the film *The Sunagawa Base*. The North Fuji Practice Range was almost entirely located in Yamanashi Prefecture. The mountain forests and fields at the foot of Mount Fuji had since Tokugawa times been open to the local people to enter and collect the straw and grasses, brushwood, trees, and mulberries to use for their livelihoods. They were even permitted to open up some of the land for cultivation.

But even without a requisition order, the situation was ineptly defined, and the lands were being used for training and practice. In 1957, the Self-Defense Forces began formally using it as a practice area. When the North Fuji Common Land Union was created, the problem of the North Fuji Practice Range became fundamentally concretized. In 1960, the Shiboku Common Land Union asked that all the common lands be returned to the people and citizens began sitting in at the practice facility.

This struggle reached its peak on October 2, 1965. On that day, as if to irritate the local farmers, who had been fighting for many years to secure the return of all the common lands, the artillery division moved its practice range from East Fuji to the "Little John" facility at North Fuji where they could fire their live artillery shells.

At that time, some of the women in the Shibokusa Mother's Group summoned up all their resolve and entered into the common lands in order to sit in at the practice range. Since mortars were landing only meters away, there were women who experienced their hats being blown right off their heads as the shells whistled by. Since they still refused to move, the American military was not able to fire a second round. As a result of this confrontation, Shibokusa Mothers all of a sudden became a household word.

In the early morning hours of July 7, 1968, in order to protest the Self-Defense Forces' artillery shell practice range, Watanabe Kimiko, who was chair of the Shibokusa Mother's group, built a small hut in which to sit in on the practice range. Just as she finished, some fifteen hundred Self-Defense soldiers beat and kicked her. It took a full ten days for her wounds to heal.

I visited North Fuji on several occasions to lend my support to the fight.

"Since I could be arrested at any moment, I like to have everything around me arranged, so I come to this little hut," Watanabe said to the women of the Shibokusa group in a weak voice.

She added, "These common lands provide many things that are essential to our livelihood. There is no way that we can sit by quietly and watch while these valuable lands are being used to practice killing people."

How well did these women of the Shibokusa Mother's Group teach us that the fight for livelihood is also the struggle for peace? To be sure, in this one respect, the solidarity these women manifested transcended many differences in points of view and extended the range of their influence. (84–88)

If Mothers Change, Then Society Will Change

A Poem I Encountered after a Heartbreaking Decision to Choose Work

> "A Wish That Mothers Who Give Life Will Also Rise and Protect Life"

> *I had a small son*
> *Tomorrow I will gently wake him up*
> *Comb his hair*
> *Soothe him and have him drink a glass of milk*
> *And I will stand in the doorway and see him off to school*
> *My son's shoulders will broaden as he walks the crowded street*
> *And the rest my golden dreams*
> *Are something to be chased*
> *I had a little son*
> *I had waited for that day*
> *When he would look after me on my deathbed*
> *With a trembling hand he would stroke my hair {and say}*
> *"Mother, please do not worry about your journey to happiness*
> *Just like the olive tree*
> *You will always live on in my heart"*
> *I had a son who would look after me this way*
> *I had a son*
> *But they killed my son*

The person who showed me this poem was a woman friend of mine from college who was a reporter. It was in early August of 1955. At that point, I was extremely depressed. I had become pregnant for the first time in my life, and as a result of feeling the pressure to choose between work and children I had been forced to make the heartbreaking decision to choose work.

In those days, the corporate world did not afford any recognition to the idea of a two-income family. Even Tôei had the customary policy that women should quit work when they got married. I had already been living with K. since our college days, but legally this was not entered in our family registry, so I had entered the company as a single woman.

Ever since I learned that I was pregnant, I had spent my days agonizing over what to do. My desire to have the baby was much stronger than I would have imagined. However, I was facing a situation whereby if I circumvented the whole "quit work when you get married" policy and had the baby, it would become clear that I had lied about my status when I joined the company and I would be forced to quit. If I were indispensable to the company, then maybe it would be possible somehow get over that hurdle, but, after all, I was just a new employee. I was in the pretty weak position of not having really compiled a record of accomplishments to speak of.

Somehow or other I had to keep working at that same workplace. I guess you could say that what made me feel attached to working at Tôei was the pioneer spirit that was being fostered in the postwar period. I was among the first women to graduate from college. If I had failed, people would have just said, "Well, that is what happens when women go to college" and the door would have been closed to other graduates coming up behind me. As one might imagine, there were still lots of male employees who would toss off careless remarks directed at me, but when women came in after me they would have to go to work in a tense, hostile environment. But, anyway, when I thought about quitting in order to have a baby after only one year and three months on the job, I kept hearing this chorus of men's voices that just could not wait to chant, "See, we told you so! Female college graduates are just not worth it!" If that were to happen, then there was the danger that, taking advantage of this kind of situation, this gate into higher education that had swung open to women would be closed. I absolutely knew that I could not be the one who was responsible for seeing this avenue into the workplace closed to the female underclassmen coming up behind me.

After fretting and feeling tormented, I decided to choose over and above the new life that was growing in my womb the path of continuing to work in the same workplace.

It seemed as though relentlessly a sharp pain, as though something had been ripped out of my body, pursued me and would not let up. The decision to have an abortion was mine alone. However, if the road to have a child and continue working had been open to me, I never would have chosen to cast the budding life in my body into the darkness. As you might think with such strong ideas, a strong sense of reproach over the fact that it felt like the child in my womb had been killed by someone assaulted me from the very depths of my heart.

When I read the poem that my friend showed me, the line "However, they killed my son" pierced my breast like an augur all the way through to my heart.

There is really no tangible difference in terms of motherly feelings between the mother who is robbed of her son in war and a mother who has her motherhood ruthlessly trampled on by a chauvinistic male society whereby the life of her unborn child is taken from her. The nationality of these precious children may be different, but they are both part of the tragedy that befalls women who are mothers. Both war and the male-centered society are products. Since I was also a woman who had been victimized by the logic of the male, patriarchal culture, I felt that I was standing in the same shoes as the author of this poem. Accordingly, I felt completely connected to that poem. (89–92)

A World Assembly of Mothers That Transcends Nationality and Skin Color

The author of the poem was the Greek poet Peredes, and it was shared at the July 7–10, 1955, World Assembly of Mothers meeting, held in Lausanne, Switzerland, in which 1,060 mothers from sixty countries participated.[11] United by the principle of "protecting the children from the dangers of war," it was historic when mothers from five continents joined together because it marked the first time in women's history that this sort of monumental occurrence took place.

The assembly was called to order by the chairwoman, Madame Cotton, who beseeched her audience, "Now is the time for peace to be protected by a mother's hand." The keynote report consisted of words of encouragement from famous women writers from around the world, and representatives from throughout the world gave reports on the actual conditions in which mothers and children found themselves.

These mothers, who overcame differences in nationality, skin color, and culture, denounced the way in which warlike policies inevitably brought hardships in livelihood, racial discrimination, and the cruel mistreatment of colonial subjects. The opinion was expressed that if mothers of the world would unite and organize, they could resolve to build a peaceful future without war.

*Women represent one-half of humankind, and we call on them,
with all the awesome love and responsibility that mothers possess,
to oppose war, call for the prohibition of the manufacturing,
testing, and use of nuclear weapons, and lead the fight to rid the
world of these weapons. Let us lead a movement to turn the huge
military expenditures required to prepare for war into funding for
housing, hospitals, and schools. Mothers who give birth to life aim
to protect that life.*

At the opening of the assembly, a verse from the Greek poet Peredes'
beautiful but heart-searing poem was adopted as a slogan for the conference.
Mothers from various countries etched this slogan on their hearts and
resolved to take the lead in peace movements when they returned to their
respective countries.

Actually, the impetus for this historic worldwide conference of mothers
came from Japan. Hiratsuka Raichô, who had been central to the movement
to protect peace, was chair of the newly founded Fudanren, and she began
preparations for a Global Women's Conference in 1953 when Fudanren
came into being by issuing the following appeal:

*To all mothers of the world, let us join together. If we do this, we
will be an invincible force fighting for women's rights, children's
happiness, and peace.*

In response to this appeal, the Women's International Democratic
Federation, in Copenhagen, Denmark, gathered some 119 people from
sixty-seven countries for a World Women's Conference, and once 10
representatives were sent, the cornerstone of the mother's movement was
put in place.

The next year, 1954, was the year that America, which had suffered
serious losses in the Korean War, wanted Japan to vastly increase its
military expenditures. The government that responded to America's request
signed the US-Japan Mutual Defense Assistance Agreement and initiated
the second Self-Defense Law, the Special Detective Law, the Police Law,
and the Second Education Law, which aimed to curtail the freedom of
teachers to investigate thought and forbid them to participate in political
movements—all of which invited the ire and opposition of the people, so
they were forcibly rammed through the Diet.

In the middle of that July, the cornerstone of a rearmament program
was put in place as, beginning with the Self-Defense Forces comprising air,
sea, and land forces, there was established a Self-Defense College and a joint
Staff Council. . . . (93–94)

As background to this kind of women's movement, more than
a central organization, the talk about some way of unifying women

progressed, so that several relevant groups, such as Sôhyô, Fudanren, the League for the Acquisition of Women's Rights, the Christian Women's Reform Organization, the Women's Democratic Club, the YWCA, the League to Protect Women's Rights, the Society to Protect the Children, and the Cooperative Society of Female Day Laborers, linked the March 8 International Women's Day with the April 10–16 Women's Week and pushed it further in 1954 to a month-long movement, under the slogan, "All women oppose war and seek to protect the peace constitution," they came together in order to make arrangements.

On March 1 of this same year, America conducted a nuclear test at the Bikini Atoll. On this occasion, the crew of the tuna fishing boat *Lucky Dragon 5*, which was 150 nautical miles away, was exposed to radioactivity, and in September, Captain Kuboyama died. This was the so-called Bikini Incident.[12]

On April 3, at the Toshima Lecture Hall meeting of the Women's Month Central Committee, a decision was made to engage in protest activities, and at the same time that people went to the American Embassy and the Ministry of Foreign Affairs to protest, while many others were gathering signatures on the streets to ban atomic weapons.

In Tokyo's Suginami Ward, for example, housewives started gathering signatures on street corners right away, and they also went door-to-door to get more people to sign up. On May 9, within the ward they worked with local women's groups, labor unions, and doctor's associations, and with the local ward representative they created a Suginami Ward Committee to Gather Signatures to Ban Atomic Weapons and played a central role in generating a nationwide cooperative organization along the same lines.

In order to let the rest of the world know how angry Japanese women were, and their determination to fight, on September 15, Fudanren and the vice chair of the International Democratic Women's League, Hiratsuka Raichô, along with five other signatories, sent an appeal to ban atomic weapons to the headquarters of the Women's International Democratic Federation and to women's organizations in each of the member countries.

Adding Japanese Mothers to the Worldwide Organizations of Mothers

For three days, on June 7–9, 1955, in places like the Toshima Public Hall and the Japan Youth Building, branch meetings and meetings of the whole organization were held. Some two thousand people came from all over Japan, and, whatever the venue, they were filled with mothers.

> *Mothers of the World!*
>
> We are responding to your call and are standing with you.
> War crushes a mother's happiness and pride, and mothers

have even been prevented from saying something that would be very natural for a mother to feel: that they hate war. We are not even supposed to shed tears when we send our children off to fight; instead we are supposed to swallow our tears and sadness. However, now we know something about the power of organizing. Mothers who have come from all over, like those from Amami Oshima, and unemployed miners have stood up for two days and joined us at this conference. With the power of these kinds of mothers, this assembly will be a success. This will mean a new page in the history of Japanese mothers.

I have no doubt that fathers and children will encourage the mothers to participate in this great parade. With this kind of support and cooperation, Japanese mothers will be able to join the ranks of those seeking to ban atomic weapons and contribute to world peace.

We are no longer individual, separate, weak women. Wherever we may be, let us always have the strength and courage of knowing we are part of the Japan Assembly of Mothers.

This declaration from the first Assembly of Japanese Mothers filled our hearts with a thousand emotions and sent our voices resounding to the rafters.

So this first assembly, which was convened by Takada Nahoko with a nod toward the International Assembly of Mothers, has since that day continued as the *Hahaoya taikai* (Assembly of Mothers).

It was never a movement led by famous women activists or a small group of women activists. It was just ordinary mothers standing up to be counted—this was the strength of this "mother's movement." But it was a threat to the government, so the Ministry of Education immediately started to set up procedures to reinvigorate its women's bureau, and the budget was expanded accordingly. Also the Liberal Democratic Party began to strengthen its policy toward women. Later it also set 70 percent of the agenda of the Mother's Assembly and started to attack the left wing as "Reds," basically obstructing proceedings. These women who had just started to make strides were horrified.

So they began the transition from the discussion phase to action by opposing the Reform of the Police Execution of Duties Law, and, for the first time, there was a large mothers and daughters demonstration in which they participated, and this demonstration played a role leading up to the opposition to the US-Japan Security Treaty (Ampo) in subsequent years.

In the 1960 Ampo demonstrations, day after day the mothers gathered under their Assembly of Mothers banner and joined hands with workers and students and marched around the Diet Building. I was demonstrating daily as a member of the United Film Workers, and I always noticed the Assembly of Mothers flag. Every time I did, I remembered the words my friend the woman reporter had spoken: "If mothers change, then society will change." Transforming themselves in the midst of struggle, boldly advancing with conviction, these mothers were developing strength born of certainty. (97–100)

Analysis

By titling her memoir *A History of Women's Movements—and My Experience of the Postwar Years*, Yoshitake Teruko made a conscious decision to situate her account of public and social events alongside her own story. The result is a narrative about the efforts of Japanese women to organize and effect social and political change interspersed with stories about her education, her involvement in student protests, her entry into the workforce, her protests against the presence of American bases on Japanese soil, and other things. Therefore, the first one hundred pages of her memoir are about Japanese women obtaining fundamental political rights in the early postwar years, the role of the democratic women's movement in that process, the place of educational reform, and the power generated by organizations like the Assembly of Japanese Mothers and Fudanren (Japan Federation of Women's Organizations). Moreover, the impact of the Korean War and later the nuclear testing at the Bikini Atoll did much to galvanize women in support of a peace movement in Japan. But it is against the backdrop of this narrative that Yoshitake tells a more personal tale of her college education, her involvement with the radical student movement Zengakuren, her job search, her employment at Tôei, and the very personal and painful struggle she endured when she became pregnant. And even when her narrative is not deeply personal, she touches on certain landmark issues of the day concerned with citizens' rights and world peace: the protests over the Uchinada and Sunagawa base incidents, and the *Lucky Dragon 5* Incident involving the US nuclear test at the Bikini Atoll, which sparked an intense reaction among Japanese citizens, especially women. It galvanized hundreds of thousands of women in a petition drive to ban nuclear testing. Yoshitake's textual strategy is to keep the reader's attention focused on the record of significant social and political events affecting women and to weave her personal story into her historical accounts of these critical moments.

Of course, we already know from the portions of her text reproduced in chapter 1 that the postwar years Yoshitake lived through were grounded in a most shocking and painful incident, her gang rape. The reader cannot fail to recognize that the narrator finds in her sexual violation a lesson for all Japanese women and also a link between her own subjectivity and identity and the outer world of social and political reality. Each woman, she seems to say, must find in herself and for herself that place where the social and cultural order imposes itself on the individual's own personal and private world of experiences. Much more about this connection is revealed in the following chapter, where she discusses the impact of the women's liberation movement on her life and her consciousness as a woman; suffice it to say here that she is suggesting that through women's organizations and participation in movements that support women's causes women can situate themselves in both history and society, and develop their historical agency. The way they do that is to become aware of that place inside themselves where the socially constructed order is reproduced, and where the difference between that constructed reality and their own personal identity and experience is painfully evident. Yoshitake finds hope in the possibility that the activism in which Japanese women engage may be sufficient to provide them with the strategies and tools they need in order to come to terms with, if not overcome, the socially constructed reality that frames and constrains their actions, and restricts women's freedom to develop and assert their own subjectivity. When she writes about women "transforming themselves in the midst of struggle," she is alluding directly to the possibility of women discovering and asserting their own sense of agency through collective action.

Even though the Left lost much ground in the 1950s, especially after the outbreak of the Korean War, which was so difficult to reconcile with the ideal of an unarmed, pacifist, neutral Japan, Yoshitake could still write confidently, "We now know something about the power of organizing." But the language of the next chapter suggests that when organization alone is not sufficient, women may need to draw on their experience of participating in the world of social and political movements to find a way to assert their subjectivity as female activists and to generate a new kind of historical agency based on a feminine consciousness.

3

RESENTING INJUSTICE

YOSHITAKE TERUKO—FROM AMPO TO WOMEN'S LIB

A t 9:30 a.m. on a rainy morning in Washington, DC, April 28, 1952, Ambassador Takeuchi Ryûji met with Secretary of State Dean Acheson and the representatives of nine other Allied nations to exchange ratifications of the Peace Treaty with Japan, which would bring the six-year, eight-month Allied occupation of Japan to an end. Immediately after the honors were done, Acheson and Takeuchi exchanged drafts of what would become the US-Japan Security Treaty, or the *Nichibei anzen hoshô jôyaku*, known in Japan as Ampo for short. The next day back in Japan, the national anthem, "Kimi ga yo," was heard on the radio for the first time in many a year, and bells could be heard ringing at the Sensôji and Sôjôji temples in Tokyo. Otherwise, things remained fairly quiet. A columnist in the newspaper *Asahi shinbun* bade "Sayonara" to the occupation but urged his countrymen not to forget and lose all that had been gained during the last six years. The next day, April 29, was the emperor's birthday, and well-wishers gathered in the square outside the imperial palace waving flags and celebrating the return of independence. But only two days later, on May Day, that same square would become a scene of carnage known as "Bloody May Day" when armed police hurled tear gas and even fired bullets to clear the square of demonstrators.[1]

As traumatic as Bloody May Day was, it would be dwarfed by the massive outpouring of protest against the renewal of the US-Japan Security Treaty that occurred eight years later in 1960. Although it has been studied only sparingly, most writers agree that it was less the actual content of the security treaty that bothered protestors than it was the manner in which the Japanese government handled the process of renewing it that raised unprecedented ire among Japanese citizens. If Japanese people were not necessarily passionate about the issues surrounding the US-Japan security relationship, they were undeniably appalled by Prime Minister Kishi Nobusuke's arrogant and "high-handed" tactics in pushing the revised treaty through the Diet. They not only found his blatant disregard for popular opinion so offensive that they felt compelled to take to the streets in protest, but they also believed that his behavior was threatening those democratic gains made under the occupation to which the *Asahi* columnist had referred. Kishi, who had close ties to colonial rule in Manchuria in the 1930s, was seen as one of the politicians most dedicated to the rearmament of Japan. In this sense, ratification of the security treaty in May of 1960 was "the culmination of years of government initiatives to reverse the democratic reforms of the Allied Occupation and revive prewar fascist institutions."[2] Therefore, what seemed to be at stake was what was often referred to as the ideal of postwar democracy.

Despite the unprecedented degree of citizen mobilization, the net result was that the treaty was signed and ratified, Prime Minister Kishi resigned from office, his successor Ikeda Hayato announced an income-doubling plan, and Japan entered the era of high economic growth during which many Japanese retreated into hard work, consumerism, and improving the material conditions of their existence. End of story. But, of course, the story never ends that simply. Significant historical events are usually followed by others. An event that looms very large in postwar history occurred a decade later when, at an international antiwar demonstration on October 21, 1970, a women's group unfolded a banner with one Chinese character emblazoned on it: "Resentment!" (怨). This unfurling heralded the introduction of the second-wave feminist or "women's lib" movement to Japan. "At long last, it is finally here," thought Yoshitake Teruko, who in this chapter finds the threads that join the tumultuous weeks of May and June 1960 with a much less heralded series of protests and demonstrations held in late 1970. Her recollections of these experiences, as recounted below, illustrate the way in which Ampo and the women's movement connected for her, and the important role that "lib thought" played in the lives of many Japanese women even though, at first glance, the movement seemed to engage only a few thousand women at most. What this chapter and chapter 4 demonstrate, however, is that some varieties of historical change may reach down much deeper into the fabric of society, deep into the consciousness and beliefs of historical actors, thus bringing about more substantial discursive and historical change than might otherwise be believed.

Women Are Stirred by the Ampo Struggle

The 1959–1960 struggle against Ampo, the so-called '60s Ampo Struggle," was the largest mass demonstration in the postwar period.

The unified movement to halt renewal of the US-Japan Security Treaty extended from April 15, 1959, to October 20 of the following year, 1960. The level of participation, according to police investigations, included demonstrations in 5,350 locations involving 4.28 million people. There were meetings in 6,300 venues involving 4.58 million people. Strikes occurred in some 86,860 workplaces, and some 900,000 police were involved, making 886 arrests.

As I think back on it now, my involvement in the Ampo struggle was pretty simple. It is not as though I knew a whole lot about the provisions of the US-Japan Security Treaty. But I guess you could say I had a feeling of distrust toward Kishi Nobusuke, who was current prime minister Abe Shinzô's great-grandfather on his mother's side, and this is how I became stimulated to participate in the anti-Ampo movement.

Kishi was a bureaucrat who in the prewar years had had several positions managing the war effort. He had been a high official in Manchuria and was a member of Tôjô Hideki's cabinet. Even though he had been designated a war criminal, here he was in the prime minister's office, trying to negotiate an alliance with the American military. A symbol of the most reactionary forces in Japan during the Korean War years, whenever he spoke, I just did not feel that I could trust a single word he said.

When, on May 19, 1960, he managed to force the renewal of the US-Japan Security Treaty through the Diet, it just fueled my anger all the more.[3] After the new treaty had been presented to the Diet, it had to be deliberated on by the House of Representatives' Special Ampo Committee. In spite of the fact that it was a military alliance that assumed Japan's rearmament, the government continued to act as though it were merely an economic alliance. Thanks to the dogged and persistent efforts of the Japan Socialist Party and several inadvertent slips of the tongue, the people gradually came to see Ampo for exactly what it was. Naturally, the movement to oppose the treaty spread widely and rapidly among the people.

Having lost all his support, around midnight between May 19 and 20, using five hundred policemen, the prime minister forcibly extended the Diet session and rammed the new treaty and security arrangement through the committee.[4]

President Eisenhower was scheduled to visit Japan on June 19. This would have been the first visit of a sitting US president to Japan. That is why the May 19 deadline was so important to the government.

After that, the Diet continued to operate in a vacuum.

Several of the leading newspapers were unanimous, printing stories with headlines like "A Reckless Defiance of Democracy" and "The Crisis of Democracy." Taking this as an opportunity, the Ampo struggle made the issue of democracy its focal point and managed to spark a wildfire that spread nationwide and ignited a mass political movement. For me, the Ampo struggle was no less than a movement in support of peace and democracy.

The revision of Ampo was something that had continued to insinuate itself into the US-Japan relationship ever since the time of the Hatoyama Cabinet. The US-Japan Security Treaty—Ampo—dates from September 8, 1951. It accompanied the San Francisco Peace Treaty and provided for the US military to continue to have bases in Japan even after the occupation ended. After the Korean War, America calculated that because of the need for bases in the Far East, Japan's existence was absolutely essential, while Japan, which desperately wanted to be independent but did not have the economic resources to support a rearmament program on its own, elected to ride on the coattails of the United States. Accordingly, the treaty was a product of the confluence of both countries' needs.

It was Japan that first brought up the revision of the treaty. According to the terms of the treaty, Japan's obligation to supply the United States with the bases it needed was clearly spelled out, but America was not equally charged with the duty to defend Japan. So it was in August 1955, under the Hatoyama Cabinet, that Foreign Minister Shigemitsu raised, for the first time, the question of the current treaty being revised so that America's obligations could be clearly spelled out. . . .

During this time, there was absolutely no evidence of any serious interest in the treaty among the populace. What woke up the sleeping child was the behavior of the Kishi Cabinet.

On October, 8, 1958, the Kishi Cabinet suddenly introduced a bill to reform the Police Execution of Duties Law in the Diet. This law placed greater emphasis on preserving the public order than on protecting individual life and property. So they wanted to greatly expand the powers of the police in the execution of their duties, which meant that the police were free to suppress mass movements in advance of the movements undertaking any action and thereby curtailing their freedom of assembly. Because there were fears that the law could be used to infringe on people's privacy, it was considered a reactionary bill.[5] Perhaps because it was introduced so precipitously and there was insufficient time to investigate the consequences of passing such a law, and to the extent that deliberations were being hurried by the government, public opposition was incapable of remaining dormant.

On October 17, in the first conference room of the House of Councillors building, an organizational meeting to launch a Women's Cooperative Association to Protect Individual Rights was held; 160 people were present. The Women's Bureau of the Socialist Party had convened the meeting and [numerous women's groups participated.] . . . On April 21, 1956, there was an Action Committee to Oppose the Resurrection of the Patriarchal System and an accompanying demonstration, and on November 7, 1957, on the Nosoto Stage in front of Shimbashi Station, there was inaugurated a group called Women who Speak Out against the Reverse Course, which succeeded in bringing an important perspective forward.

From the movement to oppose the Police Duties Execution Law, which required us to stand up and get involved, we gained the confidence to feel that if we were willing to try something we could bring about results. On November 5, 1958, at the Kyôbashi Public Hall, the Association of Mothers and Daughters Opposing the Police Duties Execution Law was established. I attended this meeting with some of my friends from the Women's History Research Group, and I headed to the Kyôbashi Public Hall on the early side. But the hall was already packed, and we had to look hard for seats; in the end, we were not even able to sit together. So I would guess that the number of participants was around sixteen hundred people. Among the participants was Kishi Teruko, who stood up and talked about her unpleasant experiences with unfair oppression.

> *Whenever I hear all the criticism directed at Kishi this and Kishi that, the sadness of sharing the same last name makes me feel that they are talking about me, which always makes my heart beat faster. I thought I might have to withdraw for the sake of my health.*

When she delivered these lines, the whole hall erupted in laughter and applause.

An appeal that reflected the movement's principles was expressed in a poem by Ema Shôko.

> *Outside, the scent of a lovely chrysanthemum*
> *Mothers and daughters have all left their homes*
> *Let us join together at today's gathering*

I do not recall the rest of the poem, but when I heard Katô Haruko beautifully read these lines, I remember even to this day how moved I felt.

It was an incredible meeting, overflowing as it was with women's sensitivity to things. I learned later that this new name for our group, the Mother and Daughter Gathering, was something thought up by Watanabe Michiko, who was the office manager and later director of the Women's Bureau of the Socialist Party.

After the meeting was over, we set out on a March of the Mothers and Daughters that went from Kyôbashi to Ginza. The leader of the march was the writer Hirabayashi Taiko. I was clutching a gold balloon in my hand as we walked slowly down Ginza's broad avenues. I imagine that such a peaceful demonstration consisting of all women, some with babies holding yellow balloons, was quite an amazing sight. Crowds gathered along the side of the road, and a few women joined us by just slipping into the procession as we marched by. In this way, our procession grew steadily in size as we proceeded through the streets.

Due to this widespread protest, replete as it was with women's ideas, and the way women's anger was focused on the Kishi Cabinet, by November 22 the cabinet abandoned the reform of the Police Duties Execution Law and the House of Representatives had to entertain a motion to recess because it could not complete its deliberations. (105–7)

Young and Old Alike Raise Their Voices in Opposition to Ampo

Our women's struggle against violence continued apace but finally, on January 19, 1960, in Washington, D.C., an agreement on the renewal of the US-Japan Security Treaty was signed, so the movement shifted from trying to prevent the signing to opposing the ratification of the treaty. In the midst of this, we put forth a slogan for the impending "women's month," which declared, "Stop the Ratification of the New Treaty, Demand that the Kishi Cabinet Resign." Especially, as the women's month was drawing to a close on April 16, we held a nationwide conference on women opposed to the US-Japan Security Treaty. Some five thousand women gathered at the Hibiya Music Hall, and there were women from all social strata and walks of life represented. From all over Japan came the old and the young, and different generations were represented along with different occupations and social classes. In other words, all kinds of different women came together in one venue. They expressed the resolve of women joined in unity and solidarity. On that day, the government and the LDP [Liberal Democratic Party] announced that they were halting deliberations on the new treaty in the House of Representatives, and they planned to complete the ratification of the treaty by mid-May. This elicited a resolve from all the women's organizations that we would inundate the Diet with wave after wave of petitions.

On April 26, the fifteenth unified demonstration and presentation of final petitions took place. All across Japan some 250,000 people participated. It was on May 14 that the national citizens' conference declared a national emergency. So, on the nineteenth, the government called out five thousand police officers, and in the ensuing chaos, the Ampo Treaty was unilaterally forced through the Diet. As soon as people heard the news, they flocked to the Diet Building, surrounded it, and in a candlelight vigil raised their voices against Ampo. On that night, as a member of the Federation of Cinema and Theatrical Workers' Union of Japan, I went with my office colleagues and we chanted "AMPO HANTAI, AMPO HANTAI" [Oppose Ampo!] until our voices were completely spent.

From that day on, the anti-Ampo movement consisted of people from all walks of life and social classes, people who belonged to organizations as well as those who did not. But they were driven to join the opposition movement as citizens with a sense of profound crisis because the Kishi Cabinet was in the process of trampling their democratic rights underfoot.

At the demonstrations in front of the Diet, the *Koe naki koe no kai* (Voiceless Voices) group came into being. It was the product of a twenty-eight-year-old teacher, Kobayashi Tomi, and others, but it was a new movement that emerged within the framework of the Ampo struggle.[6] It was an organization formed to allow people who did not belong to any other organization to participate in the marches and demonstrations. Tomi and her friends were listening to the radio broadcasts and becoming more irate, but not being part of any existing organization, they had no way to participate in the demonstration. Therefore, they just went down to the demonstration carrying a banner with the legend "Anyone can join the Voiceless Voices," placed themselves in the very rear of the procession, and started to march. By the time the demonstration disbanded they had become three hundred people strong.

The choice of a name was really a way to throw some of Prime Minister Kishi's own words back in his face because he had declared, "I want to listen to the people who have no voice. Right now all I am hearing from is the people who have a voice."

The movement to oppose President Eisenhower's planned visit to Japan reached its peak on June 10 when Ike's press secretary, James Hagerty, arrived in Japan. On that day, at Haneda Airport, some 150,000 workers and Zengakuren students had gathered at the airport for a petition demonstration. Hagerty's party was attacked in their car; swallowing their anger, they got away in a military helicopter. On the occasion of this incident, the mass media, the newspapers and magazines that had been very critical of Kishi's high-handed tactics and had supported the struggle against Ampo, now turned around and criticized the opposition movement.

Right at this point, a second General Strike was called for June 15 and 16. On this day, starting with the private railway workers, who went out on strike, some 580,000 workers participated; since this coincided with the eighteenth day in a row of demonstrations around the Diet, many unions and other supporting groups turned out to demonstrate against the government. I participated in this demonstration with my workmates from the film and theater union, but only in the evening. There was suddenly an attack by right-wing thugs armed with heavy wooden clubs on a new theater group that was marching just ahead of us. Blood flowed freely, and all hell started to break loose. Even though one after another member of the group was being knocked to the ground, the police looked the other way and pretended not to see.

At the same moment, at the south wing of the Diet Building, a police unit and Zengakuren students clashed, and around 7:00 p.m., as a result of the assault by police, a Tokyo University coed named Kamba Michiko was killed. Now this tragedy was made apparent to the entire world.

On June 16, in the name of preserving public peace, the government abandoned the idea of a visit by Ike.

On the next day, seven different newspapers joined in printing the same bold headline on their front pages: "Wipe Out Violence, Protect Parliamentary Democracy." So the true nature of newspapers and the mass media were revealed: they were still the same as they had been in the prewar years, weak in the face of the authorities. They could not find a way to respect the anger and indignation of the people and side with them.

One of the objectives of the struggle to stop Ike's visit to Japan was accomplished, but the other, to force the dissolution of the Diet by June 19, was not realized. On June 18, we had 330,000 people demonstrating around the Diet, and among them some 40,000 people began a sit-in, which continued throughout the night. But, in the end, the new treaty was passed and the curtain closed on the largest citizen movement in postwar Japan, albeit one that ended in failure. Naively, I believed in democracy and thought that if the people expressed their opposition clearly and unequivocally, the possibility of stopping something was genuine. For people who believed in this possibility, there was a depth of disappointment and disillusionment that was immeasurable. But there were also people who refused to give up.

On July 2, a nationwide meeting to refuse to recognize the new treaty was convened, and around one hundred thousand people participated. The Women's Cooperative Association to Protect Individual Rights also called for nonrecognition and demonstrated to dissolve the Diet. Even after all this, then, the women's Ampo struggle movement continued to evolve steadily. (108–12)

Working Women and the Emergence of an Affluent Lifestyle (yutaka na seikatsu)

When I entered the advertising department of Tôei, the leader in historical epic films (*jidaigeki*), movies were the leading form of popular entertainment. It was the Golden Age of Japanese film.

Even though Tôei was the acknowledged leader in these epic films, in 1961 even it was turning to contemporary dramas. And then advertising producers had to effectively promote these new films with increasingly limited budgets all the way up to the moment they hit the theaters. I guess you could say that this was done in order to combat the rise of television.

Japan became blessed with an affluent lifestyle for the first time in its history when the era of high-speed economic growth fueled by the electronics boom took off. In other words, electronic goods served as the growth engine for this period of rapid economic growth. In 1960, when the so-called Jimmu Prosperity, the consumer electronics boom, seemingly dropped on us out of the clear blue sky, there was a degree of growth in the home electronics industry that could scarcely have been imagined in the prewar era.

Within this electronics boom, the television boom was particularly striking. In 1956, in all of Japan there were about 300,000 households that owned television sets. But with the rate of diffusion doubling every year, especially in 1959 when the crown prince got married, there was a record expansion in the number of television sets, so that by 1960 there were 3.6 million in use. The number of television sets in homes had doubled in five years. By 1963, 91 percent of Japanese households had a television set.

The television boom was definitely a threat to the motion picture companies. If people were going to be lured out of their sitting rooms, where they could enjoy the pleasure of their precious little boxes, and not only leave the house but pay the transportation to a movie theater and then pay the price of admission, there was going to have to be a very grand-scale, exciting work of entertainment awaiting them there.

As the well-known producer Makino Mitsuo used to say in one of his favorite expressions, "If we do not make films that earn money, then, in the end, films will be devoured by television." Given this, all the film companies rushed to produce big, lavish productions, and even at Tôei this required the birth of a new kind of advertising producer. That I was selected as a woman to become an advertising producer was because they thought I might be able to find a way to get housewives, who had already been captivated by television, back into the movie theaters by offering them lavish productions aimed at a female audience.

After My Maternity Leave, I Return to Work Very Excited

In those days, women were covered by the Motherhood Protection Law: our overtime hours were restricted, and we were not permitted to work late at night. But this kind of protection did not fit very well with the duties of an advertising producer. After I punched my time card I would just return to my desk and continue doing what I was doing even though I was off the clock, often working long hours late into the night. One day, when I was in my second year, I collapsed in the middle of working and had to be taken away by ambulance. The result of my physical examination, though, was that I was pregnant. I had started to have a miscarriage and was extremely anemic, so not only was the fetus in danger but so was I.

I had an operation to stop the hemorrhaging and returned to work. Unfortunately, according to the guidelines of the Motherhood Protection

Law, I could no longer be an advertising producer; instead I was assigned to the public relations department.

On June 30, 1963, I safely gave birth to a healthy baby daughter. Wanting her to grow up to be a strong and supple woman, I named her Azusa (Catalpa Bow).

On the day on which my maternity leave was over, with my heart racing in anticipation, I returned to work. Feeling light and nimble, I was eager to throw myself back into my work with all the energy I could muster. I was all ready to take on the appropriate work for Japan's first female advertising producer. My heart, filled as it was with hopes, dreams, and expectations, I was thrilled and excited to a degree that surprised even me.

But, alas, I was not to be able to return to my position as an advertising producer. If you think about it, this was a company that secretly still had a system that required women to quit if they got married. Now someone had appeared who wanted to challenge this system and raise a child while working, and I guess that this was the company's response.

That was not all. Given that television was getting the better of movies, clearly the sun was setting on the film industry. I guessed that the older, established studios like Tôhô and Shochiku would survive just because they were older and established. Unfortunately, Tôei was one of the newer studios. The company president, Ôkawa Hiroshi, was, at bottom, not a film person at all. He had just thought that profits were there to be made, so he got into managing a film company.

If something did not appear to be profitable, he would turn it into something that was. With this kind of management philosophy in mind, theaters directly under Tôei were transformed into bowling alleys and hotels. If this was the case, then there was no need to make the kind of movies we had been making. Accordingly, there was no longer hardly any more overtime or working deep into the night; this meant that employees who could not really earn a living started to leave the company.

Almost all of the employees had joined Tôei because they loved movies. Then, all of a sudden, if they were going to be told to go work at a hotel or a bowling alley owned by the company, they were not about to find this very satisfying. Particularly, those who worked directly on the sets where movies were made were movie people right down to the soles of their feet, and they wanted no part of these other entities.

So at both the Kyoto and Tokyo studios there was a two-pronged labor dispute opposing inappropriate transfers and calling for an increase in base salaries. Those of us at the main office supported the strikers. The company responded by dismissing the labor union leaders from both studios. This was followed by a struggle over individual rights, and they went forward with the strike. However, before you knew it, a second union was formed, and as if we were being crushed by an avalanche, the second union people got the upper hand. I presented my resignation.

Someone I had formerly considered a friend quipped, "Women are enviable. They can get by on their husband's salary." At that time, my husband was just getting started as a scriptwriter, so he was plugging away on scripts that he could not sell. While he was doing this, we relied on my salary as the primary income. But in the spring of 1967, I became unemployed. . . . (113–16)

From the Student Upheaval to the Women's Lib Movement

Japan's women's lib movement made its appearance on the streets on October 21, 1970, at an international antiwar demonstration. In response to a call for "Women's Liberation! Preparatory Contact Meeting!" some two hundred helmeted women bearing placards with slogans such as "What the Hell Is Femininity Anyway?" (*Onna-rashisa tte nani?*), "Housewives and Whores May Appear to Be Different, but They Are Really the Same," and "Was Your Mother's Marriage Really Happy?" proceeded to attract a lot of attention as they marched through the Ginza streets.

Since the *Asahi* newspaper had made a point of signaling the event with a "Woman's Lib Arrives in Japan" headline and a big picture spread, this day when women's liberation first appeared in Japan was officially documented. Other headlines from the *Asahi* include "Women's Lib Arrives in a Male Paradise" (October 4), "Formal Accusation of [Using] Male Logic: The Language of Woman's Lib" (October 6), "Calling for Woman's Lib: A Change in Consciousness Is the Aim" (October 8), and "Women's Lib: They Made Us Say It, Too" (October 10). All of these were headlines in October of 1970. This new women's liberation movement that had blossomed in America and spread throughout the country was dubbed "women's lib" by the *Asahi* and introduced to Japanese readers; moreover, it was accurately reported that a similar movement was growing here. As these headlines clearly reveal, the attitudes toward this movement were extremely derisive.

The call for a preliminary meeting to establish connections among interested people that was issued at the time for the International Antiwar Day demonstration also included a call for an October 21 women's liberation demonstration. This call was issued by three people: Tanaka Mitsu, Asakawa Mari, and Khalid.[7] Taking their name from the occasion of the International Antiwar Day, they called themselves Group: Fighting Women (*Guruppu tatakau onna*).

In an *Asahi shinbun* photograph we can see depicted the character for "resentment" emblazoned on the Group: Fighting Women's flag as it flutters in the wind. And ever since that day, wherever women went to demonstrate, that flag was always unfurled to flutter in the wind. What sentiments or ideas were expressed by this flag?

Figure 3.1. Female demonstrators unfurl a banner. (From Mizoguchi Akiyo, Saeki Yôko, and Miki Sôko, eds., *Shiryô Nihon Uuman ribushi*, vol. 1, *1969–1972* [Kyoto: Shokadô shoten], 1992–95], 263.)

> *In the dark of the night*
> *At the edge of the earth—drip, drip*
> *Panting, squirming, continuing to burn*
> *Women's deep-seated resentment*
> *Is erupting into the air*
> *The flag of rebellion is unfurled*
> *It is women's rebellion*
> *It is a revolt . . . a woman's revolt*
> *Against the systems of control that do not allow*
> *Women to live as women*
> *We are approaching now with our straw mats and iron pots*

This is what that one, single character on the flag expresses. The women of the lib movement were mostly in their twenties and thirties. Tanaka Mitsu had been a bar hostess, but there were also many other women from the night trades such as young women working at ramen shops, go-go girls, nude models, and so on—in other words, women who were out to make and save as much money as they could in the shortest period of time.

In her capacity as leader, Tanaka Mitsu tended to respect those who dwelled in the lower strata of society, so she gave them encouragement, but there was also an age limit for those working in the night trade. While calling on women to be independent, when you looked at these women who continued working in nightclubs and bars, you might think that her [version of the women's liberation] movement was limited to the younger age groups.

But I imagine that they must have looked at me, someone who was entering her forties and had held a job in the mass media, as a member of the elite who was thoroughly enmeshed in the system. At the meetings I attended, the question was often raised in a very critical way: "Why do we have to live being held hostage to the current marriage system?" On these occasions, I would respond, "As someone born and raised in the prewar period, I would have to say that I am a product of compromise. But that is not to say that I have completely caved in to the system and lived these forty years without giving it another thought. When I was young and flexible, I, too, was able to play with radical language. Let us meet and talk again when you are all in your forties."

Nevertheless, the principles of woman's lib were fresh and exciting, and in terms of its ideology and the form that the movement took, it differed significantly from the existing varieties of the women's movement in Japan. So, without question, I was steadily drawn to this new type of women's liberation movement.

Aiming for a Revolution in My Internal "Feminine Consciousness"

One big difference with the existing form of the women's liberation movement was that women's lib, first and foremost, aimed for a revolution in the internal feminine consciousness (*onna ishiki no henkaku*) of the participants themselves. They were genuinely appealing for a revolution in consciousness. When you think about it, fundamentally, the objective of the women's liberation movement should never have been to be satisfied with just transforming the social system. It should inevitably result in an internal transformation of the movement's participants themselves, and, if you look at Hiratsuka Raichô's Seitô movement, you could say that in prewar society to participate in a women's liberation movement meant that one was clearly going against the grain of society. So, obviously, in that era, one could not have participated in the women's liberation movement without giving serious consideration to a revolution in consciousness.

However, in the postwar era, legal equality between men and women was fully established, and whatever individual men may have thought internally, externally the idea of criticizing the demand for equal rights for women on moral grounds had disappeared. As long as the constitution guaranteed equality between the sexes, participating in a movement that demanded this kind of equality was no longer any kind of deviation; it was already the norm. In fact, it was like that for me when, in the midst of these postwar social conditions—when this kind of behavior could even be considered progressive—I started working at Tôei. At that time, the postwar women's liberation movement was making comprehensive appeals on behalf of women's rights, and the emphasis was on working through labor unions and improving working conditions, trying to get better child care facilities, and so on.

I suppose it is difficult to deny the fact that in that era there was a tendency to steal from Peter to pay Paul. In other words, the individuals who sustained the system by virtue of their everyday practices—whether they supported the system or hoped to transform it—more or less abandoned any sense that they were building a new system by bringing about a revolution in consciousness.

By virtue of this process of stealing from one another, people had a tendency to be co-opted by the system and actually become supporters of an oppressive structure. So to distinguish themselves from this variety of women's liberation, "woman's lib" activists looked at themselves not as housewives (*fujin*) but as women (*onna*), and rather than working toward a revolution from within the system, they were aiming for a revolution in consciousness as the first order of business for their movement.

Tanaka Mitsu and her colleagues spoke in a very direct kind of language; even though it made me kind of wince, she would use crude terms like *brat* (*gaki*) or *punk* (*meshi*) as a reaction against the notion of femininity (*onna-rashisa*).[8]

At the beginning of the 1970s, most women still felt that they were living their lives bound up with some stereotypical image of women. At the core of women's culture, of course, was the social expectation for a woman's role, which included marriage, becoming a wife and mother and a housewife whose duties involved devoting herself to cooking, housework, and child rearing. Women internalized this notion of the ideal woman, and thus not only were they pressured into wanting to become "a good wife" (*yoi oyome-san*) but, for the vast majority of them, this goal was so deeply internalized that it became the object of their own inner wishes and desires.

Of course, it was not as though all women did get married and become housewives. But a single woman was not just a woman who did not get married but a woman who was not *yet* married (*mikon*), in other words, a woman who should eventually be married but is not married yet. Or, in the case of a society that treats her as an unmarriageable woman, most single women are just waiting to be married, so they remain firmly under the control of that desire to marry.

Also, many of the women who were in dual-income marriages, a position supported by the existing women's liberation movement, felt guilty about having been forced to do this. It was painful to read at the time about surveys revealing that, more than ordinary housewives, these women were obsessed with their salaries. And after all, I was one of those dual-income women myself.

So, if we look at it this way, it is pretty obvious that even though women's lives may appear to be multifaceted, in fact the model of the stay-at-home housewife and good wife was really, for the vast majority of women, the framework that gave their lives and behavior direction. In this sense, "femininity" or "womanliness," and the image of the "ideal woman" gradually became less something that was forced on women by the ruling class system or dictated to them by men and more something in which women themselves were complicit. So whether it is in relation to themselves or to other women, besides wanting to have the kind of nature or personality that they would prefer, they needed to find a way to free themselves from this stereotypical image of women, and they had do this not by launching an outward assault on others but by understanding the inherent contradictions and then looking inward to confront their own feminine consciousness.

In order to construct a feminine logic, then, the movement offered "Lib Camps," with topics like "What shall we do next year?" and "Let's get together and boil the problem of 'Lib' down to its basics" and so on, so that they could consciously look at women's everyday lives and, using colloquial, hypermetric language, place their own life stories at the center of the discourse and confess that the reality of discrimination against women is rooted in their own consciousness as women. By continually assessing and indicting wrongs, the woman's lib movement could be clearly distinguished not only from the existing women's liberation movement but from the new left-wing movements as well, and, in this way, the lib movement could advocate for a revolution in women's consciousness.

In the Company of Other Women, Pouring Our Hearts Out

The "Lib" Shinjuku Center—known as the Lib Cen for short—was a two-bedroom condominium located about a fifteen-minute walk from Shinjuku Station. It opened on September 30, 1972. It was launched mainly by members of two groups, the Fighting Women Group and S-E-X, both of which had members who lived there. Later on, members from Tokyo Komu-umu, the Scarlet Letter, and the Fighting Women League also became members and even though they took some different directions from time to time, they basically all continued to work together until the spring of 1977. The single most significant purpose in founding the Lib Cen was for the women who participated in the lib movement to be able to explore their collective nature and connectedness. The Lib Cen magazine, called *This Single Path*, first appeared in October 1972. In an article by Tanaka Mitsu, "Talking about the Lib Center," she wrote that they were aiming for "One large collective," and she refers to "the connectedness built by sisters based on everyday living."

In October, to mark the founding of the Lib Shinjuku Center, a meeting was held under the banner "A meeting for women who are living earnestly and want to pour their hearts out to one another while being surrounded by other women." People who recounted their stories included a part black, mixed-race woman, Tsuboi Fumiko (twenty-five years old); a Takadanobaba pawnshop owner, Suzuki Yoshi (seventy-one); sixty-year-old Maruki Toshi, who continued to draw pictures of the atomic bombings; and forty-one-year-old me. This is how my life story was recorded.

Yoshitake Teruko (critic), forty-one years old

> Was it really an accident that her character was shaped by being gang-raped by American soldiers, members of the occupying army, at the dawn of the postwar era? Just at that time, the new constitution was created, and gender equality was loudly proclaimed. It is difficult for us today to appreciate how exciting it must have been for women of her generation, who had lived through the war, to see these changes brought about.

> With this gang-rape incident as her starting point, she lived her life alone, always wondering who had done this to her and how her character was affected, so that her life was really an empty imitation.

> It was such a person who was singled out to become the first female advertising producer in Japan; she joined Tôei seven years later. . . . However, because of childbirth, she was robbed of her position. This experience convinced her that in the postwar history of women, that is, the postwar democracy that she encountered working hard on the front lines as she did, what a lie gender equality was, and how much she detested what she had been through.

At present, she is continuing to research women's history and labor problems while working as a critic. So what we have to ask ourselves is how can we deepen our understanding of the problems that she had to experience as a member of her generation? (From *Seeking Living Proof*)[9]

Just recently I saw at the Kyoto women's bookstore Shokadô a three-volume women's history work that never even made a profit when it was published called *Materials: A History Japan's Woman's Lib* (*Shiryô Nihon Ûman ribbushi*). On looking inside, I found a section called "A Meeting Where Women Who Lived Earnestly Poured Out Their Hearts in the Company of Other Women," and what jumped out at me was the recollections of four women who spoke at the meeting.

As I continued to live with the knowledge of how difficult it can be to recover one's control over mind and body after an experience of violence, it did not matter if I was at home or in the workplace, or even working with the union or being active in citizens movements—I could not get over this feeling of discomfort, this feeling of isolation, a feeling that I had no place where I truly belonged. Moreover, whenever I heard men talking in loud voices, telling people what to do, this forced me to remember the rape incident, and I would become enveloped in a sense of hatred and fear.

Trying to live my life while concealing my rape left me with a feeling of inferiority. The greater this sense of inferiority, the more I began to feel as though there was no adequate reason why I should be forced to live my life that way. When I would catch the sound of men talking, I could not help but feel sensitive to inherent violence in their sense of superiority, and, increasingly, more than men themselves, it was male society that I was growing to detest and feel isolated from. This male society was something that contributed to the whole sense of alienation that I was experiencing.

That I became able, in these circumstances, to begin to talk about my rape experience, and to write about it, was due entirely to my encounter with {the activists in} women's lib because they helped me to be aware of the existence of a feminine consciousness located inside each one of us. Why had I lived for a quarter of a century trying to conceal the fact that I was a rape victim? Why had I been constantly plagued by a sense of inferiority? As I continued to probe these questions, it suddenly became quite obvious. It was because I was, in the end, still bound up in a stereotypical image of women that defined women's happiness in terms of getting married, being a good wife, and being a good mother.

By talking about my own rape experience, and beginning to write about it, I learned that rape is not simply a violation of the flesh; it is an infringement of the respect women should have as human beings. As such, it is the worst crime against humankind. And also I learned that a violation of this sort is not a caused by animalistic instincts at all. It must be clearly recognized as a product of the culture of male superiority, and this recognition must become fully integrated into our women's logic. Learning all this was part of my healing process. It was very slow, but I gradually began to feel my confidence and pride return to life. The first step toward my own personal liberation began with recounting my rape experience and writing about it. (124–32, emphasis mine)

Encounters with "Lib" throughout Japan

The second time women's lib was sensationalized by the media was on the occasion of the Lib Camp held in August 1971.

This Lib Camp took place on August 21–24, three nights and four days at a ski resort on the Shinano Plain called the Hutte Rinsô. In the previous year, after the "10–21 Demo," with the Fighting Women Group, the Fighting Women League, S-E-X, and others at the core, "A Gathering to Discuss Women's Liberation" had been held on several different occasions. Moreover, in December there was the "1970 General Discussion Group," and in 1971 the discussions continued. Gradually a policy started to develop, and, as the range of women participants began to expand, on February 20 it was decided to hold the first Women's Lib Rally. However, because of insufficient preparations, it had to be postponed. But from among the women who did gather there, some new executive committee members were selected, and they were able to arrange a expanded summer meeting and the Lib Camps.

Women from all over Japan were widely recruited to participate in the Lib Camps. The word was spread by such minimal means as flyers, word of mouth, and so on, and there were quite a few women who, seeking a new form of women's liberation, elected to participate by themselves. The women—and this was just one portion of the women there—certainly continued to change. In this sense, one could say that the timing of the Lib Camp was really very good.

On that day, relying on just a single half sheet of newsletter, the *Lib Shinjuku News*, 257 women, some with children in tow, came from all over Japan, from Hokkaido to Kyûshû, and for twenty hours or more they introduced themselves and talked about their dissatisfaction with men, their general discontent with society, and their anger. They talked about the extremely difficult positions they had been put in because they were women and the pain they felt because there seemed to be no way out. They noted various types of behavior that could be traced to patterns internalized because they themselves had used the excuse that they were women, and so they became aware of how they constantly censored and monitored themselves. . . . These women wanted to develop solidarity with other women, so they continued to talk about the conditions in which they had been placed and how they wanted to speak frankly about all the problems that they encountered.

Although the Lib Camp was exposed to harsh media criticism and ridicule as a scandalous undertaking, the key word for this early phase of the lib movement was *encounters*. For most of the women involved, the encounters at Lib Camp were really a way to have an encounter with themselves. As they encountered other women like themselves, they came face to face with new ideas, and they came to understand that the position in which they had been placed was the result of the oppressive nature of a dual structure that was inherent in a society controlled by men. They also became aware that their feelings of being trapped, of there being no way out, were not at all a personal or individual problem; rather, they was something that also resulted from the oppressive nature of a society controlled by men. From this, they could assert that it was not divisiveness but "sisterhood" that was necessary.

In response to an appeal by the Lib Camp Organizing Committee, a nationwide lib network was created. In Kyoto a women's group demonstrated, and, in the fall during school festivals, beginning at Chiba University, discussions and lectures about woman's lib took place. Also reading groups were founded, and a little pamphlet, *Onna kara onna e* (From Women to Women), and a lib magazine, *Onna Eros* (Woman Eros) were launched.

On December 6, the *Onna iro ero shisôshûkai* (Women's Eros and Sexuality Study Group) was established, and regular weekly lecture meetings were held to debate what the content of the mass meeting would be. The next year, in January 1972, thirty women founded a group called the Association to Assist with the May Lib Meeting to undertake preparations and public relations before this next meeting, so there was a constant revolving set of activities going on.

Then, finally, it was the night before the big meeting was to commence. An evening that was dubbed a "Festival for Women and Children" offered a lecture on Kanno Suga[10] by Takarai Kinnô and a five-hour panel discussion— held without a break and attended by over five hundred women—featuring Kageyama Yûko, Higuchi Keiko, Arima Makiko, Iijima Aiko, Ozawa Ryôko, and Tanaka Mitsu.

Some nineteen hundred people attended the meeting on May 5 at the Oka Ward Industrial Building, heralded as "A Public Meeting to Examine in Detail 'Lib' Issues." The discussions were intense, with some very rapid-fire speakers, as well as skilled and extremely emotional orators who spoke with tears streaming down their faces. And everyone was contributing. In this sense, it resembled a Lib Camp discussion, yet in the opinions expressed about the direction the women's liberation movement should take, and when concrete plans were brought up, one could see how much progress the group had been making. At this meeting, some of the following suggestions were put forth: let us widen the movement to oppose weakening the Eugenics Protection Law, let us build a collective, let us build a day care center, and why don't we publish a small-circulation journal? There was also a call for, in addition to the women's movement centered on the established political parties and the labor movement, a citizens-movement-style approach to expanding the reach of women's liberation such as "No Name, Equal Floorism," "This Method of Finger Stopping," "Direct Participatory Democracy," "Self-Revolution," and "Revolutionizing Everyday Life."

However, the question remains, why did the lib movement penetrate into such a broad sphere? Most of the women who were involved with the early stages of the lib movement had participated in one way or another in the joint struggle movements, and had suffered—on multiple occasions—from being in movements dominated by male subjectivity, so they had already begun to question closely and precisely what it means to be a woman. (132–34)

Analysis

Yoshitake asks and answers an important question about why the lib movement was able to engage so many women: it was because women had already labored alongside men in all the various "struggle" movements prior to 1970, be it the student movement or the Ampo struggle. From this they learned a powerful lesson. In order to probe the question of what it means to be a woman in postwar Japan, women needed their own space, their own movement, where they would not be controlled or dominated by male subjectivity. The early postwar years were a time of genuine hope and optimism about the future. Japan seemed to be on a trajectory toward democracy and gender equality. The unprecedented outpouring of opposition at the time of the Ampo Movement was a source of inspiration to many Japanese, but it had not ended on an optimistic note. As Yoshitake observes, "I believed in democracy and thought that if the people expressed their opposition, then the possibility of stopping something was genuine. For people who believed in this possibility, there was a depth of disappointment and disillusionment that was immeasurable." There was also disappointment stemming from the fact that once she gave birth to her daughter she could not return to her former position, suggesting to her that male supremacy in the workplace still remained a powerful force.

Moreover, not unlike the "rationalization" instituted by management at the newspaper where Kishino Junko was employed (discussed in the next chapter), Yoshitake found that businessmen were now running Tôei, not people who were devoted to film, something that seemed to her to signal a turn away from the ideals of postwar democracy.

Few women writers labor as intently as Yoshitake does to explore the connections between the Ampo Movement and women's lib, and she uncovers the connection that she seeks in the way that young men and women worked together in organizations. Working alongside male students in the turbulent post-Ampo student demonstrations of the late 1960s taught women to be wary of finding room for their agendas when they shared leadership with males. But the seeds were sown for a movement in which women could own their own subjectivity and seek answers to the kinds of questions that they wanted to pose. As Funabashi Kuniko recalled, Zenkyôtô—the all-campus joint struggle committee—"began as a personal query by each individual . . . each and every student was to become the subject of the movement as an individual." It was in this sense that she believed that women's lib could occur only as a "post-Zenkyôtô movement."[11] The 1970s woman's lib movement offered women something that the radical student movement could not: a sense of community with other women. At rallies, demonstrations, meetings, and especially the Lib Camps, women had the opportunity to be with other women—even if they were hotly contesting issues that divided them. More often, though, they were "pouring their hearts out" to one another, learning about themselves and their bodies, and challenging linguistically and culturally derived definitions of womanliness and femininity. The core of Yoshitake's textual strategy is to tell the story of the women's movement from the vantage point of a transformation in feminine consciousness. She places before the reader the dilemma she had struggled with since her rape. Why did she feel the way she did? Why did she feel so inferior, and why did she hold herself responsible? It was because she had internalized a stereotype of what a woman is and what she should be from the constructed cultural order surrounding her.

By the very act of recognizing this—something she claims she never could have done without the resources and support provided by the women's lib movement—and by writing and talking about her experiences—she is able to find a way out. In spite of the painful and humiliating social realities confronting her, she was able to construct her own feminine consciousness. The very process of discovering (or constructing) that feminine consciousness enables her to find that point where the social order leaves off and her own, very personal, individual consciousness begins. Where and how to draw that line is something historians have struggled with over the last four decades, ever since Michel Foucault introduced the idea of the dispersed, decentered subject, which threw "the concepts of agency, experience and practice into disarray, since absent a purposive historical actor and any concept of intentionality, it became impossible to establish a ground from which the individual could fashion his or her destiny on the basis of his or her experience in the world."[12] But clearly events *do* happen, people participate in social and political movements, and they become engaged with the world around them. In Yoshitake's case, there is a clear link between her activism, her engagement with the women's movement, and her discovery of that "site" where the socially conditioned order clashes with her own subjectivity and agency.

Yoshitake takes her narrative a step further in this chapter, though, and sees in the development of a feminine consciousness the possibility of transcending cultural limitations by asserting her own power to write and speak for herself as an autonomous and viable historical agent, someone with her own feminine subjectivity. In her text, she is able to illuminate "the disjunction between culturally given meanings and the individual uses of them in contingent, historically conditioned ways."[13] A woman in Yoshitake's situation may rely on strategic and tactical uses of language and discourse in order to make new ways of understanding the world possible, but this also enables her to place demands on that world and the systems it embodies.[14] The following chapter echoes this one by offering a central place for a discussion of how this new kind of language, and the practices associated with the notion of a feminine consciousness, develops. Moreover, it underlines how this discourse is juxtaposed against the powerful resistance offered by internalized models of socially constructed femininity (*onna-rashisa*). Centering on the narrative of a newspaper reporter, Kishino Junko, it tells the story of how, in her struggle to create and sustain gender equality in the workplace, she felt compelled to develop her own female subjectivity and agency in the form of her *onna-ishiki*, her feminine consciousness.

4

CREATING A FEMININE CONSCIOUSNESS

KISHINO JUNKO'S "ONNA NO CHIHEI KARA MIETE-KITA MONO: JOSEI KISHA NO JIBUNSHI"

Approximately a quarter of a century before Yoshitake Teruko published her recollections about how the women's liberation movement gave her a haven and a voice that she sorely needed, newspaperwoman Kishino Junko published a moving account of her own encounter with women's lib— *Things Visible from a Woman's Perspective*—which took place around the same time as Yoshitake's.[1] There are several similarities between the two women and their experiences: Kishino was born in 1930, Yoshitake in 1931; Kishino graduated from Tokyo Women's College in 1953 while Yoshitake graduated from the considerably more prestigious Keiô University a year later, in 1954. They were both members of that first wave of women to enter four-year universities in the early postwar years, and to be permitted to take entrance examinations for some select companies as graduation neared.

Both authors write about the situation they faced as women in the workplace, but Kishino, especially, dedicates a substantial portion of text not only to the subject of gender equality in the workplace but to labor-management relations at her newspaper as well. She depicts how these relations were transformed over the years she worked there, becoming increasingly inhospitable to employees with a socially progressive outlook. And, perhaps most important, in a manner similar to Yoshitake, Kishino describes how her encounter with the women's liberation movement came at a critical moment in her life—she was just turning forty years of age—and how this encounter reoriented her understanding of the world and her place in it, leading her, in the end, to "reposition" herself in relation to society and women's place in it. Kishino adopts a textual strategy that allows her to interweave recollections of workplace conditions, excerpts from her diary, the story of her engagement with members of the company union, her participation in the Ampo protest movement, and, finally, her encounter with the women's lib movement. This strategy enables her to graft her own personal story onto the story of postwar

Japan, in much the same way that Yoshitake manifests a commitment to interweave her story with a history of women's organizations and movements in Japan.

However, Kishino's narrative includes an interesting rhetorical twist centered around a film she had seen that had a powerful emotional impact on her, a film that sparked a series of penetrating reflections on what her life had amounted to up this time. She describes sitting in a darkened movie theater, reduced to tears, as she watches a story unfold that speaks directly to her heart, a story about postwar dreams and ambitions and the heavy price that must be paid when ideals are sacrificed on the altar of "progress." The two women clearly share a similar outlook on society and politics, and while Yoshitake does talk about how the Korean War took something precious away from the Japanese, if anything, Kishino is even more explicit in her text about how her hopes and "dreams" for the ideal of postwar democracy were shattered and how disappointing, even crushing, that experience was. She opens her memoir with some of her recollections about the dream of postwar democracy.

Prologue: The Dream of Postwar Democracy

I became a newspaper reporter in 1953, so exactly a quarter century has passed since then. The place where I worked, the *Sangyô keizai shinbun* (Industrial Economic News), was located in a four-story, soot-stained building on the banks of the river. Some days the breeze from the river was heavily laden with the odor of marshy riverbanks.

In my recollections, the basement and first floor were given over to the printing facilities where a tall rotary press was in operation. The smell of printer's ink permeated the building. Up the narrow, worn stone stairway to the third floor were the editorial offices where the cultural affairs department was located. It was there, amid the noise of the printing press and the clanking of the trains that rolled by on the elevated track nearby, that I wrote my articles.

Under that bridge for the train tracks, just off to the left, was a coffeehouse we used to frequent. In the evenings, as the light from our building reflected off the dark surface of the river, the smell of *yakitori* from the shops underneath the bridge would waft up our way, beckoning to us. In those days, the other big newspapers, like the *Asahi*, the *Mainichi,* and the *Yomiuri*, which have since moved, were all down in this Yûrakuchô area, and they animated that little corner of the Ginza (which was not as brightly lit then as it is today) with their lights and the hum of their printing presses. As I sit here, these memories of sounds and smells from my youth, twenty-five years ago, which were deeply embedded in my consciousness, float insistently to the surface.

1953. A little more than seven years since the end of the war, one year after the occupation had been officially concluded by the Peace Treaty of April 1952, a time of unforgettable events. It was the era of the Yoshida Cabinets. Just what kind of period was this for postwar Japan? Reaching into a drawer where memories are kept, and checking some of those recollections against newspaper clippings detailing events from that era, an image of a truly striking period comes through.

In the year of the Peace Treaty, 1952, which led into 1953, the most unforgettable incident was Bloody May Day.[2] I was a student at Tokyo Women's University at the time, but at Waseda University they were staging a production of the Soviet playwright [Konstantin] Simonov's (1915–79) "Under the Chestnut Trees of Prague."[3] There were friends of mine who had participated in the May Day demonstrations and been severely injured. In July the government started coming down very hard on students and workers, implementing the law against destructive behavior aimed at student groups and laborers active in demonstrations, and this law was coupled with two others designed to preserve the public peace: the laws creating the Public Security Investigation Agency and a Public Safety Commission. In October, in the first election since independence, the fourth Yoshida Cabinet was established in an atmosphere of popular concern about rearmament, and by the end of the year, a large strike of charcoal makers and electric utility workers occurred.

In March 1953, Prime Minister Yoshida called the chairman of the Socialist Party an idiot (*bakayarô*) leading to a motion of no confidence being introduced in the Lower House of the Diet, which was dissolved so an election could be held on April 19. Just prior to that, the US government had announced its policy toward Japan, and even when there was a sudden and unexpected cease-fire in the Korean conflict, they guaranteed that the special procurement purchases would not be suddenly curtailed. Between June and July, there were widespread demonstrations against American bases in Japan, and in August, despite fierce opposition, antistrike legislation was passed. In October the so-called Ikeda-Patterson meeting to discuss economic and defense issues was held. Even before this, talks on the MSA [Mutual Security Arrangement] had gotten under way, and it would be completed and ratified in March of the following year, 1954. Shortly thereafter, a secrecy protection act was passed, in May. In June the second Self-Defense Law (establishing the Self-Defense Forces and the Self-Defense Agency) was passed, so by July the Self-Defense Forces came into being, which meant that, in reality, Japan had taken its first steps toward rearmament. This law meant that Japan could strengthen its defense capability and would receive US economic assistance to further that end. . . .

When we take all of these events together—the recent ending of the occupation, the onset of the Cold War dividing the world into two camps, East and West, the push to establish genuine independence while retaining a strong American presence in Japan, and the onset of an era in which serious conflicts emerged between the two camps and with those who were opposed to the Cold War divisions, with all the appropriate players lined up on the same stage—I could not help feeling that we were seeing a preview of what the coming world was going to look like.

At bottom, it was not as though I was thinking of that era in these terms at the time. Having come out of the first wave of the new university system in an unprecedented era in which graduates from both the old and new systems were competing for the few jobs available, quite by happenstance, I became a newspaper reporter. As my youth unfolded against the backdrop of the new constitution and its declaration of an era of equality between men and women, it was absolutely natural for me to pursue the path of establishing my independence as a woman. Even someone like me, who was neither completely self-absorbed nor a committed activist, just trying to establish my own independence seemed like the only thing in my world that was certain. Perhaps because I came from the rather sheltered world of a women's university, I assumed that the only two occupations in which men and women had an equal opportunity to establish their economic independence were the teaching profession and journalism. So journalism was the path I chose.

Well, perhaps to say that I *chose* this path is somewhat of an overstatement; it came about because I just happened to see a posting one day on the university bulletin board by a newspaper that I had never before read, the *Sangyô keizai shinbun*. This newspaper was just in the process of expanding its evening edition, so it was looking to add about thirty new employees that spring. Among them, five were to be women, and I became one of them. (7–10)

This passage establishes clearly the social and political context for Kishino's autobiography: the turbulent postwar years of labor disputes; the Korean War; the Cold War; Bloody May Day; the creation of the Self-Defense Forces—which was seen by many as an abandonment of the pacifist ideals of the postwar constitution—the establishment of the US-Japan security arrangement that would later spark the Ampo protest movement against its renewal in 1960; and the onset of rapid economic growth, which ensued in the next decade. Kishino hastens to add that, as a recent college graduate under the new, postwar educational system, she was primarily concerned with finding employment in a competitive job market and being able to establish her economic independence. That she became a reporter was really almost an accidental by-product, much the way Yoshitake found her way to Tôei Studios, because *Sankei* was one of the few companies that did not exclude females from applying. Kishino continues:

> From that point, for the next quarter of a century, I worked sixteen years as a reporter until 1969 when, in my late thirties, I quit the newspaper and became an adjunct college lecturer. After I had been teaching for a while I had my first opportunity to reexamine my past, a reflection that I published as an essay, "So That Gentleness Does Not Get Thrown Away" (*Yasashisa ga suterarenai tame ni*), which appeared in 1975 in *Atarashii chihei* (New Perspectives), no. 8. (9–10).

Figure 4.1. A copy of *Atarashii chihei.* (From Mizoguchi Akiyo, Saeki Yôko, and Miki Sôko, eds., *Shiryô Nihon Uuman ribushi* [Kyoto: Yûgen kaisha, Shokadô shoten], 2:226.) 1995.

There follows an extensive quotation from this 1975 essay, which opens with a clear assertion of the link between Kishino's story and the history of postwar Japan.

I was a part of that generation in which the individual stories of our youth were inextricably linked to [the story of] postwar Japan. Specifically, I entered the university in 1949 under the new system, which opened the gates of universities equally to men and women; graduated in 1953; and entered a newspaper company that was officially allowing women to take its entrance exam for the very first time. The barriers that had been erected in prewar Japan to deny women access to positions just because they were women (*onna ga yue ni*) were being swept away one by one, it seemed, and we experienced the ardor of being part of that first wave to surmount these obstacles. Perhaps for me, because "postwar democracy" was coterminus with "equal rights for men and women" (*danjo-dōken*), this latter slogan became such a meaningful part of my existence that it became a pillar on which I based my entire life course.

This postwar era, in which I began my working life as a reporter, was an incredible period marked by the "Economic White Paper" of 1956, which declared the end of the postwar period and the onset of a period of economic prosperity that would have been unimaginable in the early postwar years. In the field of education, moral education was linked to a system of efficiency ratings, a trend to which there was strong opposition. In 1960 there was the Ampo Movement, in 1964 the Tokyo Olympics, and within a blink of an eye we were heading into the era of rapid economic growth.

In 1969, after sixteen years spent working as a reporter, I quit that world and entered a new workplace, the college campus, where fierce student demonstrations and battles were still taking place. But it afforded me the opportunity to look back on those sixteen years during which I had been running frantically, like a racehorse with blinders on, unable to see anything on either side of me, only what was right in front of me. So I reflected a lot about what I had been through. What had kept me going as a reporter during those years? I discovered that there were two pillars that provided me support. The first was the energy that came from being in the first wave of women able to take advantage of the newly proclaimed equality between the sexes. No one understood better than we who were in the front lines how wide the gulf was between the ideal of working side by side with men in a open environment and the reality in which equality was largely a matter of form only. I felt it was the duty of those of us in the first wave to try and shrink that gap between reality and the ideal as much as possible. In order to have my efforts as a new, first-time female employee recognized, I felt this meant not just working as hard as men—when it came to such things as, for example, staying to work through the night like the men or overcoming the "handicap" of those who would say "She doesn't have to do that sort of work because she is a woman"—but working harder than men.

The second pillar that supported me during these years was the idea of "reporting the truth." I had many older colleagues who had been reporters during the war. They shared the resolve of people who had learned a powerful lesson from the war: if you cannot report the truth, the people will be led into war. They had no intention of ever repeating that experience. So, in addition to making sure each one of us reported the truth as we saw it, we poured our energies into making sure that any truths unearthed by colleagues did not go unreported. Unfortunately, in a strongly establishment-oriented newspaper like ours, this could mean putting up with unfairly being labeled as "Reds" or leftists. Our dream was to achieve the distant goal of socialism, which still remains unattained today.

So, supported by these two pillars—perhaps they could be lumped into the single category of the spirit of postwar democracy—I worked for the next sixteen years, from my early twenties to my late thirties. But in terms of results, the reality was that the ideals I was aiming for only continued to recede. Even as the dream of equality between men and women faded and the gap between us became all the more striking, the newspaper itself became systematically more establishment oriented. The male reporters, buoyed by their feelings of camaraderie, either got the positions in the organization that they felt they deserved or just abandoned ship. But what did I have to show for investing the best years of my youth? I could not help feeling that all I had ended up doing was becoming another cog in the wheel of Japan's high-speed economic growth machine. This was the source of profound feelings of disappointment for me.

Tormented by these kinds of thoughts, I happened to see a film that truly opened my eyes. Called *The Woman I Abandoned*, it was directed by Urayama Kiriyo and was based on an Endô Shûsaku story.[4] Perhaps one thing that attracted me to the film was a feeling of generational solidarity with the director. The main character in the film was a young student activist with a dark side. Because of his impoverished background and his deeply held ambitions, I couldn't help being reminded of some of the young men with whom I grew up. Anyway, this character became disaffected with activism and sought temporary refuge in the arms of an innocent young woman named Mitsu, probably a recent middle-school graduate just arrived in the city from the countryside. Hiding his background as a political activist, he went to work for a company. Because of his intense ambition and hard work he was rewarded with rapid promotion and even became engaged to the company president's niece. The plot, of course, becomes quite predictable as he throws Mitsu over in favor of his boss's niece. *But somewhere in the relationship between the main character and the young girl, I could see my own disrupted self (bunretsu shita watashi jishin no sugata o mi)* and somehow uncover there a clue that would shed light on what postwar democracy could have been.

It was like this. The essential nature of this young woman—who inevitably had to be abandoned by the hero, who concentrated all his efforts on moving up the ladder of success—was a femininity, a gentleness (*yasashisa*), that was expressed symbolically in the film by the image of Mitsu's plain face in a close-up, looking directly at the screen. Her gentleness marks her clearly as belonging to the ranks of the oppressed.

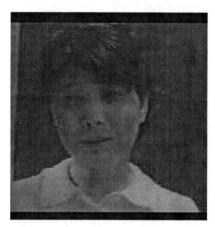

Figure 4.2. Close-up of Mitsu in *The Woman I Abandoned*. © 1999 Nikkatsu kabushiki kaisha.

It was clear to me from my own experience that postwar Japan, as it entered the period of rapid economic growth, was similarly a structure, an edifice, from which all gentleness was being excised. As someone who had placed work above all else just as male employees had, I also felt like someone who had personally thrown something away as well. Inevitably, it seemed as though it was my *yasashisa*, my femininity, that was the part of me that had become dispensable.

Yet I wonder if expressing it this way tells the whole story. At the time, I thought I was living my life consistently with the spirit and ideals of postwar democracy. But in reality my life was permeated by a duality, a *nijûsei* (二重性), because in terms of results, all that I accomplished was to feed the ambitions that supported the postwar economic miracle, exactly like my male counterparts. And all the while, what I was really doing was abandoning the part of me that was female, my feminine nature, my *yasashisa*.[5]

Just a little while after I left my position as a reporter, the so-called second wave of women's liberation, the "women's lib" movement, arrived in Japan. What I came to understand clearly from this movement was that

I needed to give up the notion that equality between the sexes was just a stepping-stone to the larger ideal of universal human liberation. No matter how hard I tried to pattern my life after men, in the end I was a woman who possessed this very "gentleness," this femininity, that was being discarded along the way. Moreover, I was startled by the enormity of what we had given up, for what we abandoned during those years was far more than just *yasashisa*. We had undermined and weakened much of the support system for postwar democracy.

This is what I believe now. I have *repositioned* (*tachi-naoshite*) myself so that I no longer stand alongside men but stand self-consciously on the side of oppressed women. I believe that we must address the faults of a structure that says that since this gentleness/*yasashisa*—symbolized by that plain, open face in the film—does not function as a force to bind people to one another, we should abandon it. I am, then, reversing my values and choosing to take up the position of women anew. As I reexamine my own short past, I believe that women's liberation must go beyond the advocacy of rights for middle-class women. For me, women's liberation must take as a point of departure the perspective of women who are oppressed, women who are expected to do the "shit work" *because* they are women (*onna de aru ga yue ni*). We need to self-consciously make this perspective our own and proceed to connect it to that part of the postwar democratic movement that is being abandoned. If we cannot move toward this kind of universal struggle for human liberation, then for what purpose was my entire youth spent?

Of course there was no way that I could have predicted it, but two years after I wrote these words I was diagnosed with breast cancer. I underwent the tortuous process of being hospitalized and undergoing surgery, and as I struggled to accept my unacceptable reality, I kept remembering the words I had written two years previously. I felt strongly that *my cancer was the inevitable rebellion of my own body against the lifestyle I had chosen*, the lifestyle that had me placing work above all else, just like men, and abandoning the part of me that was woman. *I felt that the motif that I had adopted for my essay had actually forged a connection to my life experiences and was therefore transformed into something real in my life.*

With all of this weighing down on me, I returned to my normal, everyday life, although I could never be quite sure when the cancer might reappear. Always wondering what might lie ahead for me, I began to think more and more about the task of retracing my steps along the path of life that I had chosen.

At any rate, what is now quite apparent is that my own personal history as a newspaper reporter, which corresponded to the passing of the postwar years, was actually my youth, my adolescence. Because this time period was so packed with moments—both good and bad—that it provided a direction to my life, and, beyond that, to the years that would follow. As I reflected on my past, I began to assign some clear meaning to what my own personal history—my sixteen years as a newspaper reporter—meant. Just like Japan's postwar period itself, my memories of this era are filled with regrets and remorse, and what I want to do from here on out is to probe my own experiences and create a memoir that will be shaped by the answers my questions lead me to discover. (10–15, emphasis mine)

A rich and densely packed reflection on the contours of Kishino's life, this passage points out the specific historical moments that shaped her life. Like other women of her generation, she believed that academic institutions and the workplace should offer equal opportunities for women. However, she found the atmosphere at the newspaper much less gender neutral than she had hoped, and when the Ampo struggle failed and her hopes for a neutral, pacifist—possibly even socialist—Japan faded, she began to question what she was doing and why.

The film she saw around that time made her think about what was missing in her life and what was missing in the public life of postwar Japan. She came to believe that just as Japan was losing its ideals, so she was losing her identity as a woman, her *yasashisa* or "femininity." When she was diagnosed with breast cancer, she even wondered if the disease was not somehow a consequence of the lifestyle choices she had made. In an engaging rhetorical move, she suggests that her mastectomy may have been a manifestation on the physical plane of what had been spiritually and psychically cut out of her life, and, indeed, out of postwar Japan's history. Thus, the challenges she faced in her career, the twists and turns of history, the explosion of a new mode of economic growth, the issue of gender difference, and finally her battle with cancer are all conflated to generate a compelling narrative structure. And something she makes very clear is that in the process of remembering, of creating her narrative and generating its particular structure, something profound happened. She began to experience "a connection" between what she was writing and her real "life experiences," something that, in effect, "transformed" her consciousness in the very moment that she recalled her experiences and turned them into memoir. She seems to be explicitly declaring in this single sentence that by "repositioning" herself in relation to historical events and prevailing regimes of truth, she actually transformed herself, generating a new variety of feminine consciousness, which enabled her to assert her subjectivity and historical agency.

At the outset of this study, I put forth the idea that it is possible to discover within individual subjectivities, as constructed in autobiographies or memoirs, a position—a moment—when the narrator is able to recognize that there exist differences (or tensions) between what is "given"—the historically and socially constructed reality—and how the individual might experience that reality in his or her own life.[6] In the course of becoming aware of these differences, then, it is possible for people to adapt the culturally and linguistically given terms and definitions and by putting them to new uses successfully reposition themselves in relation to historical events or present moments. Kishino Junko alludes to this point throughout the opening pages of her memoir, but she seems to make it explicit in that one italicized sentence in which she says her "motif" for reflecting and remembering forged a connection between her words and her memories and "her real life." It is not alchemy, but it is almost as powerful. It is a classic instance of someone grappling with the issues that shaped her life and undergoing a profound transformation as a result of the *process* of reflecting on and reliving those moments. While she occupies that moment of reflexivity, and gropes for a new language, a new vocabulary, that will enable her to generate her new feminine consciousness, she, in effect, not only encounters her own agency but transforms it as well.

After providing us with this powerful and tantalizing overview of the issues that her text will address, Kishino goes back to the beginning of her story and recalls her early days at the newspaper.

Early Days at Sankei: A Novice Woman Reporter

When I joined the paper in April, the morning edition was still just eight pages, but the circulation in Tokyo alone was over 650,000. From the point of view of sales, it created specialty sales operations ahead of several other newspapers, so the impetus to move from Osaka was to expand these circulation figures. . . .

In that year, five women joined the paper, and it was quite an epochal moment because bringing in five women at one time like that was sufficient to cement the paper's reputation as one with a women's financial column worth purchasing the paper for. . . .

Looking back over that period, it was a time when people were free to look ahead toward the future and dream. At that time, the general editorial principles of the *Sangyô* newspaper embraced the rather safe and noncommittal view of "reporting the news promptly, accurately impartially, and without any political party affiliation," and, coming out of the Osaka business mentality, the management believed that if the paper's reputation among the readership was strong, then the paper would sell adequately. Accordingly, I believe that the reporters felt they were free to pursue the creation of a newspaper according to what each one believed a newspaper should be without being overtly regulated by anyone. (18–24)

A great deal of *Onna no chihei* is given over to the depiction of Kishino's struggle to establish herself in the workplace, to become a successful reporter capable of competing with her male colleagues, and to establish her own economic independence. Part of her duties in the *shakaibu* (society department) were to keep abreast of developments in three of the Tokyo's principal wards: Suginami, Shinjuku, and Shibuya. This meant frequent trips to the ward offices (*kuyakusho-mawari*) to find out what issues were of concern to citizens and ward officials. During this time, Kishino wrote on such topics as vocational training for housewives seeking part-time work, worker safety issues in part-time employment situations, child care facilities, and the availability of care for the elderly in homes for the elderly. She also covered in 1955 Japan's first Assembly of Japanese Mothers (*Nihon hahaoya taikai*), something to which Yoshitake devotes considerable space as well. Impressed by their ability to voice their concerns, and with the seriousness with which they went about their responsibilities, Kishino commented that she felt she participated "more as a woman than as a reporter."

> I sat in one corner of the assembly hall not so much as a reporter but just as one Japanese woman. And I could not fail to be impressed with how these women, most shouldering heavy burdens in their personal lives, came to the meeting from as far away as Hokkaido and Kagoshima in order to attend this assembly where they laughed and cried together, as well as standing up and sharing with one another the different aspects of their lives. As a young, unmarried, and inexperienced reporter, someone who had not yet shouldered the kind of burdens that these women had, there was no way for me to really fit in with them. However, I could not help but be struck by the reality that these were not women who were going to sit back and remain silent, and this made me appreciate the steps that postwar women had taken over the previous decade. To borrow a phrase from Maruoka Hideko, "A New Women's History Is Beginning" (from the evening edition of the *Asahi* newspaper, June 10), and there I was, present at this moment of inception. (27–28)

As Kishino writes in a section of her memoir called "The First Collision over Labor Rights at *Sankei*," labor issues at the newspaper would engage her attention and interest. In search of the ideals and camaraderie that union activism brought, she found herself drawn inexorably into the tensions between labor and management at the newspaper. As she explains:

Although I was originally not very deeply interested in the labor movement, what first made me aware of the union's existence at *Sankei* was an incident in December 1954 that left a strong impression on me. The offices were still at the old building in Yurakucho, and I was a reporter crammed into the bureau covering the Tokyo Metropolitan Government Offices, spending my days trying to get used to being a reporter in the society section. One morning in December, there was a call for a limited-duration strike. I had known that occasionally at the company headquarters a union representative would stand on a desk and call for the *Sankei* union's first (and last) strike.

It was a cold morning. On that day, instead of the usual *Sankei* company flag being hoisted on the roof of the building, there was a red union flag fluttering in the breeze, and I am pretty sure that it could be seen from the Yamanote Line train as it rolled by. The *Sankei* union had been negotiating over bonuses during the past year and had secured the right to strike. It was entering the final stages of an all-night negotiation; time was running out, and in the entryway of the old building the number of picketers began to swell. Well, I called it an entryway, but we are really talking about a very small entrance—only about one meter wide—where the stairs led up to the fifth and sixth floors. It was there that young workers from the plant wearing red headbands locked arms and were standing firm. . . . These young workers, who had never participated in a strike before, stood there resolved, and even seemed to be enjoying themselves, while the contact people between the two sides ran back and forth up and down the narrow staircase. As reports of how the negotiations were progressing were ferried down to the union headquarters on the fourth floor, they were then sent out to the picketers.

How long did the picketers remain in place? Pretty soon word of a negotiated agreement was reported and the limited strike was over, so there had scarcely been a significant impact on the publication schedule of the newspaper. As far as I can recall, among the reporters working around me, this limited-duration strike was not a very big topic of conversation. Compared to other newspapers, our pay was only about two-thirds of what theirs was, which meant that without overtime pay we could barely make ends meet. Accordingly, people made fun of us, calling us the *Zangyō* (Overtime!) *keizai shinbun* instead of the *Sangyō keizai shinbun*. But I do not suppose that this was directly connected to union activities in any significant way. That December morning was just the opening act of a little drama that was being performed in an empty hall without a real audience.

However, no matter how small or modest an event it was, this limited-duration strike provided exhilaration for the union activists and most assuredly struck fear in the hearts of management. But almost everyone who recalls those years sees this event as a turning point that set the stage for the following year of the so-called "Shôwa 30 (1955) Problem" in which parties on all sides were starting to prepare their battle strategies. I guess you could say that this was the *Sankei* union's first small fire that they had ignited. . . .

So, as we entered 1955, both sides felt that these initial steps taken in the new year would set the stage for later courses of action to come. It was not only the year in which the company offices picked up and moved from the old Yûrakuchô building to the new one in Ôtemachi, but it was also the year in which the union activists who brought about the "1955 Problem" were dispersed to various regional offices outside of Tokyo. I myself also was right in the midst of all this instability, and I believe that I made choices that would affect the future direction of my life during this, my twenty-fifth year.

Actually, even though I said that I made choices affecting my future direction, it was really something that grew rather naturally as a result of my personal encounter with some of the union activists. I really cannot recall exactly when or how I met these people, or how we became friends, but it was probably just an accident of everyday life at the paper, and it was just a swirling current in which I became caught up.

Opening my heart to these people had less to do with my interest in labor problems per se than with my youthful ardor and the yearning I experienced for camaraderie, for close friendships and colleagues with whom I could walk shoulder to shoulder along the same path. . . . (29–31)

Much less than shared ideology, then, it was friendship, loyalty, and a yearning for a sense of camaraderie that drew Kishino to the labor activists. Or so she claims. However, as it turned out, the tensions generated by this 1955 action were just a harbinger of more serious problems to come. In 1958, *Sankei* founder Maeda Hisakichi was succeeded by businessman Mizuno Shigeo, who set about "rationalizing" (*gôrika*) the newspaper's management and company organization in order to make it more economically competitive. Many reporters, Kishino included, were already experiencing anxiety about their freedom to report the truth. Many of the new policies seemed designed to disperse and punish union activists. Given that this was occurring against the backdrop of growing left-wing opposition to the renewal of the US-Japan Security Treaty, there developed a considerable degree of polarization in the society at large and within many corporations and institutions. By 1960 this opposition movement had spread beyond left-wing circles to involve hundreds of thousands of Japanese from all walks of life who took to the streets to demonstrate against their government and the high-handed manner in which the governing party and Prime Minister Kishi Nobusuke rammed the treaty through the Diet, even resorting to the use of police in order to clear the socialist opposition members from the chambers.

As one of four reporters in the cultural section, Kishino had the opportunity to interview several women authors, including Hirabayashi Taiko, Ota Yoko, Tsuboi Sakae, and Kuroyanagi Fumi, as well as many well-established male authors and critics such as Ishibashi Tatsuzô, Minami Hiroshi, Mushanokôji Saneatsu, Hirotsu Kazuo, and Nakano Shigeharu, to name a few. She also developed a broader interest in figures like Agnes Smedley, the American prewar proletarian writer who had accompanied the Chinese Red Army at Yanan.[7] She linked her reflections on Smedley's life and works to some thoughts about being employed at *Sankei* as a woman reporter.

If I look back at the way my "feminine consciousness" *(onna-ishiki)* worked at that time, from the outset, I had chosen the career path of newspaper reporter because I believed that it would be possible for men and women to work together as equals *(danjo-dôken rashii to iu koto)*; it was like the golden rule for me, and the way for me to assert my rights was to let my work speak for itself, to let it demonstrate the things of which I was capable. So not just in relation to work, but in other respects as well, I wanted to show that I was the equal of the male reporters. That was how I approached things. Actually, it would be more accurate to say that because I was a woman I wanted to work harder than the men. In those days, there was not really a question about differences in treatment, and I had not yet had any experience of wanting to do a certain job but being told I could not because I was a woman. In those days, I believe that I possessed a feminine consciousness that was striving to overcome sexual discrimination. However, as I recall it now, it suddenly occurs to me that really there was this dimension to my experience in which I sometimes unconsciously felt a sense of alienation, as though this is a man's world and because I was a woman I was locked out of certain things. Clearly, I was stretching so hard, and I was so intent on pursuing my ideal of attaining equality between men and women, that I managed to close my eyes to the realities that were right in front of me.

The first thing I read by Agnes Smedley was her *Battle Hymn of China*. In March 1957, just after Mr. Takasugi Ichirô's translation of this book had appeared, a number of female reporters from the *Mainichi*, Kyôdo News Service, and *Sankei* got together and formed a book club to read this work. We also obtained her two previously published books, *The Great Road: The Life and Times of Zhu De*, and *A Woman Alone Travels to the Continent*, and I became totally fascinated with her.

In the first place, without feeling at all handicapped because she was a woman, Smedley functioned as a magnificent journalist who revealed to the world the truth about history in the first half of the twentieth century when she described all the suffering and glory that was the Chinese Revolution. Each of us women reporters etched our own idealized image of her in our hearts. I wanted to read her other works, which had not been translated yet, so I went scurrying about the used bookstores. At the same time, I was thinking that someday I would like to write a biography of her. (44–45)

What Kishino especially admired about Agnes Smedley was the way that she operated in what was essentially a man's world without any inhibitions or restraints that would limit the range of her activities because she was a woman. But Smedley's life was not without its issues and tensions. In the 1950s, she was investigated for espionage by the McCarthy committee, although no formal charges were ever brought against her.[8] Her biographers, Janice R. and Stephen R. MacKinnon, suggest some ways in which Smedley's life might have appealed to or even inspired someone like Kishino Junko.

To those who know her as a writer, a participant in revolutionary movements, and a vigorous feminist, Agnes Smedley has been an inspiration for their own struggles. She exposed prison conditions in the United States; worked to establish birth control clinics in Germany, India and China; raised funds to help organize the Indian revolutionary movement against the British; defended Chinese writers against persecution by Chiang Kai-shek; became a war correspondent of international stature; raised funds for Chinese war relief; nursed wounded guerrillas of the Chinese Red Army; and at the end of her life fought McCarthyism in the United States. What Agnes Smedley wrote and experienced now emerges with new importance to others working for self-determination and a new social order.[9]

These kinds of accomplishments clearly impressed Kishino and her fellow female reporters in Japan, and they were eager to learn more about her and possibly to emulate her. Around the same time, Kishino also wrote a substantial essay exploring some works by the proletarian writer Kobayashi Takiji (1903–33), an iconic figure who was tortured and murdered by the police in 1933. A martyr and hero in the early postwar years, Kishino was interested in critically analyzing his attitudes toward women because, despite his social progressivism and Marxism, she felt that his attitude toward women remained feudalistic. In fact, she turned her reflections on Kobayashi into a commentary on postwar gender relations.

It has been twenty-five years since [Kobayashi] wrote *Tôseikatsusha* [The Stalwart Party Man] and was murdered the following year. During the intervening years, World War II ended in Japan's unprecedented defeat; and social conditions in Japan were radically changed from the prewar years. Specifically, in the postwar period, women were given the right to participate in politics, and naturally, coeducation became a reality, so there is no comparison between the number of women in the workforce then and now. I sincerely believe that perhaps the biggest transformation between prewar and postwar Japan was in the area of women's issues. No doubt, from this very difficult shift there should have followed a major transformation in the way women were perceived. This is not only undeniable, but it was also a cause for great rejoicing.

However, in Japan there remained serious issues concerning women. When I criticized Kobayashi Takiji's perception of women as old-fashioned, I was writing as one Japanese working woman, and so I was alluding to how this was a serious problem in contemporary Japan not only for women but for Japanese men as well. I think what I was trying to do, therefore, was to say that in order to resolve these issues, in order to achieve genuine human liberation and the kind of mutual and reciprocal relationships between males and females that we wanted, we would need the cooperation of men as well as women. Also, I believe I was saying that now, after twenty-five years, we needed to reassess the contributions for which Kobayashi fought and died, and to continue to walk down that path in the direction toward which he had pointed us. The reality was quite different from the genuine equality between the sexes that I was hoping for, and this reality was something that I was experiencing directly, deep down inside of me. (46)

It is never easy to challenge the perceptions about an icon, not to mention one who is a martyr. But Kishino thought it was important to explore the attitude toward women embraced by this hero of the Left. This was the nature of the times, a moment when popular opinion was starting to galvanize around the US-Japan Security Treaty. The popular movement against the renewal of this treaty, or Ampo, as the movement came to be called, was a stunning and transformative social movement, one that affected Kishino Junko a great deal. Part 1 of her memoir contains some important recollections of the Ampo Movement, which she first brings up in a section entitled "Before and After 1960 Ampo." She writes:

Just as the 1960 Ampo Movement was highly significant for Japan's postwar history, it was a huge turning point for the newspaper as well. Thinking about those days, I think I can say this unequivocally and with intense feelings. . . . In those days reporters who opposed the renewal of the US-Japan Security Treaty, including myself, were committed to doing our jobs and reporting the truth. To that end, we maintained a militant fighting spirit that said we wanted to throw the first stone in the new road that Japan would traverse. I guess you could say that for us reporters, it was a period during which we were uplifted, albeit for a brief moment only. In the eyes of a thirty-year-old woman who loved her work, that is exactly how that moment in time appeared to me.

So, as a newspaper reporter who was deeply enmeshed in the Ampo Movement, I had never before been so interested in keeping up with what the editorial positions of the various newspapers were. In the beginning, even though there was not a single newspaper that endorsed the "oppose renewal" position, among the ordinary citizens the opposition opinion was growing rapidly day-by-day, and the papers eventually could no longer ignore their voices. Finally, in January of 1960, the [revised] US-Japan Security Treaty was signed in Washington, D.C., and the terms of the treaty were clearly set down for people to see. Concerning the content of the treaty, a very strong tone of disapproval was sounded by the *Asahi* newspaper while the *Nikkei* supported the treaty and the *Mainichi* and *Sankei* remained well disposed toward it.

On the occasion of the May 19 forced parliamentary vote, editorials criticizing the party in power appeared in several papers. Even our own paper, one that tended to be strongly progovernment, offered the following critique in its May 20 editorial.

> *When public opinion is so strongly stirred up as it is today, it is a serious problem, and just looking from the outside, it would seem that opposition to treaty revision is an extremely popular opinion. Therefore, we think that in order to persuade the majority of the people, it will require much more time and a great deal of caution and careful deliberation. This would be our hope. That is why we favor a prolonged postponement at this time. Based on this belief, we feel it is regrettable that the government acted too hastily and was overzealous and high-handed in this grave matter to the point that confidence in this important policy has been seriously undermined.*

However, during the course of a single week, at the very pinnacle of activities, we could detect a slight shift in editorial positions. Behind this shift was Prime Minister Kishi's declaration that "We cannot say that public opinion consists of what is on the radio or in newspapers. What we are now seeing on the surface is just one portion of the public's voice. We must listen to the voices of the voiceless masses. . . ."

This was a matter of the side of those favoring treaty revision putting pressure on journalists, a detailed account of which can be found in the publication *Journalists* (June 1, 1960).

The undeniable fact is, though, that the number of demonstrators who surrounded the Diet building on a daily basis continued to swell. On June 4, Sôhyô and other neutral unions, along with ordinary citizens and business owners, mobilized some 4.6 million citizens to support a General Strike, which was to be conducted in an orderly manner. I even joined one of the demonstrations that was snaking around the Diet, not so much as a reporter but as an ordinary citizen. . . .

On the evening of June 15, in a clash between Zengakuren students and police in the Diet compound, a young female student, Miss Kamba Michiko, was killed. The next morning, June 16, the morning editions rather blatantly changed their tune as they transmitted this news. If we just look at the stories from that morning, we find on the front page of the *Asahi*, "Zengakuren students force themselves into the Diet compound, a female student from Tôdai is killed, as hundreds are seriously injured when the police use tear gas"; in the society section, "More blood is tragically spilled in the vicinity of the Diet as long poles whistle through the air, stones are thrown, and numerous collisions follow; police fight back with water cannons"; and "The demonstrators light a police vehicle on fire, gas mask clad police pursue fleeing students." So with this kind of tone, the blame for the violence was being squarely placed on the students almost across the board. . . .

On the next day, June 17, when I opened the morning edition, I issued a gasp. On the front page there was laid out in bold letters a joint declaration by seven editorialists from the *Sankei, Tokyo shinbun, Tokyo Times, Nihon keizai, Mainichi, Yomiuri,* and *Asahi*, under the heading "Wipe Out Violence, Preserve Parliamentary Democracy." The newspapers that changed their stance after the June 15 incident clearly revealed their new position with this joint declaration. However, as ordinary reporters, we found this declaration to be a shocking bolt out of the blue.

In the June 17 *Mainichi* newspaper, there were two major stories with which everyone was familiar at the time. One was the government declaration that came out of an emergency cabinet meeting held in the early hours of the morning that Miss Kamba Michiko was killed. The shameless ignoring of the popular will by the government was bitterly attacked, and this placed incredible pressure on Kishi to resign. The second story was about the lament over Japan's loss of trust in the international arena because of the cancellation of "Ike's" [American president Dwight D. Eisenhower's] visit to Japan announced that same day, June 16. The sword of blame was now pointed directly toward the Socialist Party, and serious questions about whether to protect parliamentary democracy or agree to group violence and mayhem had to be faced. The first story was from the early editions, from the first to the twelfth edition, while the second followed rapidly in succession in the final thirteen editions. Moreover, from that edition we got the headline that the seven leading dailies endorsed, "Wipe Out Violence, Preserve Parliamentary Democracy," so I guess you could say that these two stories were the incidents that symbolically expressed the change in direction that the newspaper editorials took.

I would like to quote from my own diary from those days dealing with the second half of June.

> *June 16.* When the night of June 15 finally ended, the morning saw a fine rain falling. I got to work earlier than usual and conferred with the desk reporters right away. I gave up preparing manuscripts for the cultural column to appear on June 17 and phoned Mr. Etô Jun. I wanted him to write something about Kamba Michiko's death on June 15. Saying that he had barely slept a wink last night, Mr. Etô's voice on the phone was very rapid and he sounded excited. A little after noon, about an hour later than expected, he brought five pages of manuscript over by car and set out for home but was obstructed by a long line of student demonstrators on their way from Hibiya to surround the Diet Building. Carrying a soaked flag at half mast, they were singing the international student association song softly and just kept moving forward. The driver would not use his horn as he might have ordinarily done.

> That evening, I went to the darkened premises around the Diet with two of my colleagues. The student demonstrations were over, and even the regular lines of demonstrators were few and far between, though a small Buddhist memorial altar was set up at the south gate of the Diet where Miss Kamba had been killed. At the prime minister's darkened residence, a student wearing a steel helmet put his face up to the fence and screamed "Murderer!"

> *June 17.* On the front page of the morning edition there was a large banner headline proclaiming the joint declaration of the seven newspaper editors, "Wipe Out Violence, Preserve Parliamentary Democracy." Even though a commercial newspaper did not believe that it could become an ally of the people, those of us who were at the scene by no means had the feeling that the rug could unexpectedly be pulled out from underneath us either. How would the company management explain the paper's change in direction from what had been the norm up until yesterday?

> *June 18.* From 1:00 p.m. at the Kudan Grill, a student roundtable discussion chaired by Mr. Yamashita Hajime was held. (In those days, in addition to the cultural column,

I was in charge of the student affairs column as well, so I was involved in planning this roundtable discussion.) On that day, you could see the wounded right away at a glance. Mr. N., a student from Tôdai who had his head wrapped in a bandage, announced in an agitated way, before he finished what he had wanted to say, that he would have to leave early in order to go to Yokohama to visit some of his wounded friends in the hospital. After he left, Mr. T. from Rikkyô University arrived. Another Mr. T. from the Keiô University newspaper had his camera in two pieces and was about to head out to interview some of the demonstrators. So, although the roundtable was a bit of a mishmash, it did succeed in conveying the variety of different perceptions of the situation.

In the evening, there was a welcome party for a newly hired department head, Mr. Y., held at a restaurant in Tsukiji. It was past 9:00 p.m. when I left the party with three colleagues in somewhat of a hurry to head over to the vicinity of the Diet Building. The street that had previously been packed with student demonstrators staging sit-ins was now lined with little stalls selling juice and snacks, just like on Greenery Day. There was a group of four or five high-school students carrying their white school flag who had streamed toward the metropolitan police agency and were now on their way back. There were also people driving their motorcycles at top speed, so the street was very crowded. When I got home, I listened to the midnight news on the radio. On the nineteenth at midnight, the US-Japan Security Treaty would have naturally gone into effect. . . .

June 23. This afternoon, there was a memorial service organized by Zengakuren held in Hibiya Park for the late Kamba Michiko, who had been killed on June 15. Amid a sea of red and blue Zengakuren flags from various universities there was mounted a picture of Miss Kamba framed by a black border, and the podium was covered with chrysanthemums. As the students chanted, "Do Not Kill Our Comrades!" each student stood before her photograph and placed a small chrysanthemum on the pile. The line seemed to go on endlessly, and I wondered when it might be over. After 3:00 p.m. the students proceeded to the south gate of the Diet premises carrying a large flower arrangement in front of them. It took about one hour from the time that the lead group departed for the square next to the hall to be completely emptied. Among a group of Geidai students with their flag there were some who did not approve of the way the mainstream faction of the Zengakuren conducted the memorial service, so as the situation shaped up it was not clear whether they would join the march or not.

That evening, according to the mainstream faction of the Zengakuren students, there would be a demonstration outside the Japan Communist Party headquarters.

June 25. In the evening a combined editorial staff and workplace union meeting was held in the fourth-floor conference room. On the twenty-second, the company had placed its final offer for the summer bonus on the table, which was an average of about thirty thousand yen per employee. The union drew the line and claimed that it remained unconvinced and announced that it would be preparing for a strike on the twenty-fourth. The meeting was supposed to be about trying to overcome the wall that the company's response represented, but in fact Chairman Izumiyama of the executive department attended, along with Secretary Nakajima, in order to explain about the process, so it was a real show of force from the company side to get the amount of money that they were proposing affirmed, leaving the union in a very weak position. . . .

June 27. When I arrived at work in the morning I found a large crowd gathered in front of the bulletin board outside the entrance to the editorial offices. An announcement was posted saying that the people in charge of the morning edition on June 15 from the society section and the copy desk under the editor Mr. Iwasa were being punished. The reason was that that day's editorial had gone against basic company policy. However, they could not make clear precisely what aspect of basic company policy it violated. This paper was, compared to others, considered fair and had been praised in terms of newspaper labor relations and for supporting the people who went to the scene that day. Moreover, sales of the paper were good, and even after that day there were orders pouring in to the sales department from our readers. However, according to the rumors, company president Mizuno had received complaints from some of our major advertisers. . . .

June 29. The union was forced to completely swallow the company's final offer of 30,000-yen bonuses as proposed on the twenty-second. At the joint meeting on the twenty-fifth, in spite of a lot of strong opposition coming to the surface, perhaps the executive committee of the union just could not stand up to management anymore. One has to assume that they just did not have it from the very outset. The bonus that I received in my pay envelope on July 5 slightly exceeded the average at 30,243 yen. Comparable figures at some of the other newspapers were 80,451 yen at the *Asahi*, 70,218 yen at the *Mainichi*, and 76,000 at the *Yomiuri*. The summer of 1960 was a painful and difficult period. The collapse of the Ampo struggle continued, the punishments over the June 15 edition remained and our bonus was significantly reduced. The existing reality was that we seemed to be having a new employment system forced on us, one that required us to "just work!" What really completed the job and crushed our spirits was the August 4 transfer announcements for some employees that were posted hastily by management on the bulletin board. . . . In other words, key union members were being dispersed throughout the organization, in an obvious attempt to weaken the union. . . .

These [employees] were being treated unfairly. We felt that these transfers were just like the transfers [of union activists] out to the periphery during the 1955 conflict; in other words, they constituted an object lesson to the union activists who were only acting justifiably. But that was really not all, because as far as our friends were concerned, this was the initial foray in the coming decisive conflict with management.

In response to this unfair transfer of employees, those of us who supported them joined with people from other branches, and not only did we submit a complaint to the Tokyo branch of the executive committee, which declared that "This constitutes interference with union activity and unfair labor practices," but we also decided that we wanted to issue a formal complaint against the company. However, according to the company's procedures, formal complaints have to be filed within three days, and with Sunday falling in between,

> it had been four days, which the company knew full well. So
> our complaint was invalidated, and ultimately our statement
> to the executive committee was ignored. Management was
> engaging in mean and cowardly behavior. (57–69)

The labor-management conflicts in the workplace contributed to an atmosphere of disappointment and disaffection that hit very close to home. But currents were also swirling in the larger political and social arenas, which added to the sense that the postwar ideals of democracy and equality were in danger. Both Yoshitake and Kishino devote a considerable amount of space to critical moments during the Ampo struggle, but Kishino's narrative links the ratification of the treaty not only with a new attitude that prevailed in society, as citizens retreated into hard work and material prosperity, but also with events in the workplace where management was making systematic efforts to divide and weaken labor unions. Kishino continues to pursue this topic in part 2 of her memoir, where she develops the story of labor-management friction at *Sankei*, a thread with dark implications for her.

For Kishino, the labor disputes at the newspaper and the Ampo struggle were part and parcel of the same problem. The hopes and dreams of building a postwar Japan that featured genuine participatory democracy were on the verge of receding from her view. Although the precise details of her involvement with the union are omitted from her memoir, apparently management considered her sufficiently involved to assign her away from editorial duties and to the newly created "sales promotion division" (*hanbai suishin honbu*). For the next ten months, she would spend her days walking the streets, going door-to-door in order to increase subscriptions, work she found humiliating and for which she was ill-suited. After seven months of this, when most of the people assigned to sales with her had been rotated back to their regular editorial duties, Kishino was further humiliated by being kept on in sales for another three months. She claimed that she felt like a character out of Noma Hiroshi's novel *Zone of Emptiness* (*Shinkūchitai*). Part 2 contains her description of the labor-management conflicts at *Sankei,* from which I will offer a few sample comments.

Conflicts with Management

Her sojourn with the sales promotion division was a difficult time for Kishino, one she recalls with great bitterness. Not only did she languish in this assignment for ten months, but her annual bonus was reduced as well because she had so few new subscriptions to her name. But this difficult period also yielded profound insights. She observes:

At that time I finally came to see clearly the faces of the company authorities who lurked behind the new corporate structure being put in place. I finally understood in the depths of my being their regime of control (*shihai no shikumi*). I had never before thought of the workplace in terms of a relationship between those in control and those who are controlled, but in the summer of 1961, while I was in the sales promotion division, the nature of this relationship took shape squarely before my eyes. (128)

She saw the management team at *Sankei* as practitioners of a cynical theory of management: they did not believe people would work without the temptation of a carrot or the threat of a stick. They called their policy *shinshô-hitsubatsu* (sure rewards, certain punishments), but if it were effective and employees behaved as management hoped they would, they would go about their tasks with all the joy and spontaneity of robots. Although the nightmare did finally end and Kishino resumed her role as a reporter, her feelings toward *Sankei* would never be the same. In the ensuing years, she tried to immerse herself in a variety of projects as part of a process of "escaping" from a hellish blight (*tachigare jigoku kara no dasshutsu*), the focus of part 3 of her autobiography.

In Search of Projects

Part 3 of Kishino's memoir depicts some ongoing underground union activity, as well as a process of searching for other avenues through which to pursue her goals as a reporter. Frustrated by a sense of powerlessness in the face of a corporate hierarchy bent on silencing critics and punishing activists, Kishino joined with three other colleagues on the evening of August 15, 1963—the very day her newspaper ran a front-page story with banner headlines on the emperor's participation in a memorial service for Japan's war dead at Hibiya Hall—to plan an anonymous book about what was happening to many reporters. She explained their goals as follows.

What we were aiming at was a thoroughgoing inquiry into the subjective conditions and objective circumstances in which reporters have been functioning since Ampo, and to reveal the results of this probe to the public. I also felt that not only should we reporters, who must take responsibility for the formation of public opinion, make the facts of our situation clear to the public, but given the reality that our freedom to operate was severely restricted, we needed to make the question of the true role of a reporter one that we diligently ask one another. This effort took place between 1963 and 1964.

> In our concluding roundtable we took up the following issues: (1) the social responsibility of reporters, (2) the function and position of the commercial newspaper in the context of communication, and (3) what reporters for a commercial newspaper could do in the future. (169)

If these efforts did not particularly produce concrete results, they did succeed in "bringing our true sense of what the key issues were to our mutual attention."

Kishino's second strategy for coping with her difficult circumstances was to find a topic that would genuinely stir her emotions and get her involved again in functioning as an effective reporter. The topic she came upon was "youthful offenders" (*hikôshônen*).

> Along with the social changes accompanying rapid economic growth, the criminalization of youth had become a social problem. At that time, although the strains resulting from rapid economic growth were not as severe as they are today, there was something inherently false and deceptive about the call for "doubling income," something I instinctively disliked. Moreover, I felt intensely angry about the appearance of a dark underside to this growth, the criminalization of our children (*kodomo no hikôka*). . . .
>
> It may appear as though the chance to undertake this project was purely accidental, but as a reporter in the cultural affairs department, I did have responsibilities for issues relating to students and young working people, and I had consistently maintained an interest in the topic of education. Moreover, my father, as a prewar justice department official, was responsible for correctional education in the penal institutions. I was actually born in Kawagoe at the youth correctional facility. So I was led by these several threads to an encounter with youthful offenders, and they have sustained my protracted involvement with this issue. (171–72)

As she would say in another context, she "wanted to get a look at the world through the tiny aperture of each individual child's transgression" (173).

Another project with which she became involved was translating into Japanese some of Agnes Smedley's work, such as *China's Destiny* and *China's Red Army Advances*. She also translated *In Place of Splendor: The Autobiography of a Spanish Woman* (1939) by Constancia de la Mora; it appeared in Japanese as *Eikô ni kawarite*. Constancia de la Mora was born into a prominent Spanish family, studied at Cambridge, and later became a staunch ally of the communists and socialists against the fascists in the Spanish Civil War. Moreover, as a young woman, she had manifested considerable courage and independence when she defied custom and her parents' wishes, divorced her idle and worthless upper-class husband, with whom she had never been in love, and began working—scandalous for a woman of her social standing. She had a daughter to raise, and she wanted to be independent. Later she became involved with the chief of the small Republican Air Force, Ignacio Hidalgo de Cisneros. De la Mora served in the Republican government as a member of the Popular Front press service during the civil war until she fled the country.[10] As with Agnes Smedley, then, Kishino was impressed with this woman who operated independently in the field of journalism and also fought bravely for a cause she believed in.

Finally, after working on youthful offenders in general, she turned specifically to the question of female youthful offenders. In connection with this project, she read Simone de Beauvoir's *The Second Sex,* where she was struck by the statement, "One is not born, but rather becomes, a woman." As Kishino struggled to understand the sexual promiscuity of some of the young girls she was getting to know, girls who would trade sexual favors for a ride, a sweater, or a meal, she found some solace in Beauvoir's observation that "[I]t is through the eyes, the hands, that children apprehend the universe, and not through the sexual parts." Kishino saw in these girls a bizarre mixture of sexual precociousness and emotional immaturity, so she rephrased Beauvoir to the effect that "these young women experienced the world not through their eyes or their hands, but as the result of rape or some other kind of sexual victimization, through their genitals." Clearly, these girls' promiscuity was not their way of embracing the world, but it was a cry for help, an expression of something that was missing in their lives.

In the penultimate section of part 3 of *Onna no chihei,* Kishino addresses the reasons why she elected to quit *Sankei* in 1969. Although they overlap considerably, she identified three principal reasons for quitting the newspaper. First, the changes at the newspaper, especially after Mizuno took over the helm, rendered *Sankei* a place where it was no longer exciting to work. All the "rationalizations" of management had resulted in a stultifying *seitōka* (normalization), that is, a routinization, of life in the workplace. Kishino concluded that her only options were to become "normalized" herself or leave. Second, there was her overall disillusionment with Japan's postwar democratic movement and her frustration over the gap between ideals and reality in terms of women's position in postwar society. When a new system for classification was introduced into the company in 1967, Kishino was ranked in the middle tier out of three as a *shidōshoku-ikkyū* (midlevel, grade-one) employee. Most of the men who joined *Sankei* at the same time as Kishino were awarded grade-two status, the next higher rung on the ladder. Moreover, while by now they had the status of "desk" reporters, Kishino remained a regular reporter. This meant she had to work under younger and less-experienced males, and she suggests that the differences in status were quite marked. Third, the kind of warmth and camaraderie she had felt from colleagues during the struggles over union activities seemed to have dwindled by the late 1960s. Management's dispersal policies had taken their toll in terms of employees quitting or in keeping them physically separated. Also most of her male colleagues now had their "desks" or their choice assignments and were no longer prepared to rock the boat. For these reasons, although she did not feel entirely good about quitting and abandoning the fight, she resigned in order to become an adjunct lecturer at Hôsei University, where she would teach American and African American literature.

Discovering a Feminine Consciousness

The final section of Kishino's autobiography, part 4, focuses on the "discovery of a feminine consciousness" (*onna-ishiki no hakken*). It describes a path from her reading of African American writers like Langston Hughes, Richard Wright, and Maya Angelou to the feminist movement of the early 1970s. She explains it this way.

> As I look back on it now, when I first went to work, I was thinking vaguely that my options were to become either a teacher or a journalist, and so somehow I wound up a newspaper reporter. So the fact that I became a teacher later on was really a natural progression. Moreover, after the post-Ampo changes in the character of the newspaper, being forced to pass my days unable to tell the truth the way the truth needed to be told, it sparked a deep thirst in me. So I began to develop expectations that the university might be the kind of place where I needed to be. If you want to go into the concrete realities of the situation, in those days, with the lifetime employment system, it would have been difficult to move to a different newspaper, and since I did not really have the courage to become a freelancer, the only course really left open to me was to follow the model of the male reporter. The general path that I seemed to see friends and colleagues around me taking was that if they quit the paper and were not able to join another corporation, they would become teachers or maybe go to graduate school.
>
> University campuses in 1969 and 1970 were in the rather unique condition of having the student struggles still in full swing, so the lecture halls had to be guarded by helmeted police with their imposing big shields. Sometimes, in the classes I was teaching, we had to cancel class right in the middle of a discussion. One instance I can recall clearly was at Hôsei University when for some reason the students confronted me and asked

me if I had chosen the textbook by Langston Hughes, *Famous American Negroes*. Belonging to the generation that believed it was a virtue to expose oneself [to new things like this], while I may have been a little confused and inarticulate myself about my relationship to black literature, I had to address this issue in front of students for the first time.

My reason for choosing to study black literature as my next project was not only because I was stimulated by the black liberation movement that was taking place at that time in America but also because I was drawn particularly to the irresistibly fierce voice of protest that I found in Richard Wright's *Native Son*, where he seemed to speak for oppressed peoples. I may have seen in the murderer Bigger Thomas, who is the main character, the extreme version of the youthful offenders who had been occupying my attention, so I may have seen him as a conceptually unique model.[11] The students pressed me with questions, even probing my lifestyle to the point that I felt I was really being challenged and tested. . . .

I wonder if it wasn't something like this. Since I had escaped the narrow confines of the fetters that had bound me to the workplace, I felt the exhilaration of being able to breathe fresh, clean air. But, at the same time, I was not sure where I belonged or what my responsibilities were anymore. One thing was clear: I had quit the newspaper because I wanted to get past the disappointment I had experienced as a result of being unable to realize my goals there. But now how was I supposed to fulfill my goals at my new place of work? These sorts of ideas were flooding my mind around the time I had been teaching for two or three years and was starting to get used to it and was able to throw myself into it.

Then I began to search for something again. At the time, I probably was not fully conscious of it, but what I was looking for was something to which I could once again commit, something that would put direction back into my life. So I set out in search of some positive new encounters through travel, and through working with people (or participating with them in a movement).

For example, one of the benefits of being a teacher was that I could devote myself fully to travel in the summers. In the summer after I quit the newspaper, in 1970, I traveled to Korea; in the summer of 1971, I went to Okinawa; in the spring of 1972, Korea again; and in the summer of 1972, Europe. In the summer of 1973, I went to America, and in the summer of 1976, China. That was how much I traveled. Of course, as a part-time lecturer I was not eligible for any bonuses, so I really did not have the money from my lecturer's pay to do all this traveling. So I used up all my meager savings and the four hundred thousand yen of severance pay I had received when I left the newspaper.

Now that I was living in this very different period of my life, when I did not belong to any organization like a newspaper, the process of being able to see things that I had never been able to observe before turned into an experience that transformed me. To put it more succinctly, during the period after I quit the newspaper, while I did continue to do some things in the same way that I had as a reporter, at the same time, I think it had the effect of shedding light for me on how I had conducted my life up to this point.

I would have to say that, among the things I saw and learned that had the most significant impact on me was the issue of feminine consciousness (*onna-ishiki no mondai*). When the women's movement (commonly referred to as women's lib) reached Japan from the United States, it was not that long after the student movement had hit the peak of its intensity. In Japan as well, the basis for the second wave of the women's liberation movement was the student movement. The first major rally of the women's movement was held at the Sendagaya Community Center in November 1970. I was invited to participate on that day by Komashaku Kimi, a female colleague, a single woman about five years older than me.[12] I recall being impressed with the freshness and energy as speaker after speaker talked openly and honestly about their experiences as women, but I also felt a little bit uncomfortable. If I were to examine these feelings a little more closely, I would say that while I was comfortable with much of what had been written by activists in the movement (like Tanaka Mitsu, author of *Inochi no onnatachi e* [To Women with Spirit]), I was not really sure that I was fully in accord with the accompanying lifestyle. In other words, I had already been in the workplace alongside men for some years—very aware that I was perceived as a "token" or representative woman—and had developed a rather stoic approach as far as confronting male colleagues was concerned. It seemed to me that many of these women were too eager to reveal themselves and too individualistic. Compared to Ms. Komashaku, who was fully immersed in the movement, I was more cautious, more inclined to stand back a bit and keep some distance between myself and the movement.

On a cold, wintry evening, just after my fortieth birthday, I was having dinner with Ms. Komashaku at a restaurant. We began to open up to each other, to tell each other our life stories and how we had each arrived at the place where we were in our lives. As I spoke with her, suddenly I came to look at my past differently than I ever had before, a process that seemed to occur naturally.

Until this time, I had been operating in the male-centered workplace, placing priority on work, work, work, without giving it a second thought. To me, there was something natural and inevitable about this path, and, although there was no doubt some pain along the way, I also found a great deal of satisfaction. It never crossed my mind to question what I was doing. However, when I reached my forties, the possibility that I might one day have children began to surface in my consciousness. To put it more accurately, I had to start facing the harsh reality that apparently children would not be a part of my life. This hit home very hard, creating a hollow feeling, a void in my life. If I were a man, I could have both work and children. Now that I had reached a point of no return, I began to take stock of the magnitude of what I had sacrificed.

This occasion, then, became an opportunity to reexamine my past in a different light. Of course, it was not a matter of denying the validity of my life as a reporter and the intensity it involved. Moreover, although the connections might not be obvious, I believed that there was a common thread linking my work, for example, on Agnes Smedley and the female juvenile offenders, and this was the issue of women. In spite of this, I couldn't help being haunted by recurring feelings of regret that I had virtually erased that part of me that is woman—captured symbolically in the reality that I would not be having children—and had made myself just like men, for whom competition and one's success in the workplace are everything. At any rate, I began to reexamine more closely whether there wasn't something strange about discovering my feminine consciousness as the other side of the coin of a life that had been devoted to women's issues. But in the process of pursuing these very issues so energetically, I had actually succeeded in erasing my identity as a woman.

It was around this time that in a Shinjuku theater I sat through the film *The Woman I Abandoned* twice, back-to-back, unable to stop the tears from flowing. What came through quite clearly to me was that I had closed my eyes to reality and tried to bridge the gap between my ideals— rooted as they were in the postwar democratic movement's commitment to equality between the sexes—and the reality that my own efforts had been directed toward amassing an impressive success record in the workplace. I realized that, before I had become aware of what I was doing, I had scuttled anything that would interfere with work, whether it was children, who could physically disrupt my ability to work, or the notion of femininity or "gentleness" (*yasashisa*), which could dampen my competitiveness. To put it yet another way, I had erased my femininity and bought completely into the logic of the patriarchal order, with priority placed on work, and had lived my life on this basis. I had even looked at myself through men's eyes and judged myself according to male standards.

What also came to me at this time was that my position as a woman reporter was a privileged one in the sense that it was one of the few occupations that women could legitimately pursue. It was only from a position such as this that one could launch a career as a woman. When I left the newspaper and ventured out into the world, I realized how limited options were for women and was struck by how powerful the (il)logic of "Because she is a woman" (*onna naru ga yue ni*) . . . could be. Moreover, although I knew intellectually that there were lots of companies out there that would allow women an equal position at the starting line, I also had directly experienced the injustices of which many of these companies were capable. In this sense, I felt reaffirmed in that the whole reason I had pursued the dream of equality between the sexes was precisely because such conditions do, indeed, exist.

So, in an instant, a real picture of women as historically, socially, and psychologically oppressed took shape in my mind. Moreover, I experienced at the very core of my being the ways in which women's lives were oppressed. These feelings emerged in the context of [the meetings of] various women's groups where we talked about our lives, our bodies, or even how male-female relationships were portrayed in literature as seen from the standpoint of women. I think I can say that through these kinds of efforts I was able to change directions in my life as I sought a way to liberate myself and live independently among women with whom I felt the bond of sisterhood.

One more thing I became aware of about my feminine consciousness was the realization that there was a deep connection between my attraction to African American literature and the consciousness that the life I had lived was the life of an oppressed woman. I was not even aware of it myself at the time, but in discussing, for example, Richard Wright's *Native Son* with students or in something I was writing, I would refer to the main character's consciousness of himself as a black man (*kokujin de aru ga yue ni*). Not only was this something I had felt while writing on the youthful offenders, but even farther back in my mind was the strong feeling that this was a reading opened up by my own consciousness as a woman (*jibun no onna de aru ga yue no ishiki ni terashite yomi*). The women's movement in the United States had been inspired by the black civil rights movement (which, in turn, was succeeded by the liberation movements of Hispanic Americans, Japanese Americans, and other oppressed minority groups), making it evident that there is a great deal of resonance among the consciousness of oppressed groups. So I began to think it possible to nurture the concrete connections between my own consciousness and that of other oppressed classes, races, and ethnic groups. So wasn't it possible to use my consciousness as a member of an oppressed gender as a springboard to connect with other oppressed minorities, and to move in the direction of liberation from this oppression?

Be that as it may, what I really felt at the time was that *I wanted to live my life fully as a woman, at one with my body, without worrying about how I may have erased part of myself in the past.* But just at that moment, I became ill.

In March 1977, I was operated on for breast cancer. At that time, I felt that my illness was the inevitable consequence of the way I had lived my life up to that point. If I may repeat myself, it was because I had virtually ignored my existence as a woman with a body—albeit in the pursuit of equality between the sexes—and I had bought fully into the achievement ethos of a competitive society. I could not help but feel strongly that my body was in revolt against my insistence on putting work before everything else. If my life up until now had been propelling me inevitably toward my illness, then I wanted to reverse this trend and live my life in a new way. Such a change in direction could not be based on patriarchal conceptions that had been enslaving women but had to be connected with the *recovery of a feminine consciousness* capable of pointing the way to my own liberation. (226–34, emphasis mine)

This passage tells a remarkable story about the development of a feminine consciousness that can resist all the social and psychological conditioning that the cultural order brought to bear on women. As she realizes that she will not be having children—a choice she has acquiesced in silently, a choice, she recognizes, her male colleagues do not have to make—she becomes haunted by a sense of loss and erasure. Behind the sense of loss and erasure, however, is also a profound grasp of how women can be "psychologically oppressed" and their subjectivity denied them by the social constructs kept in place by the patriarchy, the very same thing she identified as a "regime of control" (*shihai no shikumi*) when she was discussing management's power to undermine the company union. When she writes about how "a real picture of women as historically, socially, and psychologically oppressed took shape in my mind," she is alluding to a subtle and powerful process that is at work on her as well as within her. To discover the "real picture" of conditions confronting Japanese women was to understand not only the cultural and political constraints women faced but *how* a transformation in consciousness could be the key to freeing oneself from these imposed regimes of truth and control.

The final two sections of part 4 take up two seemingly disparate topics: Kishino's relationship to Korea and Korean women; and her encounter with Nagayama Norio, a young man who stole a pistol from a US naval base and went on a shooting spree, killing four people. She saw in his extreme case precisely the phenomenon she had been investigating in her work on youthful offenders. Moreover, she was interested in Nagayama's prison writings and how they might relate to the protagonist in Richard Wright's *Native Son*, Bigger Thomas. Finally, she was struck by the incredible poverty and pathetic family circumstances from which Nagayama came. The connection between her interest in Nagayama and Korea was her sympathy for the downtrodden, the oppressed.

Korea was a place to which Kishino began traveling frequently and where she interviewed Korean women. Korea became for her a "mirror that could show her past and present, herself and Japan." She became interested in Japanese women who had married Korean men during the colonial period and remained there after the war and also in Koreans living in Japan. She also became quite interested in Kaneko Fumiko (1903–26), the young Japanese anarchist who, with her Korean lover Pak Yol, was convicted of treason in 1926 on trumped up charges of involvement in a plot to assassinate the emperor.[13] The product of an impoverished upbringing and an abusive family, Kaneko's life was genuinely tragic, ending with her suicide in prison. However, she left an account of her life that she wrote while in prison, and Kishino was considering writing a biography of her. This project, however, was interrupted by her hospitalization and surgery for cancer. In the hospital, she noted the feelings of young mothers who were also fighting cancer and how all they wished for was the chance to see their children grow up and be able to take care of themselves. Once again the feelings about the lack of children in her life haunted her as she realized that no amount of work she might leave as a legacy could equal the significance of a single child's life. She was plunged into darkness and depression.

In her epilogue, she writes of her surgery and recovery over the next two to three years and of her search for a new order of priorities in her life. What she came to realize about herself was that she had put far too much weight on her record of "achievements." It was now time, she reasoned, to deny her "careerism," and reclaim her life.

> At any rate, I want to listen more carefully to the voice of my own body and to live a life in which value is placed on work for work's sake, not just for careerism, and in which there is a connection between my work and my encounters with people. Would this not be the only way for me—in my weakened state of health and living in this era with its narrow range of vision—to accomplish what I have set out to do? (258)

Analysis

By concluding her text with the assertion that she wishes "to listen more carefully to the voice of my own body," Kishino was echoing her earlier claim that she wanted *"to live my life fully as a woman, at one with my body."* She points to the crux of the struggle that she had grappled with her entire professional life. She explains from the outset how individual freedom and independence were always conceived of by her strictly in terms of *danjo-dôken,* or becoming equal to (and hence like) men. Yet trying to be like men had never been fully satisfying, causing her to deny her "existence as a woman with a body." When she writes of the need to "recover a feminine consciousness," then, she is speaking to this need to reclaim not only her body but, along with it, her identity as a woman. By this time, however, a part of her body has already been lost and her sense of self, her identity, has been disrupted. It is precisely from this vantage point—the place she referred to earlier as the location of her "disrupted self," which identified so closely with the characters in the Urayama Kirio film—that she is able directly experience the need to recover her feminine consciousness.

Although there may have been no single moment that sparked her inner transformation, the darkened movie theater was certainly a catalytic point of departure. Also there was her critical encounter with the women's lib movement; her long discussions with her friend Komashaku Kimi; her participation in women's discussion groups focusing on women's bodies, their lives, and even how literature might have something to say about what is going on in women's lives; and her reading and teaching of African American literature. It was all of these things taken together that made her reflect more deeply on the position of women in Japanese society. This kind of intellectual and experiential engagement with images, texts, ideas, and movements— coming as it did on top of her participation in the movement opposing the ratification of Ampo and the labor struggles at the newspaper—as well as her traumatic fight against cancer, situated Kishino in a position from which she was able not only to rethink her life and her place in the world but also to "reposition" herself so that she could have a "a real picture of women as historically, socially, and psychologically oppressed." This repositioning situates her in that moment when she understands exactly how society sees and treats women—the regimes of truth that it insists on—but she is also learning how to assert her own subjectivity and agency to combat the socially and politically constructed reality that constitutes the water in which she must swim. She knows it is about discovering and then developing her feminine consciousness. Since part of her awareness is framed by her battle with breast cancer, her moment of discovery is deeply painful and frightening. But she can now claim knowledge that she did not fully possess before: because of what she has experienced, she now understands what it takes to be an autonomous and independent Japanese woman.

One of the remarkable things about Kishino's text, then, is how it is permeated by a sense of disruption as evidenced by the specific reference to a "disrupted self," as well as her frequent use of the term *nijûsei*—or "dual structure"—to describe the cultural episteme against which she must define herself. We also cannot fail to notice the multilayeredness of her narrative, something that Sidonie Smith suggests is typical of female self-writing.[14] Kishino's memoir is comprised of at least four distinct layers that engage the reader. First, there is the foundational one, which asserts that "*her*story" em*bodies* postwar political and economic history, that it encapsulates a process by means of which postwar Japan evolved its politically conservative social and economic agenda, callously abandoning its democratic ideals along the way. What happened to her as an employee of *Sankei shinbun* in terms of her treatment in relation to male employees, and in terms of labor-management conflicts, is a version writ small of what was occurring in the society at large.

Kishino's revelations about the impact the Urayama Kirio film *The Woman I Abandoned* had on her consciousness constitute a powerful second layer of her narrative. She suggests that this film can be read as a metaphor for the denial or repression of something deeply rooted in her own and Japan's existence. "Somewhere in the relationship between the protagonist and the young woman," Kishino writes, she is able to see her own "disrupted self." Like the ambitious young male character, she, too, has thrown herself into the fray, trying to make her mark, to become successful, in order to convince the world that women deserve equality. Another powerful thing about the film for her was the insertion of documentary footage from the Ampo protests, something that was not part of the original Endo Shûsaku novella.

The shot of the large crowd of demonstrators, arms locked, with the year 1960 emblazoned across the screen, spoke to Kishino's heart and her experiences. But it was clearly her identification with the naive young woman in the film who is so easily deceived that spoke to her, for she, too, had naively believed in the postwar constitution and the hope that Japanese men and women would become equals.

It is also obvious that the moment she enters that space—and it is simultaneously the physical space of the workplace where men and women compete and the discursive space in which she must try to reconstruct her life story—she is "disrupted," or torn apart, for she must give up something of herself both literally and figuratively. What makes this scene so pivotal—and this is reinforced by the fact that it is repeated twice in the text, once at the beginning and once again near the end—is the location of the narrator in a darkened cinema, in tears, reflecting on her relationship to the patriarchy. This becomes the rhetorical position from which Kishino reassesses the meaning of her life and grapples with the issues that have confounded her so far. The scene in the movie theater becomes a pivotal moment, then, when she reflects on and reassesses everything about her life up to this moment. She concludes

Figure 4.3. A large crowd of Ampo protest demonstrators. From *The Woman I Abandoned.* © 1999 Nikkatsu kabushiki kaisha.

that her only recourse is to attempt what she calls the "recovery of a feminine consciousness."

Kishino's encounter with the women's lib movement constitutes the third and perhaps most compelling layer of her narrative. Opening up to a close friend around the time of her fortieth birthday, and then participating in women's groups, "where we talked about our lives, our bodies, or even how male-female relationships were portrayed in literature," Kishino learned how to conceptualize women differently. She began to see women as oppressed, not unlike the characters in the African American novels she had been teaching. More important, she discovers the thread that ties together all the disparate strands in her life such as her support for the labor movement; her sympathy for Korean women; her interest in women such as Agnes Smedley, Constancia de la Mora, and Kaneko Fumiko; and her attraction to the problem of female youthful offenders. Finding her way to the women's movement and creating for herself a place within it were the decisive moves that shaped not only her text but her life as well. By drawing her readers into these historical moments, and by elaborating on not only the language and the texts that shaped her reality but the powerful social currents she experienced as well, Kishino reveals that language and memory could for her be transformational; they could make the written words on the page come alive and connect them to the real experiences of which her life was constituted. Therefore, she realizes in the very moment of recalling and writing that language is not only a means of communicating her past experiences "but a structure of objective relations that constituted the condition of possibility for both the production and deciphering of discourse."[15] She had confronted in both her own world at the newspaper and again in the larger world of social movements such as the Ampo protests and the women's lib movement the conditioned social reality in which she had to exist. *Danjo-dôken* was never going to be more than window dressing unless the content of these words could have real social meaning. The only way to bring this about, she realized, was to "reposition" oneself and bring about a transformation in consciousness from within.

Finally, the fourth layer of her text is constituted by her encounter with breast cancer, a layer that is the occasion for a rereading of the basic questions with which her narrative began. What does it mean for a woman to work alongside men in the bastions of male power and authority? What does it mean to be perceived "as a woman" or to take on certain responsibilities (or to be denied others) "because she is a woman?" As Kishino reexamines her life in response to her crisis, it becomes an opportunity for her to "reposition" herself in relation to her text and her life so that she *"no longer stand{s} alongside men but stand{s} self-consciously on the side of oppressed women."*

As she concludes her memoir, Kishino finds that she wants to live her life fully— *"without worrying about how I may have erased part of myself in the past"*—but the grim reality is that the costs of that erasure have come back to haunt her. Knowing that she must submit to a frightening excision in order to rid her body of cancer, she comes to see breast cancer as the "inevitable consequence of the way I had lived my life." The recognition that permeates Kishino's *Things Visible from a Woman's Perspective* is that the conditioned social reality in which she lived required the sacrifice of something valuable in her life, something intangible but tied to her whole identity as a woman. In the workplace, in her labor and social activism, and in her teaching, she continually came up against silence and repression, and she was drawn to figures in life and history who had bravely tried to resist these forces. Perhaps in a manner similar to Yoshitake's penchant for blaming herself for her rape, Kishino began to wonder whether her own body wasn't rebelling against the life course she had chosen, even though, ironically, this path was rooted in the ideal of attaining equality with men in the workplace. By addressing these kinds of questions in her memoir, though, Kishino leaves behind distinct textual traces of her struggle that point her readers to that space—that site—where a change of consciousness born of sustained reflection can allow a writing subject to forge a new identity and subjectivity that contains the potential for a new form of historical agency. The social and cultural constraints with which Kishino grapples are formidable, but they are never able to fully prevent her from mounting a form of resistance nor from discovering her feminine consciousness. It was this discovery, in turn, that allowed her to "reposition" herself and conceptualize women and their place in history and society in a new way. In the end, this discovery was the only weapon she knew how to wield against the regimes of truth and control (*shihai no shikumi*) that were aligned against her.

5

FRAMING GENDER QUESTIONS

KANAMORI TOSHIE'S "WARATTE, NAITE, ARUITE, KAITA: JOSEI JYAANARISUTO NO GOJÛNEN"

As Jill Ker Conway notes, "By the second half of the nineteenth century, women's access to education and the emergence of the women's professions provided a new social territory from which women could examine the meaning of their lives and comment upon their society."[1] Japanese women in the prewar period clearly did experience some of this improved access, but it was often limited and conditional. But in the postwar years and under the new constitution, women did have, in name, equal access to education and employment, although the previous chapters illustrate how elusive and frustrating this quest for equality proved to be. Kanamori Toshie (1925–) was another newspaperwoman who joined the staff of the *Yomiuri shinbun* as a reporter in April 1952, just a year before Kishino joined the *Sankei shinbun* (even though she was five years older than Kishino) and two years before Yoshitake entered Tôei. All in all, it seems that she was treated somewhat better at the *Yomiuri* than Kishino or Yoshitake were at their workplaces because Kanamori eventually became the first woman to be named a department head when she was appointed to lead the woman's department (*fujinbu*). Nor did either the massive Ampo protest and the women's lib movement seem to make the same kind of significant impact on her that they did on Yoshitake and Kishino. At least her memoir does not reveal any information about how either of these movements may have affected her. Moreover, she has nothing to say about being disappointed over what became of the ideal of postwar democracy. And yet her narrative does not exult in unequivocal triumphs and successes.

Kanamori was extremely interested in women's issues when she was a reporter, and after she retired she worked tirelessly with local women in Kanagawa Prefecture to create the Kanagawa Women's Center located in Enoshima. So, while she may not have written anything in her memoir about a "feminine consciousness," nor discussed her disappointments over the fate of postwar democracy, she does take on gender issues that were central to women's lives: education, equality in the workplace, and the effect of aging and elder care on women's lives. Her memoir—translated as *I Laughed, Cried, Walked and Wrote: My Fifty Years as a Female Journalist*—which consists mainly of excerpts from published articles that appeared throughout her career—does not contain much in the way of the intensely personal revelations that we find in Kishino's and Yoshitake's texts, with the possible exception of passages dealing with the care and eventual death of both her mother and her husband. Nevertheless, in her own words, she wrote articles criticizing discrimination against women and consistently offered insights into contemporary Japanese society from a woman's perspective.

Preface

Beginning in 1952, and for the next thirty years, I worked for the *Yomiuri shinbun* as a reporter in the Tokyo editorial offices in charge of the women's department. These days, the women's department has evolved into the lifestyles and information department, but the *Yomiuri* has a long history of targeting women readers with a section on women and lifestyles, which was handled by the women's department. On April 3, 1914, during the Taishô fascination with "cultural life," when the number of young women graduating from high school and continuing their education was on the rise, the *Yomiuri* led the newspaper world by being the first to create a single page aimed at attracting female readers. However, on entering the Shôwa period, with the shortages of materials, newspapers had to reduce their number of pages, and once they were reduced to a single-page edition, the women's page was eliminated altogether.

Then, in the postwar period, when the number of newspaper pages expanded again in an era of rapid economic growth, they brought back an evening edition of the paper in 1950, and the women and lifestyles section made its reappearance. For this reason, they needed to recruit female reporters, so the next year, for the first time, they opened the employment examination to women as well as men. Although I did not know if I would be successful, I considered it a challenge to take the exam and eventually got the unofficial word that I had passed.

When I received that news, I was more surprised than overjoyed; my mind went blank, and I felt as though I were walking on clouds. But you have to realize that at that time I had already been a full-time housewife for several years, and really the whole idea of working full-time was more like a dream to me than anything else.

In March of 1945, in my third year at a girls school, I had entered an arranged marriage after being introduced by someone in my neighborhood. At that time, late in the war, almost all the young men had already been shipped off to war, so there were very few remaining in the home islands.

But my husband was someone who periodically spent time in China working with the military, and when he was back in Tokyo for a two-week period, we held the *omiai* meeting (a formal meeting between prospective partners in an arranged marriage)

We married in a hurry, and he was sent right back to China while I remained living with my parents and continued attending school just as before. But in April, the school was destroyed during an air raid, and the following month our family home was burned to the ground as well. Eventually, my family had to be evacuated to relatives in the countryside until, finally, the war ended. Our family returned to a burned-out barracks, and the following year my husband returned safely from China. It was then that we started living together. What an extremely busy time!

In time my husband joined the ranks of the "salarymen," and I started to learn all the skills that a bride should learn but I had not had the leisure to pursue during the war years—things like cooking, sewing, and so forth. My husband was in the first generation of "worker bees," so he never returned home until very late at night. Even though I cooked the best meals that I could with the limited foods available to us, and waited up for him to come home, he would often arrive home late and just say, "I already ate."

Plagued by gloomy thoughts that all I was doing was simply seeing my husband off in the morning and waiting for his late return while my own life just slipped away before my eyes, my father unexpectedly made the observation, "The world is in the midst of big changes. It is an era in which even women can graduate from college!" My father's alma mater, Takushoku University, was nearby, and he recommended me to it. As a result, I became the first woman and the first housewife to become a student there. Two years later, when I realized that I had no desire to return to the life of seeing my husband off and waiting for him to return, I was fortunate enough to have the door opened to become the first woman to take the *Yomiuri* employment examination. So I became a reporter for the women's department.

In the decades of the 1960s and 1970s, the norm for a division of labor along gender lines was based on the belief that "Men go to work, and women stay home take care of the household." Specifically, for women who did join the workforce, they confronted the very thick wall of discrimination that assumed that a woman quit when she got married, had a baby, or reached the age of thirty. But women began to appear who were willing to take cases to court as violations of the constitution, which guaranteed equal access to employment.

After about my tenth year with the newspaper, I began writing articles with a byline criticizing and censuring this kind of discrimination against women. In fact, in this book, I will be drawing on the articles written during these years, so I think you could say that they represent a footnote on one woman's experience rooted in the history of this era.

However, even if I wrote some pretty harsh commentary in my articles, I always enjoyed seeing my male reporter colleagues the next day. In those days, out of about a thousand reporters in the editorial division, there were only about 5 female reporters. Of course, we did become pretty frustrated with our male colleagues from time to time; but we worked very closely with them from morning until night, so we did not hold back in our criticisms of them. But once evening rolled around and we went out for drinks together after work, I enjoyed the frank give-and-take with them. In those days, the paper was located in Ginza, where there were lots of little bars and drinking spots, so reporters always could be found hanging out and having a good time.

I can recall one incident that might be worth recounting. In those days, the editorial writers who were in charge of the editorial pages were all men. However, even they recognized that on April 10, which was designated as Women's Day, it was necessary to write articles on women's issues. (Note: April 10 was the date when women got to cast their ballots in an election for the first time, so from that day on, for one week, it was declared Women's Week.) Since they were pretty bewildered most of the time, I was often asked to help them out and provide them with a brief background lecture.

However, on one occasion, they went ahead and ran their editorial without soliciting my thoughts. When I read it, it seemed to hang together well, and the headline was "Destroying the Myth That Men Work and Women Stay Home to Tend to the Family." I was delighted and called out to M-san in the editorial writers' room. When M-san came out he was beaming, and I offered him my right hand and said, "This morning's editorial was great! Let's shake hands." He replied, "You guys are scary. I decided to write about women's issues only in a token fashion." My eyes opened wide, and I said to him, "Really, well, aren't editorials always written pretty superficially?" He just said, "Damn you, you little rascal!" and he made as if to punch my arm and we both laughed until I took my leave.

There is no doubt that the times do change and eventually women did begin serving as ambassadors, cabinet ministers, and heads of political parties. Then one year on New Year's Day, when I received a New Year's card from M-san, he had added a line to the effect that "the tokenism has actually become the reality." I realized that he had remembered what we said that day, and it made me laugh out loud. It was a very happy New Year's Day for me!

In March 1982, I retired from the newspaper, and, in November of that same year, I went to work for ten years at the Kanagawa Prefecture

Comprehensive Women's Center located in Enoshima. After that I worked as an educator for Kamakura City, and then, in my late seventies, I quit public service altogether. Finally, in the fall of last year, as I approached my eightieth birthday, I began to distance myself from both work and studying and just enjoyed reading and spending time with friends. One regret I had was that I always wanted to take some of the articles I had written under my byline during my years as a reporter and use them as some sort of proof that I had actually been alive. Thanks to Kashima Mitsuyo of Domesu Publishing, and with unparalleled support and help from Yano Misao, I was able to get three volumes of my articles published, *Challenge Is Interesting, Let Us Sing of Caring for the Elderly*, and *More Than Material Riches, We Need Riches in People and Friends*. And now I have to express my deepest gratitude for their support with this book. Also, having lived such a long life, I have many friends who have supported me along the way that I wish to thank. (1–5)

It is interesting that both Kishino and Kanamori reminisce fondly about the atmosphere near Ginza in the early postwar years when reporters hung out together after work having drinks and socializing. Although Kanamori clearly experienced some frustrations and faced her challenges in the predominantly male workplace, it seems that she did not have to put up with the same kind of hardships that Kishino did. The next section of Kanamori's memoir takes up the question of education and how the International Year of the Woman in 1975 was a starting point for new ways of thinking about the place of women in Japanese education.

Expectations for Education: The Image of Women in Textbooks

Once again it is the time of year when our children get their hands on their new textbooks. But what kind of image of women is depicted in these texts? Last year (1975) was the International Year of the Woman, and a large international conference was held. A "Global Action Plan" was adopted by the United Nations and many of the member nations to cover the next decade, and this year is the time when each country is supposed to start implementing the plan.

Eleven to Zero

Makino Tomitarô was born over a century ago in the town of Sagawa in Takaoka-gun of Kôchi Prefecture into a wealthy sake-brewing family. . . . Tomitarô later became an outstanding botanist. He became so famous that his name, rendered as Tomi Makino, became widely known even among foreign scholars.

> Benjamin Franklin was born approximately 270 years ago
> in America. . . . Devoted to improving himself since he

was a little boy, Franklin later made many discoveries and inventions. He also helped found a university, published newspapers, and worked hard to make the world a better place. (*Atarashii Kokugo*, third grade, second half, Tokyo shosai)

Japanese-language textbooks prepared for elementary school students are published by five publishers, and each one includes one individual's biography for the students to read. . . .From the first grade through the sixth, there are about twenty people whose biographies are included in these textbooks. Among these twenty, nine are foreigners, and only one woman is included: Madame Curie. However, among the Japanese people included, all eleven are males. Not a single woman is represented. . . .

So, the ratio is eleven to zero, even though in the classroom the number of girls is just about equal to the number of boys. I put the question of why this should be the case to a Ministry of Education official in charge of examining and certifying textbooks, one Harada Chikasada. The specific criteria for certifying textbooks are spelled out in three sections of the Fundamental Education Law and the School Education Law, particularly "The Purpose of Education," "The Government Curriculum Guidelines" ("The Objectives of the Curriculum" section), and, concerning politics and education, the "Impartial Position" section.

So, based on the Government Curriculum Guidelines, the publishers have the authors and editors assemble appropriate materials, and then they apply for certification. "We respect the rights of the editors and authors, and we do not interfere with content. If there is a violation of the Government Curriculum Guidelines, we may tell them to change something, but we do not tell them how to change it or what to change it to. The opinion that it is strange to include not a single biography of a woman is reasonable. But we would ask you to communicate that concern to the authors and the editors. Of course, I never have said anything like we should not include biographies of women."

Next, when I asked textbook publisher Gotô Yasuo of Kyôiku Shuppansha, he replied:

> *Of course we are not discriminating against women. Even if the main character in the biography is a man, we emphasize that they accomplished whatever they did with the support of their family. Perhaps it is because among the authors of textbooks, there are so few women, that we could consider getting more women to write textbooks in the future. And we would appreciate recommendations if there are appropriate women to feature.*

Somehow there was a kind of careless, absent-minded quality to his response. So, when I asked historian Nagai Michiko about this, she replied as follows.

Are there appropriate biographies of women? That is ridiculous!
Of course there are! I can think of fifty or sixty right off the top of
my head, for example.

She went on to elaborate on such women as Nakajima Utako, who set her sights on academics in the tumultuous transition from the late Tokugawa to the early Meiji periods and opened her own poetry school in Hagi, where Higuchi Ichiyô was among her students. Likewise, there was Tenshûni, who was Toyotomi Hideyori's daughter. Residing at Tôkeiji, a temple in North Kamakura, she protected women who would not submit to authority, and so her temple became known as a refuge for women and also as Midorikiri Temple. Inoue Den was the inventor of Kurumegasuri, a kimono fabric pattern. Wakamatsu Shizuko was the first student to enter the Ferris Girl's School in 1870. Later she married Iwamoto Kenji, principal of Meiji Girls School. She worked tirelessly for the education of women and, with love and affection, translated *Little Lord Fauntleroy* into refined and elegant classical Japanese, so she contributed to the development of many young women over the course of nearly a century.

In addition, there were educators like Tsuda Umeko, who studied abroad when she was only eight years old and founded Tsuda College on her return, as well as one of the founders of Tokyo Women's College, Yasui Tetsu. Likewise, there was also the grandmother of the popular rights movement, Kusunose Kita of Tosa, who raised her voice in 1878 calling for women to be granted the right to vote.

However, Miss Nagai did go on to say:

Nevertheless, we cannot say that Japan ever produced a woman
like Mme. Curie, whose individual abilities allowed her to
overcome gender barriers. {This was} around that time during the
Meiji period when the "respect men, despise women" philosophy
was in full swing, so Japanese society was incapable of producing
a woman like Mme. Curie. I guess we cannot say that Mme.
Curie acted uncharacteristically as a woman when she discovered
radium. So perhaps this missing piece is one of the reasons that the
textbooks lack biographies of women.

The textbook publishers themselves confirmed that their whole process of creating textbooks was under the control of men when they lined up all the signed endorsements on the back cover. A Tokyo meeting of the Women's Issues Group looked into the authors of 34 textbooks for elementary school years 1 through 6, and they found that while there were

714 male writers, there were only 8 women. Moreover, among the Ministry of Education's 42 textbook investigators, there were just 2 women who were responsible for books for the home economics curriculum. Under the Minister of Education's advisory committee for questions and inquiries, there is a textbook certification and authorization committee made up of citizen academics numbering some 80 people of whom exactly 3 are women. This is the case even though half of the consumers of these textbooks are female. (16–21)

Revisiting Women's Education: Realizing "Life and Independence"

How can we improve women's education? On January 13, 1981, for the next four days, at the Japanese Teacher's Union's thirtieth annual meeting of the educational research committee, one of the twenty-six subtopics that were taken up was this question of women's education. About three thousand teachers debated these issues for three straight days. But now let us talk about why women's education should have become such an issue.

It was actually four years previously that the research committee of the Japan Teacher's Union first took up the question of women's education, but this was the first time the topic was granted its own independent forum. From all across the country, the Teacher's Union assembled some fifty-two reports and set about in earnest fashion to tackle how teachers need to approach girls' education.

From the statements made by the teachers at the meeting, there were three main pillars supporting the way in which they wanted to tackle the question of girls' education. The first was to actually survey the state of awareness among the students, the faculty themselves, and the mothers. The second was to reexamine the textbooks themselves. Finally, there was the element of the actual experiences of the teachers in the classroom.

As far as the survey is concerned, it was hardly surprising to learn that a rigid attitude toward girls that was rooted in the past quickly came to the surface. Of course this was true of the children and their mothers, but these attitudes could be found among the teachers as well. For example, in high schools where the number of male teachers is very large, the vast majority's image of a girl's future was "to get married and have a happy family," and in terms of expectations for their own daughters, their aim was "to raise a feminine daughter." (From the Kagoshima High School Teacher's Union.)

Next, taking a look at the textbooks, we can see that there were very many issues. Whether it was language arts textbooks, society, family, or English, women were consistently depicted in a supporting role from within the family while the man was the one going out to work. Moreover, in a middle-school Japanese history textbook, for example, there were only six women including the likes of Himiko and Murasaki Shikibu. While an elementary school textbook for social studies did present the tragic circumstances of the female textile millworkers, it wound up undercutting the point by observing that "Japanese industry was able to develop and prosper thanks to the efforts of these people." . . .

There may have been some women who had received a girls' education that was designed to rear them to be feminine (*onna-rashii shitsuke no kyôiku*). However, in the 1975 International Year of the Woman, when issues surrounding women's education came in for a great deal of discussion, the impetus to rethink existing traditional attitudes toward girls' education was launched. The traditional view that little girls should be cute and grow up to be good wives that permeated society to such a great extent in the olden days was still very strongly rooted and took the form of the "good wife, wise mother" approach to education, which emphasized training a girl to become a good wife and mother. However, don't these kinds of expectations and attitudes, which are so deeply rooted in society, crush individuality and erase some of the potential available to each young girl? When a woman marathoner who is a housewife establishes an amazing new record, or a woman passes the difficult legal licensing exam, these stories become news, and to the extent that they come as a surprise to society, doesn't that tell us that all the various abilities that women possess can be imprisoned in this one, narrow interpretation of the word *housewife*? (22–24)

Changing Expectations for the Home Economics Curriculum

Even though society may look like it is changing a great deal, sometimes it really does not change much at all. . . . With the new constitution proclaiming equality between men and women, and with progress being made toward democratization, in 1947, the government guidelines for teaching established an "Education for Constructing a Household" curriculum to be taught at the elementary, middle, and high school levels. Two years later, in high-school, the "General Household" course was established as an elective class. However, by the time we entered the 1950s, there occurred a movement within the government to revive the old family system (*kazoku-seidô*) and moral education. Moreover, as we entered the 1960s and the era of high-speed economic growth, which was dependent on rapid technological advancement, expectations grew for women who could take care of the home while the kind of workers that were needed to fuel the high rates of economic growth could devote themselves to building the new society.

In such an era, the Ministry of Education began to place emphasis on the special characteristics of women and their responsibility for the household, and in the 1970s it sent out notification that four courses in the home economics curriculum would become compulsory.

Women's Participation in Society: A Favorable Global Wind

After entering the decade of the 1970s, I would often refer to "The 'LL' [Long Life] Era for Women's Lives." In the old days, it was assumed that the lifespan of Japanese people was right around 50 years. But with the advance of modernization after World War II, not only did lifestyles improve but longevity was extended, especially for women. In 1975 the average lifespan for women was 76.8 years (71.3 for men), and by 1985 this figure had surpassed 80 years, signaling that the era of "Long Life" had arrived.[2] On the one hand, the number of children Japanese women would bear in a 50-year lifetime was 3.65, but with the decline in the birthrate, this number fell to 2.0 in the 1970s, and in 2001 it fell to an all-time low of 1.33. So, not only did the period of child rearing grow shorter, but the amount of time given over to housework also continued to shrink. Therefore, women now were allowed plenty of time to enrich their lives with a variety of activities other than just child rearing and housework.

And, on the other hand, with the postwar equality of opportunity in education, along with the importance being placed on one's academic record, the number of facilities offering lifelong education increased as we entered the information age as well. I guess we could say that we entered an era in which the possibilities for developing one's individuality and increasing one's abilities were expanding, so that we were also entering the era of the "Large Life." It was a natural and necessary progression toward the "LL era of women's lives," wherein opportunities for women to participate more naturally and normally in society grew.

However, the sexual division of labor based on gender and the assumption that "Men work and women take care of the household" had very deep roots, ensuring that the wall of inequality between the sexes would remain very thick. This, in turn, meant that women's ability to fully participate in society, especially in the form of working productively, was rendered problematic. As economic development progressed, the industrial world needed the labor power of women, but they were primarily in either one of two categories of lower paid employees: young, unmarried women or part-time housewives. Ever since the 1960s, there have always been women from a variety of locales who brought suit against corporations for their policies requiring women to resign upon marrying or having children, in other words, against the entire system that required young female workers to quit upon marriage or childbirth. In those days, it was my direct experience gained from many interviews as a reporter that "More than a matter of being a labor problem, it is a matter of basic human rights."

It was also during the 1960s that the movement to expand public child care facilities arose in response to women needing to continue working after marriage and childbirth, but this was also obstructed by the thick wall of belief in the notion that "Women should stay at home and take care of housework and raising children." But, over and above the desires of these women, a favorable wind began to blow from what was taking place on the world stage.

With the UN support, 1975 became the International Year of the Woman, and that year the first Global Women's Conference, embracing the themes of "Equality, Development, and Peace," was held. Including Japan, some 133 countries sent government-supported representatives to participate in the conference, where a policy was settled on by several countries to have some concrete follow-up in terms of an "Action Plan." Of course, there were some male reporters who saw fit to teasingly imply that, especially for Japanese women, who were not privy to very much information from outside of Japan, this conference was just an opportunity for women to sit around and gossip. However, as far as the movement to bring an end to discrimination against women was concerned, it had its roots back in 1946, the year after the end of World War II, when the committee on the status of women was created. Following this was the 1948 "World Human Rights Declaration" and then the 1967 "Declaration on the Abolition of Discrimination against Women," from which flowed a current that culminated in the 1975 International Year of the Woman.

So it was in such an era, then, that Japan, now the second-ranked country among economic superpowers, along with many of the developing nations, finally joined the movement, and the government launched in 1977 the "Domestic Action Plan." After that time, numerous plans all over Japan were created to correct the division of labor based on gender and establish gender equality, which emboldened women all the more. The Convention on the Elimination of All Forms of Discrimination against Women (CEDAW), a treaty meant to eradicate all forms of discrimination against women, was adopted by the UN General Assembly in 1979 and came into force as a treaty in 1981, but in order for Japan to ratify this treaty in 1985, it needed to adjust its domestic laws so that they conformed with the treaty. The result of this was the Equal Employment Opportunity Law for Men and Women and an act that bestows Japanese citizenship on any child born in Japan regardless of which parent is Japanese (previously, citizenship was transmitted only through the father). Also home economics courses would be required of both boys and girls. Thereafter, spanning three different international women's conferences that grappled with these issues, the Fundamental Social Law for Joint Male-Female Participation in Planning was passed and implemented in 1999. (27–31)

Families, the Aging Society, and the Declining Birthrate

I alluded earlier to the fact that the number of children that Japanese women bear in their lifetime declined in 2001 to its lowest level to date,

1.33, which we can see as a result of the phenomenon of women postponing marriage and pregnancy until later in life.[3] The average age of a woman's first marriage in 2001 was 27.2 (in 1975 it had been 24.7), so women are marrying later than men. Accordingly, the old value system, which held that women's happiness was rooted in marriage, is changing, and women want to find their happiness not only in their role as wives and mothers but also in other outlets for self-expression as a way to realize their potential. The difficulty of working and raising children at the same time definitely causes women to hesitate about having children and often results in postponing birth; one could also mention the costs of educating children and maintaining a home mortgage as influencing factors. I suppose we could say that another influential factor would be the lack of adequate day care facilities and the paucity of cooperation that one can expect from spouses. The percentage of women who can get time off for child rearing stands at 56.4 percent while only 0.42 percent (in 1999) of the husbands whose wives have just given birth are able to take time off, a pathetically low figure. So, in addition to providing some needed social support in terms of more child care facilities, there was a desire to see the corporate side acknowledge that it has an obligation to revise the system, which requires long working hours for males and prevents them from cooperating more around the household.

Recently, in various locations, groups of fathers have been putting together movements to deepen the quality of their relationship with their children. I heard one such father say with deep regret, "They say that we are in our prime as workers, but if you think about it, it is the children who are in their prime for growth and we should be in our prime as fathers." I would love to see this point of view become more widely adopted and expressed.

A special characteristic of Japan's aging society is the speed with which the transition has occurred. If the percentage of people sixty-five and older is 7 percent of the population, this constitutes an aging society, but when it reaches 14 percent, this means the society has become an aged society. In Japan, the 7 percent mark was reached in 1970 and the 14 percent mark in 1994. In other words, in just twenty-four years Japan went from being an aging society to an aged society. Among Western European nations, where aging occurred simultaneously with modernization, the comparable period in England was forty-five years, and in Sweden, where it took the longest, it was eighty-five years. This means that Japan's transition was the most rapid in the world, but by 2000 those over sixty-five years of age reached 17.3 percent, so it is predicted that by 2050, the figure will become 35.7 percent, which means that among the citizenry one in every three Japanese people will be sixty-five years old or older.

Another special characteristic of Japan's situation is that care of the elderly has fallen heavily on families and especially on women. According to a 1998 survey conducted by the Women's Committee to Improve the Aging Society (founded by Higuchi Keiko and others), in 93 percent of the cases where families were performing elder care, women were the primary caregivers. With one in every four persons being over sixty-five years old, this elder care will be needed for both sets of a couple's parents, as well as for elder siblings, meaning that instances of multiple elder care will be on the rise. It is clear that there are real limitations to the capacity of families, and especially women, to provide elder care.

My own mother died eight years ago at age eighty-nine. During her final three years, I worried that both of us might collapse from the stress on both our minds and our bodies. But during those difficult days, I had an unexpected experience. My once robust mother suffered dementia, and she would smile up at me as her caregiver just like a little child and call me "Mother," and, in turn, I would hold her like a little baby and sing her songs, and I could not help feeling how precious a thing was this life that was ebbing from her frail body. Child rearing and elder care both involve a tremendous amount of pain and effort. However, at the same time, the joys of raising a young, new life and caring for a life that is waning can both give rise to warm and gentle feelings. Is it not an unfortunate thing that men who consider both child rearing and elder care to be a woman's function miss out on this dimension of the human experience?

Since there was no such thing as elder care insurance eight years ago, the financial burden as well as the toll it took on my mind and body was very great. In the year 2000, elder care insurance became a reality; just like with health insurance, by paying premiums you become entitled to some elder care services, so there have been some thoughtful improvements made. By having such social supports, families can have a little room to breathe in terms of the mental and physical stress. I became an advocate for the principle that "Society should provide care for the elderly while families supply the love and men and women cooperate and share the burdens."

The Diversity of the Family: Moving Toward a Period of Change

In 2001 the average life span of a Japanese person was 84.93 years for women and 78.07 for men, which placed Japan at the top of global longevity tables. Along with the advancement of the aging society, the number of households with only elderly couples, and of households of single older people living by themselves, has grown substantially, making the question of social support for them an increasingly important topic. On the one hand, along with the growth in dual-income families, as well as the number of unregistered marriages, same-sex couples, single-parent families, and friends of families who have no other blood relatives, the notion of "family" has continued to grow ever more diverse. There are even those who believe that the terms *kazoku* [family] and *katei* [home] should be differentiated and that the modern family should be defined simply as a group of individuals who live together.

Moreover, with this kind of transformation in the family and the home, we have also seen a rise in the level of such things as domestic violence, child abuse, elder abuse, and so on. The victims of domestic violence are almost always wives, and the main reason is that the long-term division of labor based on gender has created a hierarchical, unequal relationship between husband and wife. The notion that a wife must obey her husband has created social acceptance for the idea that if she fails to obey it is acceptable to hit her, something intrinsic to an unequal society based on discrimination against women. And in the overwhelming number of cases, the wives are not able to establish their own economic independence, so even when they are victimized by violence they feel they have no choice but to endure it.

At the kinds of housing referred to earlier, where only old couples live, stories of murders and double suicides make the news, but the perpetrators are almost always the husbands. When the husband collapses, the wife somehow does what is necessary to take care of him and manage everyday life, but if the wife collapses, the husband is not even capable of making a satisfactory meal for himself, much less take care of someone else, so there have been many cases where only tragedy ensued. I think it is time to renew the call for women's financial independence, an independence of lifestyle for men, and adequate social support.

Also many of the instances of abuse of children or the elderly occur when there is a young mother raising children or a daughter-in-law taking care of an elderly person, everyone living in close quarters. So, along with increasing the level of responsibility and burden sharing for the men, we need to be able to expand the field of vision and the range of observation for women, and to allow them to have friends with whom they can talk freely, and to have available both here and in the countryside the necessary support system from the wider society.

In addition, there are many other challenging issues, such as the way housewives' pensions are taxed; the way women are relegated to part-time, detached employee status with low wages; the rapidly rising rate of suicide among middle-aged and older men; and, due to developments in reproductive technology, such things as in vitro fertilization, embryo transfer, surrogate birth, and on and on. Moreover, we can look beyond these issues to see how the transition from an industrialized society, in which the small family became the norm, to a postindustrial society, in which the family did not end up being destroyed exactly but continued to change so that a real gap between the existing consciousness and traditional practices, emerged and placed stresses and strains on the family. To that extent, without getting caught up in individual phenomena, I think we want to reinforce the principles that emerged from the 1994 International Year of the Family, confirming once again that we are heading into the twenty-first century.

To begin with, we need to actively encourage fundamental human rights and liberties within the family, equality between men and women within the household, equality between men and women in terms of both family responsibilities and employment opportunities outside the home, and, finally, the opportunity for independent activity. From the viewpoint of the former large-family model, it appears that the functioning of the family is weakening, so individuals will have to work hard in order to establish a humane family environment in which individuality for both men and women can be nurtured. Societal support will be indispensable to achieve this, and the government is going to have to pour some energy into developing policies to support child rearing. (32–36)

Thinking about the Family and Childrearing: Changes in the Nuclear Family

I had been born and raised in Tokyo, always used to living in a cramped space with virtually no yard for many years, but twenty-three years ago I moved with my family out to Kamakura. There were four of us: my husband, myself, our daughter, and my mother. I pictured the four of us enjoying quiet, endless early afternoons together, but before very long my daughter got married and left home, my husband got cancer and died at the age of fifty-eight, and finally, after living together with my mother for sixteen years, I ended up living there alone.

I guess our family was somewhat of an anomaly, but, if you think about it, it could be the pattern that the typical nuclear family of a husband and wife with two children may follow. In this four-person family, it seems that the children marry and join the workforce, so the unit is reduced to three and then two, and then, after a certain time, the older couple usually ends up with the wife outliving the husband by another nine years, or so the statistics on life span would tell us. Therefore, women living in this age of declining birthrates and an aging society must think about this kind of life cycle and, indeed, must plan for it.

Two Pillars: Preparing for Old Age

In 1970, when I was working as a reporter in the women's department of my newspaper, I was in charge of a series of articles under the title "The Era of the Husband and Wife." The point was to compensate for the overemphasis placed on the vertical relationship between parents and children and look more closely at the horizontal relationship between the couple and how the modern family needed to change in order to recognize this. The case was made that it was necessary to recognize that, as opposed to couples as parents, couples have various forms of independence that need to be recognized and they need to be able to deepen the warm connections between them.

In that year, the percentage of the Japanese population that was over 65 years of age had reached 7 percent; in other words, Japan had become an aging society. However, 24 years later in 1994 this figure had doubled to 14 percent meaning that Japan had made the transition from an aging to an aged society. Comparing this transition to the developed nations of Europe where it took between several decades and even up to a century to come about, in Japan the change has occurred at warp speed.[4] Accordingly, whether privately or publicly, there is an urgent need to develop some policies.

The above-mentioned series of articles predicted these kinds of social changes and presented a plan, and I included the phrase "two pillars." Most of the childbearing and child-rearing activities are completed by the time a woman reaches her fifties, and since women these days experience many long years after they "retire as mothers," in addition to the pillar of the family and home, they are free to pursue another pillar—the pillar of participating in society in some manner.

The first thing is that by having a job, people who formerly worked can continue to raise their knowledge base and skill level. There are two avenues open to housewives. If they are not pressured to find a job for economic reasons, they can get some education or training in order to have a better, more fulfilling job. But another route is to build on the skill she has developed raising children and managing the household, or a skill developed pursuing a hobby, so that she can find something that is half for fun, but something she can get serious about as well. I have often thought that the age when the housewife can market her skills is on us, or that if "one pursues a hobby for ten years or more, you can find a way to make it your profession."

Second, by working, one can acquire economic power, and, in order to avoid poverty in one's later years, this can be very important. In my case, when my husband died, for the long years that were waiting ahead of me, I had the resources in terms of my income to somehow live my life and still take care of my mother, and that was a great source of relief for me. Moreover, a job can be a way to develop one's individuality and abilities, as well as a vehicle for self-expression. And, third, contemporary women blessed with the opportunity offered by a long lifespan and the importance placed on education, can through their work play a significant role as members of society, something I think they should be able to do for a long period of time. . . .

Do Not Make Elder Care Exclusively a Woman's Job

Of course, everyone knows that the advent of the aging society means that "elder care" has become an important topic. Men and women's average life span is roughly seventy-six and eighty-three years, respectively; therefore the majority of the burden of elder care falls on women. On the one hand, over 80 percent of the care for the bedridden elderly that takes place in the home is performed by women—wives, daughters-in-law, and daughters. So elder care, whether it is the caregivers or those being cared for, is a huge issue for women.

In the case of women, the aging society phenomenon has only just begun. The percentage of the total population occupied by those over sixty-five years of age currently stands at 15 percent, but at its peak in 2025 it is predicted that it will exceed 25 percent. This means that the number of people with serious disabilities among the aging population will rise, and the burden of care for them will grow heavier. At the same time, the statistics show that the women who will be asked to perform this care will also be aging, so aging wives, daughters-in-law, and daughters will have to take on an ever increasing burden of caring for others. Moreover, since women's social progress will naturally be a trend of the times, the number of older women living alone or households comprised of only an elderly couple—in other words, people who have no one to take care of them—will also be growing, just as I suggested earlier. Therefore, we will continually be pushing the limits of what is possible in terms of people caring for the elderly themselves, within the family. Everyone knows, therefore, that this is why the government has put forth new "Gold Plans," creating public insurance programs and seeking to build lots of facilities, and there is a great deal of popular interest in these issues.

This is why I have argued for some years for a system of "cooperative, joint efforts to bring together one's own contributions, along with public assistance and mutual cooperation, including the cooperation of men." Of course, the elderly themselves need to make an effort, and the primary role of their families is extremely important. But at the same time, the support of the central government, as well as local organizations and agencies— in other words, public support—must become regularized. All of these resources need to be brought together, and with help from neighbors and local support agencies we can make progress. Moreover, we need the support of men in all these areas. They must help share the burden so it is not just the wife, but sons and sons-in-law, dorm "fathers" and male nurses, male helpers and volunteers—all of these pieces have to be part of the picture. When I was taking care of my elderly mother for the last three years, I often thought how wonderful it would have been if there had been some kind of helper who could have come in and made night rounds, or if there had been some way to have some public assistance for me because there were many times when I felt I needed "a man's help."

Women themselves need to get rid of the "curse" that makes them feel that it is their role to perform elder care and get used to accepting some public help. If caregivers can get a little relief now and again, they will be able to provide much better care. At the same time, I really want to urge men to become a part of the caregiving process. This is not solely to reduce the burden of child care falling on women. Rather, it is also a wake-up call for these males who know nothing but work so they can have the very human experience of understanding how fragile and precious life can be, which comes with the act of caring for another.

To take all these things together, in order to prepare for old age, men's lives and their perspectives must be included in the mix so that they can do their share of cooking and laundry and acquire the basic skills of independent living. Because we know that there are many instances in which the wife is the first one to suffer a collapse, then these inexperienced husbands do not know how to do anything for themselves and they may wind up tragically ending their spouses' and then their own lives.

More Than Material Wealth We Should be Rich in Friends

Previously, I argued that in addition to the pillar of the family women should have another pillar to support them, that of work and having an occupation. But if our lives have only work and family, that is not enough either. Beginning with the greenery and water found in the natural environment, we need to have our garbage disposed of, welfare for the elderly and the disabled, and any number of other things necessary in any given locality. When localities are where we need to establish our quality of life, I want to see people participating in local movements. Moreover, another necessary condition for a rich and fulfilling "senior life" is to have access to hobbies and classes that one can join. For someone like me, who had become a "woman worker bee," this was a very significant issue.

Family, work, one's local area, and oneself—aren't these four things where one's hopes for a meaningful life in a mature society, a life that could put a smile on an individual's face, might begin? I guess you could say that in order to prepare for one's later years, a rich diversity of human interactions would be very important. I personally was able to avoid the sadness of living by myself by being able to enjoy living freely and just for myself, not only enjoying times with my daughter and my grandchildren but also spending time with all the friends with whom I became close over the years. Many people worry about money after they get older. But I think that more than having money you should have people around you; you should have friends to be with. (58–66)

Welfare and Eldercare: From Today to Tomorrow

What kind of conversation would one expect to hear these days from men who are in their fifties? No doubt they will speak mostly about golf and their work. Once they enter their sixties, the topic of health may be added. But as individuals, their interests and enjoyments are few and far between, so even if they do speak it is not always very interesting. In contrast to this, consider women talking during the last two or three years. They are trying to construct a culture. I feel that it is precisely here that a gap has begun to appear between men and women.

In the case of women, the issue of compatibility between work and family is both an old and a new theme. Therefore, when I think about the fundamental ways in which human beings live, I think it is less a matter of compatibility between two opposites. I would like to advocate for bringing four parts into harmony. What would these four parts be? In order to see individuals become more active and engaged, I would see these four components become integrated in people's lives: family, work, local community and leisure. These four areas combine to establish a complete or total way of living.

If we consider this notion that human nature is comprised of these four major parts, naturally they have different weights depending on the different stages in one's life. For example, men in their forties and fifties naturally put most of their weight on work. However, that is not all there is to it; there is also one's role in the household, and sometimes one may take part in a local gathering. . . . In such instances, the relative weight placed on work is less. For example, even if it drops all the way down to zero, the remaining weight can be apportioned among local activities, family, and the individual's freedom. These people's lives are not likely to become like the wet leaf that sticks to one's back, or the blank space.

What is necessary is to understand that our lives are comprised of these four different segments. And, if we were to in some way add something to the mix, to state the conclusions in advance, it would be possible, then, to achieve a full life. To argue that these four components comprise a total life is, in effect, a way of nudging older people toward a "soft landing. . . ." (68–69)

Checking for Something That Might Be Missing

Once I was watching a documentary on television about an old folk's home, and the following scene struck me. The old women were patting each other on the shoulder, rubbing each other's backs, and just being friendly. By contrast, the old men were just plopped here and there, like birds roosting in a tree. Somehow, their appearance, just sitting on the sofa with their chins resting on their hands, seemed so lonely . . . [that] it really made a strong impression on me.

I suppose this was the result of men coming out of a world where they could only communicate with people whose title and status they knew. In other words, in a world where someone's official position and title means nothing, they did not seem to know how to even begin a conversation. In order for this not to happen, I believe there must be a change from this existing vertical society—where the myth of position and status dominates—to the values of a more horizontal society. I think this is a key point in bringing about the idea of a life rooted in the four different dimensions. Is it not the case that men are at a complete loss when it comes to functioning appropriately in the family or local area?

Recently, among that generation that is younger than the baby boomer generation, there is a growing number of men who do not covet the high positions that will require them to sacrifice their individuality and their family life as well. These people grew up in an age of abundance, so they are familiar with pastimes like sports and music. Moreover, they have absorbed a consciousness of equality toward women, so they are willing to help with child-rearing and chores around the house. I guess we just have to acknowledge the fact that people born in the Shôwa era lack this element in their character and have no intention of living their lives this way. To begin with, perhaps people could evaluate themselves in terms of the four dimensions of life and see how they turn out. If ten were a perfect score, and, say, work earned eight points, the local area was valued at zero, and the family came in at, say, two points, how high would the enjoyment of individual pursuits be rated? Then, maybe, people could get an idea of what is lacking in themselves and their lives. . . . (67–73)

The Human Experience in the Decade of the 1980s and Women's Responsibility

"Mom, let's start eating better food beginning tomorrow. It will be alright!"

I suddenly closed the household account book and called to my mother in a loud voice. This happened one day about three months after my husband passed away, so it was more than twenty years ago. But I still remember it very clearly.

My husband was an employee of a small to medium-sized enterprise, but he died of cancer in June of that year at the age of fifty-eight. Apart from the sadness about his loss, beginning with the next month, July, his paycheck stopped coming. A two-income family for twenty-six years, I had grown used to managing our household finances based on two incomes. But, be that as it may, I thought that there was no way that I would not be able to live on my own salary. After all, all my male colleagues were doing it, right? So, filled with anxieties and concerns, I set out to do just that.

I had forgotten how many years I had kept these household account records, but I started to make entries for daily expenditures. July, August,

September—I made a conscious effort not to make wasteful purchases, and perhaps because I was sensitive to the high price of good quality fish, I kept our account in the black. Feeling relieved, that was when I called to my mother that we could start eating better food.

Since I was the only daughter who had gotten married and moved to Tokyo with my husband, where we both worked, we started living together after my husband's death. If we had tried to live on my husband's pension from his company, we would have run through it in about three years. Since I was over fifty years old at the time, it probably would have been difficult for me to get a part-time job. Women's old age lasts for a long time. However, while taking care of my mother, I knew that somehow we would be able to make a life for ourselves. It was really fortunate that I had my own job, and that I had my own independent income! I felt that strongly, very deep in my heart.

Of course, full-time housewives find happiness, too. However, because I had spent many long years as a newspaper reporter interviewing people, it seemed to me that two conditions were necessary for nonworking housewives to be happy, and I felt strongly they had to be 100 percent guaranteed. The first was that the husband remains a healthy breadwinner throughout his long career. The second was that the husband continues to love his wife.

No matter how good a husband might be, an unexpected traffic accident, a natural disaster, or a long, complicated illness, even culminating in death, can always occur. The place where one works might go bankrupt or undergo a restructuring as well. Moreover, even a husband who has married for love may, over a long period of time, find his affections drawn toward another woman. It is hardly a rare occurrence that the husband might turn his back on his wife or even leave her. Whichever is the case, the wife who is left behind will find herself immediately facing a difficult financial predicament.

Drawing on my own personal experiences, and my years of observation as a reporter, I would just like to say that a woman trying to live without her own income is a kind of lifestyle that feels like you must walk naked and alone across a barren field when a cold wind is about to blow, a prospect that anyone would find difficult to bear. Having to live your life economically dependent on someone else means having to give up some of your own right to make decisions. I had no interference or meddling from my late husband's family members or from neighbors, so I was able to live my life freely. I had a respectable job and my own income and was able to make a decent living, so it came through strongly to me that because I was economically independent I was able to guarantee my spiritual freedom.

Expanding One's Abilities

Whenever I have this sort of conversation, housewives are always quick to tell me, "Well, you have skills so you are different." I just shake my head from side to side. I had taken the examination for the newspaper on a whim with no expectations for success, so I hardly had any qualifications to be a newspaper reporter. Ever since I was a child, I had loved to read, and I always felt that reading was a close relative of writing. But as a recent female graduate in an era well before the equal opportunity employment law, I had to look for enterprises that were willing to open their doors to women.

When I would finally complete the draft of an article, I would frequently only have it crumpled up and thrown away. I would rewrite them so that there was hardly a trace of the original remaining. I was often ordered to rewrite them not just once but two and three times. Finally after one, three, maybe even five years, I finally was able to write something decent. During the twenty-five years before I got into management, every day, rain or snow, I was out there with my little reporter's notebook and pencil taking notes as I walked around the towns, the villages, and the mountains, continuing to walk and write.

One year, I was ordered to begin a series on New Year's Day around the theme of "future living." I enthusiastically started going around consulting with scholars and researchers in the areas of clothing, food, and lodging, and I worked very long and hard on my manuscript. However, when I read it over, it was just not at all interesting! Even rewriting it did not help. It was still bad. Not knowing what to do, I went and visited my boss at his home. He was staying home resting with a cold, so while coughing frequently he looked over my manuscript and said:

> What if we bring in just one housewife and introduce her
> to our readers by following her for one day, from morning
> until night. And interweave the story about how her life is
> changing. Like you could start with "One morning in year
> X of the twenty-first century, Mrs. A woke up and . . ."

I felt like the scales were falling from of my eyes! I had focused too much on the data I had collected and had tried too hard to work it into my story. That is why reading it was so painful and just not interesting at all! So I returned home immediately and set about rewriting the manuscript. The next day it passed through the editor's hands with no objections and was safely ensconced on the special New Year's page. In terms of my feelings, I felt as though I had done a great job providing a real gem for this edition.

Ability, then, is something you develop and extend by continuing to work, by accepting assessment and criticism, by doing some self-reflection. I guess you could say that it is a matter of simultaneously learning how to extend your efforts and continue to grow. So even though I may have at times felt that I was unsuited to the work, that I was no good at it and would never succeed, by maintaining my "nothing ventured, nothing gained" spirit it really worked out exceedingly well. Ability is something that you sometimes have to draw out and discover. Raising children is also very important, but I would have to say that for the human experience of the 1980s it is also important to nurture and develop yourself. . . . (85–89)

Pride in One's Profession: "The World That Lives at Night"

It is now 9:15 on a Monday, May 30, 1977. I am in a private room on the twelfth floor of the new wing of the "J" hospital in Ochanomizu, sitting on a cot tucked in next to the wall, writing in this diary. I had come the previous day, Sunday, with my little Boston Bag, planning to stay a little while.

This is one little paragraph from my old diary. Prior to that, I had not kept a diary, and even nowadays I do not. However, beginning with the day my husband entered the hospital, I decided to start keeping one. I knew that these would be my husband's final days.

It was exactly three years ago, in May, that my husband had been diagnosed with a stomach ulcer and had undergone surgery at this same hospital. After the surgery, the doctor told me privately that my husband had stomach cancer, which had already entered stage three. All of a sudden, a scene that I had only seen happening to people in television dramas was now happening to me. I will refrain from revealing any further details at this point. I am sure there are many other wives who have been through experiences like this.

Two years later the cancer reappeared; he was hospitalized and had another operation. The cancer had spread to his peritoneum. About three months after he returned home from the hospital, he became extremely weak and was readmitted to the hospital. However, they discovered that he had a serious herpes condition, so after some treatment he was sent home again. In May 1977, just at the start of Golden Week, he was readmitted to the hospital for the fourth time.

Three weeks after he reentered the hospital, I heard from the nurse in charge that my husband was starting to press the call button in the middle of the night constantly, so they wanted a family member to come and stay with him. My husband's increasing discomfort and the lack of sufficient nursing care were the reasons given.

My husband was basically a sincere man with a strongly developed sense of responsibility, but he also had his stubborn side. Apparently he would ask the nurses if they were not reducing the flow of the IV drip to fit better with their working hours, although that would confuse the order of things and interfere with his injections.

One day I was told by the nurses, "The things your husband says are not far from the truth, but he does not understand that the nurses' working situation is very strictly monitored and they do not have a lot of flexibility." I also learned that they considered my husband to be pretty well feared, so the younger nurses felt uncomfortable around him and were starting to distance themselves from him.

At any rate, after passing many days like this, I came to move into his hospital room and stay with him. At that time, I was working in the Otemachi district in downtown Tokyo as a newspaper reporter. During the day, in addition to a practical nurse, I had requested help from my mother and younger sister, and I would come in the evening and spend the night. I would head out for work the next morning. During the day, I would weave my way through the workday, and then I would go to the hospital where I would usually start out by changing his diaper and performing various other tasks. As I think back on it now, it was as though my mind and body were being chilled to the point of numbness.

Although I am very slender and weigh less than forty kilos, perhaps I am strong at my core because I have never once had the experience of being hospitalized for a surgery. Therefore, it was only through my husband's hospitalization that I could enter this world of hospitals, where they say "it is a world where even the night is alive," and I was really able to experience what hospitals are all about.

As I lay there on my cot, the nurse would come around with a flashlight in one hand, making her rounds. From my cot I would just raise my head and say politely "Thank you" for all that she was doing. My husband would say things like "Could you raise my body up some? I would like a drink of water please. Could you turn me over?" And I would have to change his diaper during the night as well. Not only was it difficult to get enough sleep, but being that my husband's room was near the nurse's station, we could hear the sound of the call buttons going off from neighboring rooms and the nurse's voice asking what was wrong, and finally the sound of feet rushing off to a patient's room. This notion that hospitals are a world in which the night is truly alive was something I experienced directly. I also came to appreciate how difficult was the job of the nurses who worked in this world.

Solidarity with Friends Who Also Work

After two weeks of sleeping in my husband's hospital room, I decided to ask permission to absent myself from work during his last few days. My husband looked happy when I told him, but the next morning he fell into a coma, and five days later, on a cold, rainy evening, his life ended at fifty-eight years of age.

The doctor asked permission to conduct an autopsy, and I agreed. Finally, after his corpse had been moved to the morgue, I sat through the night with him in the company of family members. Just a little after dawn, the head nurse and two other nurses joined us at the funeral. In the pale morning light, as I watched the three women emerging from the mist in their white uniforms, I could not help but feel, "Ah, how beautiful!"

After the funeral was over I gave the head nurse a standard greeting: "Thank you for all your help. I feel much obliged." But then, somewhat unexpectedly, I grasped her hand rather forcefully and said, "Let's keep on working hard together." It was a strange thing for a patient's wife to say. However, I think what it revealed was that I was thinking of both of us as female colleagues who were working, and, in that sense, we shared a feeling of solidarity as women who were pursuing careers with some social meaning and significance in which we could take some pride, yet which also were accompanied by a fair share of trials and tribulations.

The Job That Sustained Me

After learning about my husband's cancer, other than telling him and a couple of other relatives, there was really no one else with whom to share the news. Therefore, after he died, I heard from a number of people around me, who seemed to be surprised, words to the effect that "You really hung in there while continuing your busy job as a reporter!" However, something that I felt deeply was that "I was able to hang in there precisely because I had a job!"

These are the kinds of memories I have.

Just before my husband entered the hospital for the last time, we were heading into Golden Week in May, so I decided to just continue to work and manage as best I could. I knew I would need to be by his side night and day during his final days, so I thought I could hang in there until the long holiday commenced. However, before we could even get to the first, second, and third of May, my husband and I were both feeling that we had fallen into a deep, bottomless well.

When healthy, my husband's weight exceeded seventy kilos, but now he weighed only about forty. He always cared about his appearance so much that he would not even entrust the pressing of his slacks to the cleaners and would do it himself, but now he looked so thin. . . . I did not want my husband to see my reaction so, in order to hide the tears that overflowed, I was always running to the bathroom and washing my face. One day, when I had an appointment at work that I could not miss, I went to meet a friend in a coffee shop in the neighborhood. After we discussed what we needed to, we kept on talking—losing complete track of time—about women's issues as pertained to work, education, and welfare.

Then all of a sudden I noticed that I felt a surge of energy flowing through my entire body. I was like a dry sponge that soaks up water. That was it! I knew that I still had a lot of work that I needed to undertake. It was like a ray of light that was reaching me in that bottomless well into which I had fallen.

So, OK! On my way back home my heart let out a big sigh of relief. Even though there was no way to prolong my husband's life, I knew that I at least had the power to send him off on his journey under the best conditions imaginable. I was suddenly overcome with a feeling that I wanted to wave both of my arms around in the air. My work gave me courage, and my courage provided me with a support I desperately needed. I believe that to this very day. (131–36)

Living and Loving Both Work and Family: Women and Work

Until the year before last, I worked as a part-time adjunct instructor in the literature department of a private university in Tokyo for about twelve years. So what was someone like me, who was neither a scholar nor a researcher, teaching? Well, I guess you could say it was a type of women's studies because I used works of modern literature to examine women's lifestyles, their relationship with men, and how the institution of marriage should work. At one point during the first term, on the subject of "women and work," I asked the students—both male and female—to do some reading over the summer break, especially novels and autobiographies, and to write a paper for the beginning of the second term.

During the first class in September, I asked the students to report on the contents of their papers, and the first one to raise his hand and speak was a male student. He had selected *Hanauzumi* by Watanabe Junichi, a novel based closely on the life of a real historical woman who was a pioneer female physician, Ogino Gin.

To give a brief overview, Ogino Gin was born in 1851 into the family of a village headman in Saitama Prefecture. At eighteen years of age she married a man from the neighboring village. However, she contracted gonorrhea from her husband, divorced him, and returned to her home where she had to get treatment. However, it was very difficult for a young woman to have that part of her body treated by a male physician, so it caused her a lot of anguish.

Then one day news of something came to her ears that sounded like a dream: in the West there were female doctors! Really? Women can become doctors? Well, that is it, no matter what it takes. . . So, in the year of 1871, when she was twenty-one years old, she made up her mind to become a doctor. However, medical schools in those days were the sole preserve of male students and women were excluded.

However, she burned with a desire for knowledge and was tenacious, so she entered in the first-year class of the established Tokyo Women's Normal School. She must have been very bright, but she also had a tremendous capacity for hard work. She was able to graduate from this esteemed school, which had brought together the most talented women in all of Japan in five years, and after graduating she finally got permission to enter a private medical college. But she was the only woman admitted, so she suffered shouts and verbal insults from the male students who surrounded her. They yelled at her to go home and even pushed her around on occasion.

Finally, however, she did graduate and then had to face the second thick wall that was obstructing her path. Since there were no examples of women being allowed to take the qualifying exams for practicing physicians, she was told that no one could license her. After persisting, however, she did finally get to take the exam, and thankfully she passed with the highest marks. The year was 1885, and she was thirty-five years old.

The student who was presenting basically outlined the facts as described above and added an explanation of the conditions of discrimination faced by Meiji era women in terms of their legal standing and in terms of education.

I continued by asking one more student to present. The next presenter was a female student, and the work she had selected propelled us forward to present times with a consideration of Okifuji Noriko's *The Day Women Leave the Workplace* (*Onna ga shokuba o saru hi*).

An autobiographical work, it tells the author's story of her career as a female corporate manager, and her deepening love for her job, but also of her husband's transfer [while she remained in the family home] and the death of her elderly father, who lived with them, of a disease he contracted and how this affected her two adolescent daughters, who were shaken and suffered continually. Feeling that her family was inviting destruction, she broke out in tears and knew she had to quit her job. So she did. She took her two daughters and moved back in with her husband.

The female student who presented added some discussion of trends in recent years in terms of progress for women in the workplace, the rise in the average age, and years of continuous service. However, on the other hand, the number of housewives working part-time has increased markedly, so instead of developing greater continuity of work on the whole, people are seeking to affirm the model that would require women to resign on the occasion of giving birth and then return to the workplace in middle age.

Unintentionally Putting Resources In

That these two students gave their reports on that day was purely an accident, but as I listened to them, I recall feeling my heart sink. On the one hand, we had a concrete example of an early Meiji woman who with tremendous effort, along with blood, sweat, and tears, pioneered the path into a new specialized profession for women. And then, on the other hand, we have a woman who loves her job but at the same time loves her family, so, after shedding a lot of tears, she agrees to abandon her job in favor of familial need. Separating these two stories are more than one hundred years, a long time period filled with burdens and struggles. I said to the students:

> *You will be graduating soon and heading into the workplace, but I want to impress on you female students that the pathway to balancing work and family has a long and deep history.*
>
> *In the olden days, women's lives were very short and impoverished; they bore lots of children, and raising children and managing the household inside and out required a lot of physical labor. However, as time passed, the amount of time and physical effort required to raise children and maintain the home would change completely. Contemporary women are blessed with "long" lives in terms of time and "large" lives in terms of ability. In order for women to realize this "LL" life, the family not only needs to play a role but the companies also need to play a positive role in terms of local residents in the countryside as we move toward an era in which participating in the broader society is something that becomes a natural occurrence, if not to say an inevitable one.*
>
> *I also want you male students to think about these changes occurring in women's lives and become good partners when the opportunity presents itself.*

Perhaps I had struck a chord; perhaps I had managed to put some energy in the right place at the right time as the students seemed to listen with amazed and docile expressions on their faces. (137–40)

Analysis

Sometimes, small successes like these are their own reward. Kanamori suggests that it is possible that she may have changed a few people's lives in the course of trying to educate them. During her career as a writer for a major newspaper, she also did her best to have an impact on her readers, perhaps suggesting how people think about women, gender relations, families, and what the most fair and equitable response should be to the dilemmas of an "aged society." If Kanamori's narrative lacks some of the drama and intensity that we find in those of Yoshitake Teruko and Kishino Junko, in giving thought to how families of the future should be constituted, and how they should function, Kanamori asks her readers to consider new ways of thinking about not just women's roles but men's roles as well. In this sense, her critique is radical. In calling on both men and the corporate system in Japan to become more participative in the caregiving process—whether for infants or the elderly—Kanamori wants something beyond just a more equitable burden-sharing arrangement. She wants to see Japanese men who have buried themselves in their work and the corporate culture participate in both a wider and deeper dimension of the human experience. Should people heed Kanamori's call and start thinking about more flexible working arrangements for Japanese males, the result would be a revolutionary transformation of both Japanese society and Japanese culture.

Though never quite finding herself at the vortex of a personal crisis in the manner of Yoshitake and Kishino, Kanamori shared with them an awareness that women needed to ask themselves some hard questions about what drove them to feel that they had to do everything by themselves. She refers to the "curse" that women impose on themselves that makes them feel that they must be the ones to perform elder care. Kanamori tells women that they need to get used to accepting help, both public and private. She has some important things to say about end of life care that she confronted when her husband was dying of cancer. Experiencing the world of Japanese hospitals as she spent the night near her husband's sickbed, she writes very frankly and appreciatively of the value of retaining her job and of maintaining a commitment to her career and her colleagues. All of this—not to mention the income and medical insurance—were significant components of her life that sustained her during this dark time. By recollecting and reconstructing this experience, and how she related to the head nurse as a fellow professional with a job to do, she is telling women in Japan that it is a valuable asset to have a profession, a job—something that people can both respect and appreciate—and that women should not feel guilty about continuing to work. If that means that other people in the society and community, including the government, have to take on a greater role, then so be it. One might wonder, as well, whether a woman writing in the prewar period would dare to have asserted the value she placed on her work and her profession and how she would not abandon them as her husband faced his final months and weeks.

Finally, in writing about her commitment to local history and local women's groups, her discussion of the leadership and efforts that went into the establishment of the Kanagawa Prefectural Women's Center leaves a textual trace that calls attention to the value of grassroots community organizations for women. Therefore, Kanamori has also found a place in her recollections and memories where women find connections to the local community, as well as the society and culture at large. In doing this, she not only documents the establishment of her own subjectivity and agency but points other women in a direction that will allow them to discover their own as well.

6

CONCLUSIONS

I began this book with an assertion that women's postwar memoirs and autobiographies are of interest to historians because they help us understand how the end of the war affected Japanese women and what the experience of the early postwar years was like for them. I also suggested that the narrative structures and strategies that female autobiographers adopted operated to pinpoint the spatial and temporal locations in which they managed to transform their "feminine" consciousness. I posed a series of questions about how Japanese women reconstructed and reordered the events of their lives and turned them into coherent narratives. To what extent were they able to resist the social and cultural forces that were aligned against them, forces that obstructed their development of a sense of female identity and historical agency? How effectively were they able to reconstruct that moment of resistance in their memoirs, and how did that process of reconstruction help them to establish their historical agency?

In the preceding pages, I have argued that the kinds of self-referential narratives explored in *Changing Lives* offer valuable insights into the social and political movements in which postwar Japanese women participated. The movements in which these women were enmeshed are important because they put them in touch with the social conditions and regimes of thought that shaped their identity, subjectivity, and agency. Many writers on autobiography believe that women do not readily come to terms with their own agency, but *Changing Lives* makes it clear that agency is an issue with which postwar Japanese women struggled doggedly. The important thing is that these women *were* able to find venues in which to struggle, establish their identity, discover their own voice, and assert their historical agency. I submit that this is something that requires a great deal of courage and determination.

Winston Churchill allegedly remarked after World War II, "Of all the amazing deeds of bravery of the war, I regard MacArthur's personal landing at Atsugi the greatest of the lot."[1] This act was perceived as courageous because no one knew for sure what awaited the general when he stepped, unarmed, from his aircraft. The stories contained in *Changing Lives* are also very much about women who were courageous and brave, women who stood up for themselves under the most challenging of circumstances. One can argue that it takes a certain amount of courage just for women to take up the pen and write their own stories. This is because women's voices have often been silenced and their opinions on important matters have been neither sought nor valued. Most women grow up in cultures created and dominated by men; they are not usually able to see themselves reflected in those cultures, and they do not find it easy to discover their authentic selves within the confines of their structures and governing ideologies. Consequently, women tend to construct a different kind of autobiographical narrative than men do. Although it is a gross oversimplification, men often tell tales of overcoming tremendous obstacles in order to become the successful person they are today. Whether their triumphs are religious, secular, or expressed in terms of a quest for authenticity and identity, their narratives tend to embrace a trajectory appropriate to someone who has power and agency. Women, lacking power, position, and agency, and often denied a voice in the culture, are more inclined to create narratives that raise questions or seek solutions to problems they have encountered in their lives.[2]

As we have seen, the narrators in *Changing Lives* looked deep inside themselves in order to better understand how they came to accept the prewar ideology and what they should do next, once the war ended and it was time to build a new life. For many the end of the war was a shock, a trauma; it represented a stark rupture with the past. As we have also seen, though, narratives are one way to cope with trauma and come to terms with deep-seated change. Okabe Itsuko, Shinya Eiko, Sawachi Hisae, and Yoshitake Teruko all looked into their hearts, reflected on their past experiences, and directly confronted how the moment of the emperor's radio broadcast turned their world upside down. Shinya and Okabe yearned to feel ordinary again; Yoshitake needed to retreat into deep sleep for thirty-six hours and then had to face her future and figure out what to do next. Unfortunately, she also had to learn how to cope with the trauma of being gang-raped by members of the occupation forces. Sawachi Hisae's perspective was that of a young girl returning home from Manchuria. She watched the once vaunted Kwantung Army abandon the civilian population, and it made her wonder about the whole decision—spearheaded by elites from this military unit—to fabricate an incident and invade Manchuria. She also found out what it was like to be a returning immigrant. This made her think about the whole act of immigration and wonder why her family chose to take that step.

By their own admission, Yoshitake, Kishino, and Kanamori were part of that first wave of women to attend four-year universities in the early postwar years—something that their mothers and grandmothers were not able to do so easily. Prewar women did attend four-year universities and earn degrees but rarely on the same footing as males. Yoshitake, Kishino, and Kanamori graduated and sought employment in organizations where women were allowed for the first time to take qualifying exams and be interviewed. All three were hired by media companies, but Yoshitake and Kishino struggled to establish themselves in their careers in a fully satisfactory manner. This was not because their work was of less than the highest quality but because rules about compensation, promotion, and regulations regarding family leave frustrated their experience in the workplace and, at times, hindered their career advancement. Kanamori Toshie's case was slightly different. She joined a very well established newspaper and was seemingly more successful than Kishino and Yoshitake in negotiating her rise to a position of responsibility at the *Yomiuri shinbun*. In her narrative, she testifies to the importance having a good job when her family was in crisis. To have an occupation, a profession, and colleagues who supported her kept her energized and helped her to cope with the death of her spouse and later her mother. To write about these feelings openly required some measure of courage. Despite what the postwar constitution proclaimed, equality between the sexes in the workplace was hardly a given; it was something to be negotiated, and it remained elusive for most. There was still a powerful cultural expectation that women were supposed to manage the household and be caregivers. In their narratives, by probing issues about work, equality in the workplace, the place of family, and the role of women within the family, these writers all interrogated gendered norms and redefined the spaces and roles normally assigned to men and women.

Okabe Itsuko's narrative ventures into places that many memoirs do not. The death of her fiancé, Kunio, at the Battle of Okinawa changed her life. She entered a marriage that was different from the one she wanted and was emotionally abused by her husband. She left that marriage and took care of herself (and her mother) by becoming a writer. But all this was long behind her when she decided to revisit Kunio's short life and death. She did not have to do this, and it was no doubt a painful process for her. But just as Kunio had confided in her, she felt compelled to share her experience truthfully with the reading public. In doing so, she took on the forces in prewar society that had buffeted and controlled her, and she indicted them. The prewar education system, the neighborhood associations, the propaganda and hypocrisy underlying it all—all of these pieces of the prewar regime of truth were exposed in her narrative. Who could speak the truth? Unexpectedly, it was a young man who was just entering military service who whispered the truth to Okabe in the most unambiguous terms, and she was so shocked that she did not know how to deal with his revelations. The process of exploring the context of Kimura Kunio's beliefs pushed Okabe's narrative into a compelling portrait of the prewar years. She did not need to make those personal revelations, but she did, and that took courage.

If Okabe was disappointed in herself for believing everything that had been taught to her in school and preached to her by the neighborhood association, how much more chagrinned did the younger Shinya Eiko feel? A "loyal imperial daughter," she had joined a women's auxiliary unit after high school and seemed to be eagerly anticipating the emperor's call to engage the invading Allied army in a final, cataclysmic battle. But she soon turned her life around completely and this took courage. After dabbling in a variety of left-wing activities, Shinya discovered theater. She soon found that parts for women were few and far between unless you wrote and produced your own material, which she began to do. For some thirty years she played a Zainichi Korean woman who stood onstage and told tales of discrimination and abuse. Later she would add the story of a *buraku* woman to her tales. By inhabiting characters that had been utterly marginalized by prewar society, she learned things about herself and how ideologies penetrate one's soul and distort one's being. Acting enabled Shinya to get outside herself and transcend racial, ethnic, and national boundaries, and to experience the viewpoints of people different from herself. This, she believed, leads to a deeper understanding of history. She rarely had the opportunity to play on the big stage, but she persisted, performing nightly in the smaller venues, without ever giving up. This took great courage and determination.

The two women whose courage perhaps stands out the most are Yoshitake Teruko and Kishino Junko. The tone of Yoshitake's narrative is strikingly restrained. In almost the same breath in which she exults over the sight of Japanese women casting their vote for the first time in history she leads readers into the darkness of her gang rape. In passages that are rhetorically powerful, she explains how the lib movement provided her with the necessary tools to process her experience more than two decades later. She comes to understand how the patriarchal culture silenced her and left her to fend for herself. She could have made the case for the power of the lib movement without such personal revelations, but they make her narrative more compelling. Much of her story is nestled within a narrative of the women's movements during the postwar years. We learn about her admission to Keiô University, her membership in the theater club, her affiliation with Zengakuren, and her sense that the Korean War did much violence to the ideals of postwar Japan. She also writes of her decision to join Tôei Studios, despite an inauspicious interview process, and of her job promoting a documentary film for Tôei that opposed the presence of American bases in Japan. She then explains how she came to support the women who rallied to oppose land expropriations at Sunagawa and Uchinada. The story of the *Lucky Dragon 5* incident near the Bikini Atoll, and how that mobilized thousands of women to protest against nuclear armaments and testing, is also a part of her narrative. These are all instances in which pieces of her narrative intersect with larger social and political events going on around her. Coming to see Prime Minister Kishi as anathema, creating a context for understanding the Ampo movement, and, finally, describing how Ampo and the student protests of the 1960s set the table for the women's lib movement in 1970—all of these were important moments in postwar history that Yoshitake either witnessed or in which she directly participated. And while this narrative thread is unfolding, Yoshitake describes for her readers the conflicts she was facing in the workplace, her unwanted pregnancy, later the birth of her daughter, and, finally, her defiance of expectations that she would not return to work. At the heart of her narrative is her depiction of the Lib Camps and the consciousness-raising sessions that, despite not offering her everything she wanted, provided her with the vocabulary and venue she needed in order to develop her feminine consciousness. This makes for a very rich and insightful narrative, one that took great courage to construct.

Kishino shared much with Yoshitake, but she never married or had children, and this came to bother her. She felt the sting of choices that she had to make while her male colleagues did not. She tried to work alongside men as an equal, but that only led to frustration. She identified with the young girl who was abandoned in the Urayama Kirio film that made such a strong impression on her, a young woman whose innocence—like the ideals of postwar Japan— was sacrificed on the altar of rapid economic growth and material gain. She began to identify with characters in African American literature as she felt increasingly that Japanese women and blacks had something in common: they both experienced discrimination and repeated transgressions. Although, like Yoshitake, Kishino had her moments of discomfort with the younger, more outspoken, sometimes blunt, and even crude advocates of women's lib like Tanaka Mitsu, in the end, she, too, immersed herself in the movement and took from it what it could teach her. It taught her that she had the capacity to discover and nurture her feminine consciousness and, on the basis of that discovery, "reposition" herself in relation to her narrative and life experiences.

And then everything began to make sense. Now there was a way to reclaim the spirit and ideals of postwar Japan, but it began with each woman's interior life. Like Yoshitake, Kishino discovered that Japanese women had to come to understand who they were and why society chose to see and treat them as it did. Women had to learn which part of them was genuinely their own, and which part had been created or distorted by the patriarchy. These are not easy things to confront, and the lessons they taught these women were not easy to learn. It takes great courage to confront reality the way these two women did.

Kanamori Toshie's narrative does not seem at first glance to have the emotional depth of Yoshitake's or Kishino's. But it should not be sold short. If Kishino and Yoshitake sometimes felt older and out of step with the lib movement because they had coexisted with men in the workplace for decades—and, in Yoshitake's case, had married and started a family—Kanamori was even more out of step. She had been married very young, an arranged marriage, but soon learned that it was not her destiny to keep house and wait for her husband to return home from work. She entered college as a nontraditional student and then qualified by examination to join one of Japan's most prestigious news organizations. Once there, she had her trials, but she persevered and, over time, became the resident expert on women's issues. Throughout her career, she wrote about the inequality that women experienced in education, in the workplace, and in the family. She understood well that the graying of Japanese society posed a serious problem for Japanese women because in addition to the burden of child and spousal care housewives were now likely to have to bear most of the burden of caring for both sets of aging parents. Since the burden would not fall equally on sons and daughters, Kanamori wanted corporate Japan to sit up, take notice, and adjust its expectations so that husbands, too, could help raise their children and care for their aging parents.

One of her most revelatory passages, I think, is her description of being in the hospital with her husband, who was dying of cancer. Not only did she feel a bond with the nurses who cared for him (and were subjected to his verbal abuse) on a professional level—as working women with careers in a profession—but she positively exulted at the importance of her job in helping see her through her husband's death. It was not just having the salary and benefits, although they were extremely important; it was also the fact that she had an *identity*, that she was somebody with a career, colleagues, and a workplace in which she felt a sense of belonging. This, she writes, helped sustain her through the darkest hours, and I think it took great courage to go against the grain and express these feelings openly.

The history of an era cannot be constructed by simply stringing together a series of individuals' personal accounts of their experiences. Yet it is clearly in these individual accounts that the details of the era come alive. To be "allowed *inside* the experience of another person who really lived and who tells about experiences which did in fact occur" is a privilege that provides the historian with rich details and a nuanced version of history.[3] Whenever we read accounts of how women managed to negotiate their identity and enhance their self-awareness against an internalized cultural code that dictates how they should conduct themselves and how their lives should be lived, we learn something about those individuals, about the times in which they lived, and about ourselves. For example, on the occasion of the November 14, 1970, meeting in Shibuya Ward that was dedicated to a discussion of the meaning of women's liberation for Japan, which attracted approximately five hundred women from many walks of life, at least one author, Akiyama Yoko, admits how fearful she was initially. In her *Notes for a Private History of 'Lib'* (1993), Akiyama describes how she felt drawn to the women's movement but as a young working mother did not have the courage to attend the first demonstration, on October 21, 1970, because she was worried about the potential for a violent clash with riot police. When the November meeting was scheduled, however, Akiyama overcame her fears and attended. Impressed by the age range of the participants—from young students to sixty year olds—and the depth of the questioning that took place, Akiyama soon became a committed participant.[4] Five hundred women is not an overwhelmingly large number, but the narratives examined in *Changing Lives* testify to how deeply felt the experience of the lib movement was for so many Japanese women.

The energy and the grassroots nature of the movement eventually brought results. The years 1976–85 were officially declared the Decade of Women by the United Nations. In 1979, the General Assembly adopted the Convention on the Elimination of All Forms of Discrimination against Women. The convention defines discrimination against women as "any distinction, exclusion or restriction made on the basis of sex which has the effect or purpose of impairing or nullifying the recognition, enjoyment or exercise by women, irrespective of their marital status, on a basis of equality of men and women, of human rights and fundamental freedoms in the political, economic, social, cultural, civil or any other field."[5] Signatories were supposed to bring their domestic laws and practices into compliance, so the 1980s in Japan was a time when the government and women's groups were scrambling to put things like the 1986 Equal Employment Opportunity Law on the books. Generally felt to provide guidelines that were not easily enforceable, the law was revised and strengthened considerably in 2007. But, in the end, laws are only laws; the culture of Japan's male-dominant society seems to change only very slowly. In terms of the "gender and empowerment measure," Japan was ranked fifty-seventh among 109 countries in 2009, far below most of its industrial and economic peers.[6]

The stories that are recorded in *Changing Lives* belong to the generation that came of age in the early postwar years. Despite the fact that Japanese women still earn less than half of what men do, the opportunities for education and employment are substantially better now. In that sense, some of what Yoshitake, Kishino. and Kanamori went through are not things that most young women face today. Yet the experiences of these women remain instructive. If nothing else, they teach us something about having the courage to stand up and speak out. As Shinya Eiko put it, postwar Japan was a time for women to start seeing with their own eyes and thinking for themselves. The stories in *Changing Lives* also remind us that subjectivity and agency are essential components of historical understanding. To overlook them is to fail to grasp the real dynamics of an era, and it is to miss out on important stories that enrich our knowledge.

It is clear that agency is much more a process being negotiated than it is a state of being. But, as Joan W. Scott points out, "[B]eing a subject means being '*subject to*' definite conditions of existence," and how can we be aware of these conditions if we do not explore them?[7] The women whose voices appear in *Changing Lives* used their narratives as a way to cope with disruptive change and to better understand the conditions in which their subjectivity and agency were being negotiated. The power of their self-writing is that their narratives became sites where authors stop or at least slow down the flow of time while they reflect on and assess how social and political conditions shaped their identities. The process of reflecting on events in their lives enabled these women to understand who they were at the time, as well as who they are now, now that they have reflected on the historical moments they experienced and the social movements that shaped them. This, in turn, helped generate in these women a sense of their own agency. As they reflected on and wrote about these social conditions and movements, their agency and subjectivity were (re)created in the act of writing, ensuring that they would come through the reflective process with a deeper understanding of their own lives and their relationship to the times. Isn't that precisely why Kishino Junko was able to describe the process of stepping outside of her reflections on her experiences and "repositioning" herself in relation to both her text and the world? The stories that Kishino, Yoshitake, Kanamori, Okabe, Shinya, and Sawachi tell are stories of survival, commitment, and courage that have a great deal to teach us. It is up to us to learn from them.

NOTES

Chapter One

[1] John Dower, *Embracing Defeat: Japan in the Wake of World War II* (New York: W. W. Norton, 1999), 45–46.

[2] Ibid., 22.

[3] Sharalyn Orbaugh, *Japanese Fiction of the Allied Occupation: Vision, Embodiment, Identity* (Boston and Leiden: Brill, 2007), 9–10.

[4] An interesting note is that when conducting her research, Orbaugh was struck by how few women writers contributed to this outpouring of literary expression. There are numerous possible explanations for this lack of representation of female writers—for example, many of the women writers were either ill or exhausted in the years following the end of the war—but chief among the reasons was the fact that it fell to women to provide for families in the absence of fathers and sons who did not return from the war. Sata Ineko wrote fiction because she needed to support herself and her children, but it was not the same ideologically oriented proletarian fiction that she had been writing in the late 1920s. Moreover, at least three well-known women writers, Tamura Toshiko, Miyamoto Yuriko, and Hayashi Fumiko, died before the occupation period was over. Personal narratives such as memoirs and autobiographies are, of course, very different from novels and short stories, but clearly female autobiographers and memoirists did recall that day (August 15) in 1945 very well, and many reconstructed their recollections of that day in their narratives. See ibid., 349–55.

[5] See Kano Masanao, *Gendai Nihon joseishi: Feminizumu o jiku to shite* (Tokyo: Yuikaku, 2004), 5.

[6] See, for example, Jill Ker Conway, *When Memory Speaks: Reflections on Autobiography* (New York: Alfred A. Knopf, 1998), 14, where she writes that models of the heroic woman in the West still demonstrate "no agency, no power to act on her own behalf." This is in marked contrast to the typical life script for a man for whom "Life is an odyssey, a journey through many trials and tests, which the hero must surmount alone through courage, endurance, cunning and moral strength. . . . His achievement comes about through his own agency, and his successful rite of passage leaves him master of his fortunes." From this model of an autobiographical heroic figure evolves the "self-created economic man," that "successful accumulator of wealth, who makes the journey from poverty to worldly success and triumphs through the economic disciplines of thrift, industry and deferred gratification." (7–9).

[7] See William H. Sewell, Jr., *Logics of History: Social Theory and Social Transformation* (Chicago and London: University of Chicago Press, 2005), 143.

[8] See Ronald P. Loftus, *Telling Lives: Women's Self-Writing in Modern Japan* (Honolulu: University of Hawai'i Press, 2004).

[9] For the notion of regarding feminists and social activists as "sites—historical locations or markers—where crucial political and cultural contests are enacted," I am indebted to Joan W. Scott's work, especially *Only Paradoxes to Offer: French Feminists and the Rights of Man* (Cambridge, Mass.: Harvard University Press, 1996), 16. See also Loftus, *Telling Lives*, 17. On the "linguistic turn" in general, see Gabrielle M. Spiegel, "Introduction," in *Practicing History: New Directions in Historical Writing after the Linguistic Turn*, edited by Gabrielle M. Spiegel, 1–31 (New York: Routledge, 2005) ; and Elizabeth A. Clark, *History, Theory, Text: Historians and the Linguistic Turn* (Cambridge, Mass.: Harvard University Press, 2004), 1–8. As Geoff Eley notes in his book *A Crooked Line: From Cultural History to the History of Society* (Ann Arbor: University of Michigan Press, 2005), "History is also a site of difference; in the loose sense of the term, it offers contexts for deconstruction. History is where we go for defamiliarizing our ideas and assumptions; it is our laboratory, where we question the sufficiencies of apparently coherent and unified accounts of the world, and where the ever-seductive unities of contemporary social and political discourse may also be named, de-authorized, and upset." (9–10).

[10] See Gabrielle M. Spiegel, "Comment on *A Crooked Line*," *American Historical Review* 113, no. 2 (April 2008): 411–12. I believe that Spiegel's position, which she refers to as a "return to a modified phenomenology," is a compromise position that recognizes the socially conditioned nature of reality but still allows room for human action and agency. As she expresses it, "[T]he reinsertion of the agent as an effective social actor has been achieved by highlighting the disjunction between culturally given meanings and the individual uses of them in contingent, historically conditioned ways." Sewell, in *Logics of History*, acknowledges something similar when he notes, "[H]istorians implicitly assume that social life is fundamentally constituted by culture, but by culture in the widest possible sense—that is, by humanly constructed practices, conventions, and beliefs that shape all aspects of social life." (9–10). This view would also clearly allow a substantial role for the human agent in historical change.

[11] Conway, *When Memory Speaks*, 7.

[12] Handô Kazutoshi, *Shôwashi, Sengohen, 1945–1989* (Tokyo: Heibonsha, 2009), 12–18. The five individuals he cites are novelist and essayist Uchida Hyakken, banker and cabinet member Kobayashi Ichizô, Tôdai professor Yabe Teiji, poet Saitô Mokichi, and novelist Yamada Fûtarô.

[13] This term also commonly appears as Anpo, an abbreviation of the Japanese term *Anzen Hoshô Jôyaku*, or the Mutual Security Treaty.

[14] Kano Masanao, *Gendai Nihon joseishi*, 3–4. Kano also notes on p. 3 how *ribu* came to be known as "the demon child" (*onigo*) of the Left, a point echoed by Shigematsu

Setsu in her important study *Scream from the Shadows: The Women's Liberation Movement in Japan* (London and Minneapolis: University of Minnesota Press, 2012), 112.

[15] Some of the material in this section, and in the later section on Shinya Eiko, first appeared in my "Finding New Pathways: Japanese Women's Memoirs at the End of the Pacific War," *Japan Studies Association Journal* 8 (2010): 146–64. I appreciate being able to reproduce the material here with the journal's permission.

[16] Okabe Itsuko, *Yuigon no tsumori de* (Tokyo: Fujiwara shoten, 2006). Page numbers are provided in parentheses in the text.

[17] Yoshitake Teruko, *Onnatachi no undôshi—watakushi no Ikita Sengo* (Tokyo: Mineruba shobo, 2006).

[18] On the RAA, see chapter 2; and Dower, *Embracing Defeat*, 127–32.

[19] The incident is discussed in chapter 2, 46–47.

[20] The International Antiwar Action Day was an outgrowth of the anti–Vietnam War movement in the United States, which was planning an antiwar protest in Washington, D.C., for October 21, 1967. Well over one hundred thousand protestors turned out in front of the Lincoln Memorial. The protests continued annually after that in various cities around the world.

[21] On "Khalid," see chapter 3, note 7.

[22] See Debbie L. Kralik and Antonia M. van Loon, "Transition: Moving through Life's Adverse Disruptions," http://72.14.253.104/search?q=cache:cqtU6UTJnEoJ:www.rdns.org.au/research_unit/documents/RDNS_transition_poster.pdf+becoming+ordinary&hl=en&ct=clnk&cd=4.

[23] Shinya Eiko, *Joryû Shinya Eiko: Watakushi no rirekisho* (Osaka: Kaihô shuppansha, 2005).

[24] See Yoshitake, *Onnatachi no undôshi*, 5.

[25] Initially the occupation encouraged unionism but by 1946 MacArthur had become increasingly suspicious of all forms of labor militancy as being primarily the result of communists plots. Even though the proposed General Strike, set for Feb. 1, 1947, had the support of both procommunist and non-communist unions, representing some 3 million workers, at the last moment MacArthur issued a directive saying that he would not permit the general strike to take place. See Dower, *Embracing Defeat*, pp. 268–270 where he writes that the "suppression of the general strike marked the beginning of the end of the possibility that labor might be an equal partner in the sharing of 'democratic' power." (270)

[26] For their advice and for arranging permission to use the photograph, I wish to thank Mr. Kawase Kôji and Mr. Kobashi Kazushi.

[27] Sawachi Hisae, *Watashi ga ikita "Shôwa"* (Tokyo: Iwanami Shoten, 2000).

[28] See Owen Evans, *Mapping the Contours of Oppression: Subjectivity, Truth, and Fiction in Recent German Autobiographical Treatments of Totalitarianism* (Amsterdam and New York: Rodopi, 2006), esp. 325–28.

Chapter Two

[1] William H. Sewell Jr. *Logics of History: Social Theory and Social Transformation* (Chicago: University of Chicago Press, 2005), 10.

[2] See John Dower, *Embracing Defeat: Japan in the Wake of World War II* (New York: W. W. Norton, 1999), 89–97.

[3] For background on Oku Mumeo and her prewar activities, see Ronald Loftus, *Telling Lives: Women's Self-Writing in Modern Japan* (Honolulu: University of Hawai'i Press, 2004), 32–81.

[4] Yoshitake refers to Hiratsuka as being in her eighties, but, born in 1886, she was only sixty-four in 1950.

[5] The reference here is to the May Day celebration in 1952 when labor union members, students, and others marched into the "imperial plaza," which had been declared off-limits to protestors by Prime Minister Yoshida, who recalled very well the riot that had erupted there six years earlier during Food May Day, when it had earned nicknamed the "people's plaza." Placards on Bloody May Day in 1952 were against remilitarization, the presence of US bases in Japan, the retention of Okinawa by the United States, and the deteriorating economic circumstances facing Japanese workers. The demonstrators spontaneously decided to march from the Meiji Shrine area to the imperial plaza, and when they arrived they were met with police, and a violent altercation ensued. See John Dower, *Embracing Defeat: Japan in the Wake of World War II* (New York: W. W. Norton, 1999), 554–55; and Kenji Hasegawa, "Experiencing the 1952 Bloody May Day Incident," *Stanford Journal of East Asian Affairs*, available online at http://www.stanford.edu/group/sjeaa/journal3/japan2.pdf.

[6] In her autobiography, *Ahinsa o ikiru: Kôra Tomi jiden* (Tokyo: Domesu shuppan, 1983), Kôra writes extensively of the influence Tagore had on her, calling him her teacher for life. The word *ahinsa* is spelled out phonetically in her title alongside the Chinese characters *hisen* (非戦) or "renunciation of war," suggesting that the lasting commitment to peace she learned from Tagore was one of the grounding forces for her existence. She also met Jane Addams in Chicago on her way to study at Columbia University in 1917, and she listed her as an important influence as well. In 1919 she was sent as a delegate to the first meeting of the Women's International League for Peace and Freedom, held in Vienna, where she was reunited with Jane Addams, who led the organization. She would later accompany Addams on her travels around Japan and act as her interpreter, something she did for Tagore whenever he came to Japan as well. Perhaps the most compelling scene in her autobiography depicts her 1935 trip to India to see Mahatma Gandhi in order to seek his advice on how to keep Japan from heading into a full-scale war. She stopped in China on the way, met the

writer Lu Xun, and visited with Tagore before proceeding to meet with Gandhi. Gandhi startled her with the fierceness of his reply to her question about stopping the Japanese military from invading China. He raised his voice and told her that she and Christian peace activists like Kagawa Toyohiko were not doing enough to stop the military. "It's because you—Kagawa and Kôra—aren't willing to die that you are unable to halt the militarists!" he said. See *Ahinsa o ikiru*, 91–93.

[7] Sekigawa Hideo (1908–77) was a well-known, leftist director. However, the film in question was most likely issued under the title *Bakuon to daichi*, or "Explosions and the Land" (1957). An extensive search at the National Film Center in Tokyo failed to uncover any mention of a film called *Sunagawa Kichi*, but reviews and articles about *Bakuon to daichi* suggest that this, indeed, was the film to which Yoshitake refers. See, for example, Sato Tadao's review, "*Bakuon to daichi*," *Eiga Horizon*, October 1957, 102–3; and Tsugenama Tadao, "*Bakuon to daichi* no kako to genzai," *Eiga Geijustsu* 5, no. 12 (1957): 65–66. A biographical sketch, Okada Shin, "Sekigawa Hideo," in *Nihon Eiga no Kaikô Jôei* (Tokyo: Film Library josei kyôgikai, 1963), pp. 258–260, includes a complete list of his films, and no *Sunagawa Kichi* title appears there. A copy of the screenplay reveals that *Bakuon to daichi* is a semidocumentary film based in part on the novel *Chôkan* (Director General) by Akae Yukio. See *Nenkan daihyô shinario shû* (Tokyo: Mikasa shobô, 1957). 194–224. See also Ogura Shimbi, "*Bakuon to daichi*," *Kinema Junpo* 186 (1957): 54; and Iijima Tadashi, *Sekai no eiga* (Tokyo: Hakusuisha, 1957), 278–281.

[8] The Uchinada Incident of 1952–53 and the Sunagawa case of 1955 were, along with the Girard case, named for the American servicemen who shot a Japanese woman who was salvaging expended cartridges on a base firing range, were among the three most celebrated incidents of popular opposition to the presence of US bases in Japan in the early postwar era. A Tokyo District Court had agreed with citizens in a 1959 ruling that the presence of the American base at Sunagawa constituted a violation of the principles of the peace constitution, but, as recently released documents demonstrate, the United States intervened to ensure that the ruling was reversed at the Supreme Court level. See Gavan McCormack, "Ampo's Troubled 50th: Hatoyama's Abortive Rebellion, Okinawa's Mounting Resistance, and the US-Japan Relationship," *Japan Focus*, http://japanfocus.org/-Gavan-McCormack/3365. It is interesting that Yoshitake was involved with promoting a documentary film on the protest movement against the Sunagawa base and also chose to write about the Uchinada Incident as well.

[9] Also known as *jika-tabi*, these are a type of traditional Japanese sock that may also have rubber soles and are worn outdoors by construction workers and farm laborers.

[10] See note 7 above.

[11] I have been unable to correctly identify this Greek poet, and my rendering her name as "Peredes" is just a guess based on the katakana included in Yoshitake's original.

[12] The Daigo Fukuryû Maru or *Lucky Dragon 5* Incident, touched important sensitivities among Japanese people. It occurred at 6:45 on the morning of March 1,

1954, when the United States detonated a bomb code-named "Bravo" on the atoll of Bikini. The bomb was equivalent to seventeen megatons of TNT, thirteen hundred times the destructive force of the bomb dropped on Hiroshima; it was specifically designed to create a significant amount of fallout. The US government had issued a general warning referring to a danger zone around Bikini, but there was no specific warning indicating the timing or location of the test. The *Lucky Dragon 5* was some hundred miles east of Bikini when the bomb was detonated, but it was affected by fallout when the wind changed direction. The crew members suffered from radiation sickness, and one of them died of liver and blood damage on September 23. Today there is a small museum dedicated to the *Lucky Dragon* in Tokyo near Shinkiba Station where you can see the wooden tuna trawler. Recently an account of one of the crew members, Ôishi Masashichi, was translated into English and published. Excerpts have appeared in the *Asia Pacific Journal: Japan Focus*. Here is a sample.

> *6:45 a.m., March 1. A yellow flash poured through the porthole. Wondering what had happened, I jumped up from the bunk near the door, ran out on deck, and was astonished. Bridge, sky, and sea burst into view, painted in flaming sunset colors. I looked around in a daze; I was totally at a loss.*
>
> *"Over there!" A spot on the horizon of the ship's port side was giving off a brighter light, forming in the shape of an umbrella. "What is it?" "Huh?" Other crewmen had followed me onto the deck, and when they saw the strange light, they too were struck dumb and stood rooted to the spot. It lasted three or four minutes, perhaps longer. The light turned a bit pale yellow, reddish-yellow, orange, red and purple, slowly faded, and the calm sea went dark again.*

See "The Day the Sun Rose in the West: Bikini, the *Lucky Dragon* and I," http://japanfocus.org/-Oishi-Matashichi/3566. The book is Ôishi Matashichi, *The Day the Sun Rose in the West: Bikini, the Lucky Dragon, and I* (Honolulu: University of Hawai'i Press, 2011).

Chapter Three

[1] This account is based on Kano Masanao, *Nihon no Gendai* (Tokyo: Iwanami shoten, 2000), 12–15.

[2] Wesley Sasaki-Uemura, *Organizing the Spontaneous: Citizen Protest in Postwar Japan* (Honolulu: University of Hawai'i Press, 2001), 16.

[3] There is a story that as early as 1956, the veteran political strategist Miki Bukichi, who was terminally ill at the time, summoned Kishi to his bedside and tried to tell him that this was no time to press for rearmament or a new security treaty with America. The *Lucky Dragon* Incident was fresh in people's minds, and antinuclear sentiments were growing. He reportedly said to Kishi, "*Kishi-kun, muri-oshi o surun janai yo. Muri-oshi to iu no wa isshô, ichido shika toranai monda* (Kishi, now is not the time to force the issue. Forcing an issue is something that you can get away with only once in your career)." Kishi was in no mood to listen, and Miki passed away

the following day. See Handô Kazutoshi, *Shôwashi Sengohen, 1945–1989* (Tokyo: Heibonsha, 2009), 439–40.

[4] The socialist opposition had packed the hallway outside the office of the speaker of the Lower House, preventing him from getting to the floor to call the Diet into session. The police forcibly cleared the Socialist Party members out of the hallway and escorted the speaker to the podium.

[5] This bill touched a nerve with people who had lived through the prewar years when police could stop and question citizens at will. It was nicknamed the "Oi kora Police Bill" because *kora* is a crude way of saying "you," and *Oi* is an abrupt way to get someone's attention. This would be equivalent of a police officer calling out to someone, "Hey, you, get over here!"

[6] On the "Voiceless Voices," see Sasaki-Uemura, *Organizing the Spontaneous*, 148–94.

[7] The name Khalid, spelled phonetically in katakana, is not found in many documents but, according to a personal communication from Miko Sôko, she was a young Japanese woman, probably about twenty, who was an activist at the time.

Yumi Doi (aka Sayama Sachi), who was a member of *Gruppu Tatakau Onna*, also recalls Khalid as an active feminist who joined *Gruppu Tatakau Onna* and later *Re-gumi*, a lesbian feminist group. Ms Doi speculates that the name "Khalid" was her "activist" name taken in reference to Palestinian militant, Leila Khaled. (From personal correspondence with Ms. Doi in May 2012.)

At the time I was reading these memoirs and researching the individuals involved, there was very little published about Tanaka Mitsu. As this manuscript entered its final stages of preparation, Setsu Shigematsu's book, *Scream from the Shadows: The Women's Liberation Movement in Japan* (Minneapolis and London: University of Minnesota Press, 2012) appeared and she has provided extensive analysis of Tanaka's role in the women's lib movement, especially in Chapter Three, "*Ribu* and Tanaka Mitsu," where she refers to Tanaka as "an agitator, activist, and organizer, spokeswoman, philosopher, writer, and leader." (p. 103) But Shigematsu understands very well the ambiguous nature of the position in which Tanaka found herself: leader of a movement that did not want leaders. As she effectively argues, Tanaka was most interested in a movement without leaders because that was the only way to achieve the true liberation on *onna*; yet she was constantly recognized as the leader of the *ribu* movement and became its unofficial spokesperson. Although there were times when Tanaka tried to "share decision-making and to push responsibility onto the other members," ironically, this only disappointed many of the other *ribu* women. Therefore, all too often, Tanaka wound up appearing "ambivalent…uneasy, frustrated, and inconsistent in how she dealt with her position of power." (125) And yet she brought such a fresh perspective to the movement, and her voice was so unique and powerful that it is hard to conceive of the *ribu* movement without her.

[8] Yoshitake in this chapter and Kishino Junko in the next both express some discomfort with what Shigematsu refers to as the "shocking, bold, and moving" discourse that Tanaka practiced. A kind of *"ecriture féminine,"* she wanted women to express themselves in *"onna kotoba,"* or women's language. As Shigematsu writes: "Tanaka's ability to speak in relation to existing political discourses enabled *ribu* to derive its politicality and relevance. Suddenly, a voice who referred to herself as *onna* began sarcastically questioning and exposing the shortcomings of Marxism. In a voice full of insolence and irreverent laughter, she mocked the notion that women would be liberated after a socialist revolution...In "Liberation from the Toilet," she refers to the dominant system that renders women's sexual function into 'toilets' for men whose sexuality is also reduced to 'excrement'." (Shigematsu, *Scream from the Shadows*, pp. 110–11). Yoshitake and Kishino were just turning forty years old, had established themselves in their careers, and therefore were not fully comfortable with such a shocking, abrasive and confrontational approach. Yet they were drawn in by the power of Tanaka's message: women need to understand themselves, they need to see why they are the way they are, and they need to join forces in order to take liberation into their own hands.

[9] See Mizoguchi Akiyo, Saeki Yôko, and Miki Sôko, eds., *Shiryô Nihon Uuman ribushi,* (Kyoto: Yûgen kaisha, Shokadô shoten, 1992–95), 2:60–61, for the original text.

[10] Also known as Kanno Sugako (1881–1911), she was arrested for her part in the "High Treason Incident" of 1910 and was executed the following year, the only woman to be hanged on that day. Born in Osaka, her mother died when she was only ten years old and her stepmother mistreated her. Kanno was raped by a miner when she was fifteen years old, and she moved restlessly from Christian reform groups to socialist and other leftwing groups in the ensuing years. In 1908, she took part in the Red Flag incident for which she spent several months in prison. After she was released from prison she met Kôtoku Shûsui and became very interested in anarchism. Many see her as the prime mover behind a plot to throw a bomb at the Meiji Emperor's carriage for which she and twenty-three other leftwing activists were arrested. Eventually, twleve people were hanged, including Kanno and Kôtoku Shûsui. For details, see Mikiso Hane, *Reflections on the Way to the Gallows*, pp. 51–58.

[11] Quoted in Muto Ichiyo, "The Birth of the Women's Liberation Movement in the 1970s," in *The Other Japan: Conflict, Compromise, and Resistance since 1945,* edited by Joe Moore (Armonk, N.Y.: M. E. Sharpe, 1997) 148. See also, Onnatachi no ima o Tôkai, comp., *Zenkyôtô kara ribu e* (Tokyo: Impakuto Shuppankai, Hatsubaimoto Izara Shobo, 1996.

[12] Gabrielle Spiegel, "Comment on *A Crooked Line*" (from the *American Historical Review* forum on Geoff Eley's *A Crooked Line*), *American Historical Review* 113, no. 2 (April 2008): 406–16.

[13] Ibid.

[14] See Miguel Cabrera, "On Language, Culture, and Social Action," *History and Theory* 40, no. 2 (December 2001): 82–100.

Chapter Four

[1] Portions of this chapter appeared earlier in the *U.S.-Japan Women's Journal*, English Supplement 11 (1996): 23–46. Used with permission.

[2] See chapter 2, note 5.

[3] Simonov was an award-winning Russian poet, novelist, and playwright. His poetry is considered some of the most beautiful in the Russian language. This play, *Pod kashtanami Pragi*, was written in 1945. Simonov served as a member of the Soviet mission in postwar Japan, so presumably his name and works were familiar to many Japanese.

[4] See Urayama Kirio, dir., *Watakushi ga suteta onna* (1969), reissued on video by Nikkatsu kabushiki kaisha in 1999. For the story, see Endô Shûsaku, *The Girl I Left Behind*, translated by Mark Williams (New York: New Directions, 1994).

[5] I take Kishino's use of *yasashisa* as very comparable to Yoshitake's use of *onna-rashisa*, or "womanliness," a term that many feminists rejected as something defined by the patriarchy. In the very first 'lib' demonstration, women carried placards asking "What the Hell is 'Womanliness' Anyway?" (*Onna-rashisa tte Nani?*). *Yasashisa* refers to a specific feminine or womanly quality, *gentleness*, but it has multiple meanings to be sure. Some elements of *yasashisa*, Kishino accepts—or at least she regrets having to see them fall by the wayside—but other parts she realizes must be rejected because they incorporate assumptions about femininity that are rooted in the patriarchy.

[6] See chapter 1, 3–4.

[7] Agnes Smedley (1892–1950) was born in Missouri, grew up in poverty, and became an activist in such causes as Margaret Sanger's birth control movement, the Indian independence movement, and the Chinese Revolution. She became a writer and reporter and moved from Germany to Shanghai in 1929, where she remained until 1941. She wrote for the German magazine *Frankfurter Zeitung* and later for the *Manchester Guardian*. She traveled with the Eighth Route Army (later the People's Liberation Army) and spent time at Mao Zedong's headquarters in Yanan.

[8] See Janice R. MacKinnon and Stephen R. MacKinnon, *Agnes Smedley: The Life and Times of an American Radical* (Berkeley: University of California Press, 1987) for details. The most recent biography of Smedley to appear, Ruth Price's *The Lives of Agnes Smedley* (New York: Oxford University Press, 2005), concludes that Smedley may indeed have been involved in espionage activities throughout her career. Although the documentary evidence is fragmentary and circumstantial, it was convincing enough to persuade the author to alter her assumptions and acknowledge that the rightist, McCarthyist charges against her were not entirely bogus.

Apparently Smedley worked for an Indian revolutionary organization in San Francisco and the Comintern in China and can be linked to various Soviet agents in the Far East. Price does write, however, that "In her finest moments (and even in some of her worst) Agnes Smedley acted from a truly generous heart. Inspired by an abiding love and faith in ordinary people, she resisted with all the force of her being the misery and evil she saw around her and did what she could—in her own headstrong, often damaging fashion—to move humanity forward. More than fifty years have passed since Smedley's death. The Cold War is over. Maybe we can begin to see her as someone larger than the sum of her actions. In recovering Agnes Smedley, perhaps we can find our own roots in our shared humanity." (10)

[9] Agnes Smedley, *Portraits of Chinese Women in Revolution*, edited with an introduction by Janice R. MacKinnon and Stephen R. MacKinnon (Old Westbury, NY: Feminist Press, 1976), ix–x.

[10] See Patricia V. Greene, "Constancia de la Mora's *In Place of Splendor* and the Persistence of Memory," *Journal of Interdisciplinary Literary Studies* 5, no. 1 (1993): 75–84.

[11] For a collection of essays on Wright's protagonist, see Harold Bloom, ed., *Bigger Thomas* (New York and Philadelphia: Chelsea House Publishers, 1990).

[12] Komashaku Kimi (1925–2007) was a professor of modern Japanese literature and women's studies at Hôsei University, which is probably where Kishino came into contact with her. She was the author of numerous books on topics ranging from modern writers such as Akutagawa Ryûnosuke, Natsume Sôseki, Tanaka Kôtarô, and Yoshiya Nobuko to a critical analysis of Murasaki Shikibu's feminist message in the *Tale of Genji*. She has authored several collections of critical essays from the literary perspective of the *majo* or "witch."

[13] See Kaneko Fumiko, *The Prison Memoirs of a Japanese Woman*, translated by Jean Inglis with an Introduction by Mikiso Hane (Armonk, N.Y., and London: M. E. Sharp, 1991). The original Japanese title is *Nani ga watakushi o kô sasetaka* (What Made Me Act This Way?). See Saeki Shôichi, Kano Masanao, comp., *Nihonjin no jiden* (Tokyo: Heibonsha, 1980), 6:75–334, for a version of the original. See also *Reflections on the Way to the Gallows,* translated and edited by Mikiso Hane (Berkeley: University of California Press, 1988), 75–124.

[14] See Sidonie Smith, *The Poetics of Women's Autobiography: Marginality and the Fictions of Self-Representation* (Bloomington: Indiana University Press, 1987) where she notes:

Often, projecting multiple readers with multiple sets of expectations, she responds in a complex double-voicedness, a fragile heteroglossia of her own, which calls forth charged dramatic exchanges and narrative strategies. . . . To write an autobiography from that speaking position does not become tantamount to liberating woman from the fictions that bind her; indeed, it may embed her even more deeply in them since it promotes identification with the very essentialist ideology that renders woman's story a story of silence, powerlessness, self-effacement. (53)

It is part of Smith's argument that as males partake of the universal human subject, they develop a sense of a disembodied self—an individual in search of his soul—while women, designated as 'Other,' remain trapped or "embodied" in a very different kind of self, "harbor[ing] no unified, atomic, Adamic core to be discovered and represented" (15). As Smith notes:

[T]he subject of traditional autobiography marshaled the vagaries of his unique history under the banner of the universal subject. Through this practice he reaffirmed, reproduced, and celebrated the agentive autonomy and disembodiment of the universal subject, valorizing individuality and separateness while erasing personal and communal interdependencies. As he did so he reenacted the erasure of the feminine that facilitates male entrance into the public realm of words, power, and meaning. (19)

[15] Gabrielle Spiegel, "Introduction," in *Practicing History: New Directions in Historical Writing after the Linguistic Turn*, edited by Gabriele Spiegel (New York and London: Routledge, 2005), 5.

Chapter Five

[1] See Jill Ker Conway, *When Memory Speaks: Reflections on Autobiography* (New York: Alfred A. Knopf, 1998), 15.

[2] The figures for 2010 were approximately 79.5 years for men and 86.5 years for women.

[3] Japan's fertility rate has continued to fall; although it stood at 1.37 in 2008, it dropped in 2009 to approximately 1.20 births per woman.

[4] According to the International Longevity Center of Japan publication *A Profile of Older Japanese, 2011*, this process took 114 years in France and 40 years in Germany. See http://www.ilcjapan.org/agingE/index.html.

Chapter Six

[1] Quoted in D. Clayton James, *The Years of MacArthur*, vol. 2, *1941–1945* (Boston: Houghton Mifflin, 1975), 785.

[2] Sidonie Smith makes this clear when she writes that "the ideology of gender makes of woman's life script a nonstory, a silent space, a gap in patriarchal culture," and that a woman's "'natural' story shapes itself not around the public, heroic life but around the fluid, circumstantial, contingent responsiveness to others that, according to patriarchal ideology, characterizes the life of woman but not autobiography." A woman who writes an autobiography, Smith finds, is "resident on the margins of discourse, always removed from the center of power within the culture she inhabits.

See Sidonie Smith, *The Poetics of Women's Autobiography: Marginality and the Fictions of Self-Representation* (Bloomington: Indiana University Press, 1987), 50–51.

Jill Ker Conway echoes Smith's point by posing a question: Given that Western language and narrative forms have been developed to record and explicate the male life, how can a woman write an autobiography when to do so requires using a language which denigrates the feminine and using a genre which celebrates the experience of the atomistic Western male hero? Jill Ker Conway, *When Memory Speaks: Reflections on Autobiography* (New York: Alfred A. Knopf, 1998), 3. Even though women inherited a different tradition from the Western canon than men did, they did write their lives, though often without sufficient consideration of their historical agency. If men's narratives rely on the classical Greek myths in which an Odysseus-like character undertakes an epic journey of adventure, achieves his goals, and can thereby assert that his success is due entirely to his own agency, women, by contrast, typically downplay their sense of agency in their own lives and successes because they are not convinced that they have control over their own destiny and accomplishments. See Conway, *When Memory Speaks*, 14–18.

[3] Conway, *When Memory Speaks*, 6.

[4] See Akiyama Yoko, *Ribu Watashi shi Nooto: Onnatachi no jidai kara* (Tokyo: Impakuto Shuppankai, 1993), 7–9.

[5] For the text of the convention, see http://www.un.org/womenwatch/daw/cedaw/.

[6] See *Human Development Report, Overcoming Barriers: Human Mobility and Development* (New York: Macmillan Palgrave, 2009) 186, cited in http://www.wa-pedia.com/statistics/japan_world_ranking.shtml.

[7] Joan W. Scott, "The Evidence of Experience," *Critical Inquiry* 17 (1991), quoted in Gabrielle M. Spiegel, "Introduction," in *Practicing History: New Directions in Historical Writing after the Linguistic Turn*, edited by Gabrielle M. Spiegel (New York: Routledge, 2005), 12.

BIBLIOGRAPHY

Primary Texts

Kanamori Toshie. *Waratte, naite, aruite, kaita: Josei jyaanarisuto no gojûnen.* Tokyo: Domesu shuppan, 2006.

Kishino Junko. *Onna no chihei kara miete-kita mono: Josei kisha no jibunshi.* Tokyo: Kawade shoten, 1980.

Kôra Tomi. *Ahinsa o ikiru: Kôra Tomi jiden.*{Living Peace: The Autobiography of Kora Tomi]. Tokyo: Domesu shuppan, 1983.

Mizoguchi Akiyo, Saeki Yôko, and Miki Sôko, eds. *Shiryô Nihon Uuman ribushi* {A History in Medieval of the Japanese Women's Lib Movement]. 3 vols. Kyoto: Shôkadô shoten, 1992–95.

Okabe Itsuko. *Yuigon no tsumori de.* Tokyo: Fujiwara shoten, 2006.

Sawachi Hisae. *Watashi ga Ikita "Shôwa."* Tokyo: Iwanami shoten, 2000.

Shinya Eiko. *Joyû Shinya Eiko: Watashi no rirekisho.* Osaka: Kaihô shuppansha, 2005.

———. *Enji Tsuzukete Hitori Shibai Shinse Taryon.* Osaka: Kaihô shuppansha, 1991.

Yoshitake Teruko. *Onnatachi no undôshi—watakushi no Ikita Sengo* [A history of women's movements—and my experience of the postwar years]. Tokyo: Mineruba shoten, 2006.

Secondary Sources

Akiyama Yoko. *Ribu Watashi shi nooto: Onnatachi no jidai kara.* Tokyo: Impakuto Shuppankai, 1993.

Bloom, Harold, ed. *Bigger Thomas.* New York and Philadelphia: Chelsea House Publishers, 1990.

Cabrera, Miguel. "On Language, Culture, and Social Action." *History and Theory* 40, no. 2 (December 2001): 82–100.

Clark, Elizabeth A. *History, Theory, Text: Historians and the Linguistic Turn.* Cambridge, Mass.: Harvard University Press, 2004.

Clayton, James, D.. *The Years of MacArthur.* Vol. 2, *1941–1945.* Boston: Houghton Mifflin, 1975.

Conway, Jill Ker. *When Memory Speaks: Reflections on Autobiography.* New York: Alfred A. Knopf, 1998.

Dower, John. *Embracing Defeat: Japan in the Wake of World War II.* New York: W. W. Norton, 1999.

Eley, Geoff. *A Crooked Line: From Cultural History to the History of Society.* Ann Arbor: University of Michigan Press, 2005.

Endô Shûsaku. *The Girl I Left Behind.* Translated by Mark Williams. New York: New Directions, 1994.

Evans, Owen. *Mapping the Contours of Oppression: Subjectivity, Truth, and Fiction in Recent German Autobiographical Treatments of Totalitarianism.* Amsterdam and New York: Rodopi, 2006.

Greene, Patricia V. "Constancia de la Mora's *In Place of Splendor* and the Persistence of Memory." *Journal of Interdisciplinary Literary Studies* 5, no. 1 (1993): 75–84.

Handô Kazutoshi. *Shôwashi sengohen, 1945–1989.* Tokyo: Heibonsha, 2009.

Hane, Mikiso. *Reflections on the Way to the Gallows.* Berkeley, CA: University of California Press, 1988.

Hasegawa, Kenji. "Experiencing the 1952 Bloody May Day Incident." *Stanford Journal of East Asian Affairs,* http://www.stanford.edu/group/sjeaa/journal3/japan2.pdf.

Iijima Tadashi. *Sekai no eiga.* Tokyo: Hakusuisha, 1957.

Kano Masanao. *Gendai Nihon joseishi: Feminizumu o jiku to shite.* Tokyo: Yûhikaku, 2004.

———. *Nihon no Gendai.* Tokyo: Iwanami shoten, 2000.

Kaneko Fumiko. *The Prison Memoirs of a Japanese Woman.* Translated by Jean Inglis with an Introduction by Mikiso Hane. Armonk, N.Y., and London: M. E. Sharp, 1991.

Kralik, Debbie L., and Antonia M. van Loon. "Transition: Moving through Life's Adverse Disruptions." http://72.14.253.104/search?q=cache:cqtU6UTJnEoJ:www.rdns.org.au/research_unit/documents/RDNS_transition_poster.pdf+becoming+ordinary&hl=en&ct=clnk&cd=4.

Loftus, Ronald P. "Finding New Pathways: Japanese Women's Memoirs at the End of the Pacific War." *Japan Studies Association Journal* 8 (2010): 146–64.

————. *Telling Lives: Women's Self-Writing in Modern Japan*. Honolulu: University of Hawai'i Press, 2004.

MacKinnon, Janice R., and Stephen R. MacKinnon. *Agnes Smedley: The Life and Times of an American Radical*. Berkeley: University of California Press, 1987.

McCormack, Gavan. "Ampo's Troubled 50th: Hatoyama's Abortive Rebellion, Okinawa's Mounting Resistance, and the US-Japan Relationship." *Japan Focus*, http://japanfocus.org/-Gavan-McCormack/3365.

Mizoguchi Akiyo, Saeki Yôko, and Miki Sôko, eds. *Shiryô Nihon Uuman ribushi.* vols. Kyoto: Yûgen kaisha, Shokadô shoten, 1992–95.

Muto Ichiyo. "The Birth of the Women's Liberation Movement in the 1970s." In *The Other Japan: Conflict, Compromise, and Resistance since 1945*, edited by Joe Moore. Armonk, N.Y.: M. E. Sharpe, 1997. 147–171.

Nenkan daihyô shinario shû. Tokyo: Mikasa shobô, 1957.

Nornes, Abe Mark. "Pôru Ruta/Paul Rotha and the Politics of Translation." *Cinema Journal* 38, no. 3 (Spring 1999): 91–108.

Ôishi Matashichi. *The Day the Sun Rose in the West: Bikini, the Lucky Dragon, and I.* Honolulu: University of Hawai'i Press, 2011.

Ogura Shimbi. *"Bakuon to daichi." Kinema Junpo* 186 (1957): 54.

Onnatachi no ima o Tôkai, comp. *Zenkyôtô kara ribu e.* Tokyo: Impakuto Shuppankai, Hatsubaimoto Izara Shobo, 1996.

Okada, Shin, "Sekigawa Hideo," in *Nihon Eiga no Kaikô Jôei* (Tokyo: Film Library josei kyôgikai, 1963), 258–260.

Orbaugh, Sharalyn. *Japanese Fiction of the Allied Occupation: Vision, Embodiment, Identity*. Boston and Leiden: Brill, 2007.

Price, Ruth. *The Lives of Agnes Smedley*. New York: Oxford University Press, 2005.

Rotha, Paul. *Documentary Film*. New York: Hastings House and Communication Arts Books, 1953.

Sasaki-Uemura, Wesley. *Organizing the Spontaneous: Citizen Protest in Postwar Japan.* Honolulu: University of Hawai'i Press, 2001.

Sato Tadao. *"Bakuon to daichi." Eiga Horizon*, October 1957, 102–3.

Scott, Joan W. *Only Paradoxes to Offer: French Feminists and the Rights of Man.* Cambridge, Mass.: Harvard University Press, 1996.

————. "The Evidence of Experience." *Critical Inquiry* 17 (1991):4. 773–797.

Sewell, William H. Jr., *Logics of History: Social Theory and Social Transformation.* Chicago and London: University of Chicago Press, 2005.

Shigematsu, Setsu. *Scream from the Shadows: The Women's Liberation Movement in Japan.* Minneapolis and London: University of Minnesota Press, 2012

Smedley, Agnes, *Portraits of Chinese Women in Revolution.* Edited with an introduction by Janice R. MacKinnon and Stephen R. MacKinnon. Old Westbury, NY: Feminist Press, 1976.

Smith, Sidonie. *The Poetics of Women's Autobiography: Marginality and the Fictions of Self-Representation.* Bloomington: Indiana University Press, 1987.

Spiegel, Gabrielle M. "Introduction." In *Practicing History: New Directions in Historical Writing after the Linguistic Turn,* edited by Gabrielle M. Spiegel, 1–31. New York: Routledge, 2005.

————. "Comment on *A Crooked Line*." *American Historical Review* 113, no. 2 (April 2008): 406–16.

Tsugenama Tadao. "*Bakuon to daichi* no kako to genzai." *Eiga Geijustsu* 5, no. 12 (1957): 65–66.

INDEX

CPSIA information can be obtained at www.ICGtesting.com
Printed in the USA
BVOW040546240413

318830BV00007B/4/P